EARTH SYSTEM EVOLUTION

EarthComm®

EARTH SYSTEM SCIENCE IN THE COMMUNITY

Michael J. Smith Ph.D.
American Geological Institute

John B. Southard Ph.D.
Massachusetts Institute of Technology

Ruta Demery
Editor

Developed by the American Geological Institute
Supported by the National Science Foundation and
the American Geological Institute Foundation

IT's ABOUT TIME™

Published by
It's About Time Inc., Armonk, NY

Earth System Evolution

Published in 2002 by
It's About Time, Inc.
84 Business Park Drive, Armonk, NY 10504
Phone (914) 273-2233 Fax (914) 273-2227
Toll Free (888) 698-TIME
www.Its-About-Time.com

Publisher
Laurie Kreindler

Project Manager	**Project Coordinators**	**Design**
Ruta Demery	Emily Crum	John Nordland
	Matthew Smith	

| **Studio Manager** | **Senior Photo Consultant** | **Photo Research** |
| Joan Lee | Bruce F. Molnia | Caitlin Callahan |

| **Creative Artwork** | **Technical Art** | **Creative Artwork** |
| Tomas Bunk | Stuart Armstrong | Tomas Bunk |

| **Safety Reviewer** | **Production** | **Physics Reviewer** |
| Dr. Edward Robeck | Burmar Technical Corporation | Dr. John Roeder |

All student activities in this textbook have been designed to be as safe as possible, and have been reviewed by professionals specifically for that purpose. As well, appropriate warnings concerning potential safety hazards are included where applicable to particular activities. However, responsibility for safety remains with the student, the classroom teacher, the school principals, and the school board.

EarthComm® is a registered trademark of the American Geological Institute. Registered names and trademarks, etc., used in this publication, even without specific indication thereof, are not to be considered unprotected by law.

It's About Time™ is a registered trademark of It's About Time, Inc. Registered names and trademarks, etc., used in this publication, even without specific indication thereof, are not to be considered unprotected by law.

© Copyright 2002: American Geological Institute

All rights reserved. No part of this publication may be reproduced, stored in a retrieval system, or transmitted, in any form or by any means, electronic, mechanical, photocopying, recording, or otherwise, without the prior written permission of the copyright owner.

Care has been taken to trace the ownership of copyright material contained in this publication. The publisher will gladly receive any information that will rectify any reference or credit line in subsequent editions.

Printed and bound in the United States of America

ISBN #1-58591-059-7

1 2 3 4 5 QC 06 05 04 03 02

This project was supported, in part, by the
National Science Foundation (grant no. ESI-9452789)

Opinions expressed are those of the authors and not necessarily those of the National Science Foundation or the donors of the American Geological Institute Foundation.

Table of Contents

1
Astronomy...
and Your Community

2
Climate Change...
and Your Community

3
Changing Life...
and Your Community

EarthComm

Photos and Illustrations

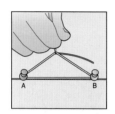

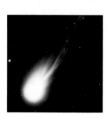

E175, photo by Cody Arenz, Nebraska Wesleyan University

E10, E11, E20, E22, E24, E29, E30, E31, E33, E34 Fig. 4, E50, E52, E59, E64, E71, E75 Fig. 2, E100, E103, E106, E107, E108, E109, E111, E113, E114, E118, E119, E121, E129, E130, E131, E140 Fig. 2, E149, E150, E151 Fig. 1, E184, illustrations by Stuart Armstrong

E85, illustration by Stuart Armstrong, source: Köppen Climate Map

E97 (top and bottom right), illustration by Stuart Armstrong; source: R. S. Bradley and J. A. Eddy based on J. T. Houghton et al., Climate Change: The IPCC Assessment, Cambridge University Press, Cambridge, 1990 and published in EarthQuest, vol. 5, no. 1, 1991.

E100 Fig. 1, by Stuart Armstrong, source: redrafted from Muller and MacDonald, Ice Ages and Astronomical Causes, Springer-Praxis, 2000

E101 Fig. 3, E132, E169, illustrations by Stuart Armstrong, source: Jouzel, J.C., et al, 1987, Nature 329:403-8; Jouzel, J.C., et al, 1993, Nature 364:407-12; Jouzel, J.C., et al, 1996, Climate Dynamics 12:513-521; and Jouzel, J.C., et al, 1999, Nature 399: 429-436

E114, illustration by Stuart Armstrong, source: Skinner and Porter, The Dynamic Planet, John Wiley & Sons, 2nd Edition, February 2000

E126 Part A Table, illustration by Stuart Armstrong, source: Global Historical Climatology Network 1701-07/2000 (meteorological stations only) and Hansen, J., Sato, M., Lacis, A., Ruedy, R., Tegen, I. & Mathews, E. (1998) Climate forcings in the Industrial era, Proc. Natl. Acad. Sci. USA, 95, 12753-12758.

E126 Part B graph, illustration by Stuart Armstrong, source: Methane data: Chappellaz et al, Nature, v. 345, p. 127-131, 1990; CO_2 data: Barnola et al., Nature, v. 329, p. 408-414, 1987; Change in temperature data: Jouzel et al, Climate Dynamics, 12:8, p. 513-521, 1996.

E139, redrafted by Stuart Armstrong from a diagram by John Woolsey of Woolsey Studio, Boston, source: Stanley Chernicoff

E159, illustration by Stuart Armstrong, source: Tom Crowley and Consequences Magazine E161

E166, illustration by Stuart Armstrong, source: Gastaldo, Savrda, Lewis. Deciphering Earth History. Page 13-11.

E66, Figs. 4, 5, Dana Berry, Space Telescope Science Institute

E4, E14, E28, E37, E47, E58, E69, E105, E117, E125, E136, E148, E156, E165, E173, E182, illustrations by Tomas Bunk

E176 Tyrannosaurs Rex, University of California Museum of Paleontology

E51, photo by Digital Stock Corporation Royalty Free Images: Backgrounds from Nature

E18, E43, E54, photos by Digital Stock Corporation Royalty Free Images: Space Exploration

E9, E19, photos by Digital Vision Royalty Free Images: Astronomy and Space

E157 desert, photo by Digital Vision Royalty Free Images: North American Landscapes

E161 Fig. 2, photo by Digital Vision Royalty Free Images: American Highlights

E75 Fig. 4, E76 Figs. 5A, 5C, photo by European Southern Observatory

E176, Archaeohippus, Florida Museum of Natural History

E176 Wolf skull, Bill Forbes, Biology Department, Indiana University of Pennsylvania

E180, image courtesy of Geological Survey of Canada

E76 Fig. 5B, photo by Pat Harrington at University of Maryland

E77, photo by Jeff Hester and Paul Scowen, Arizona State University, NASA, and National Space Science Data Center

E34 Fig. 5, International Astronomical Union

E97 (top left), photo courtesy of Laboratory of Tree Ring Research, University of Tennessee

E92, E102 Fig. 4, E140 Fig. 3, E152 Fig. 3, E157 grassland, taiga, photos by Bruce Molnia

E187 Fig, 5, photo courtesy of the Morton Arboretum, Lisle, Illinois.

E7, photo by NASA and European Space Agency, A. Dupree and Ronald Gilliand

E8, E13, photos by NASA and the Hubble Heritage Team

E41, Photo by NASA and National Space Science Data Center

E42 Table 1, E44 Table 2, data from NASA

E45, E65 Fig. 3, photos by NASA

E53, photo by NASA Goddard Space Flight Center

E83 (top right), image by NASA

E2, E3, E25-27, E32, E40, E55, E68, E84, E96, E82 (left, bottom), E110, E122 Fig. 4, E135, E146, E147, E157 tundra, chaparral, mountain zones, E160, E161 Fig. 1, E163, E171, by PhotoDisc

E187 Fig. 4, from a painting by Alice Prickett and published in black and white in Phillips and Cross (1991, pl. 4) Phillips, T.L., and Cross, A.T., 1991, Paleobotany and paleoecology of coal, in Gluskoter, H.J., et al., eds., Economic Geology: U.S.: Boulder, Colorado, Geological Society of America, Geology of North America, v. P-2, p. 483-502.

E168, photos courtesy of F.W. Potter and D.L. Dilcher, Florida Museum of Natural History

E116, photo courtesy of T. Rimmele, M. Hanna/NOAO/AURA/NSF

E93, E133, E151 Fig. 2, E152 Fig. 4, E154, E158 tropical rainforest, temperate evergreen forest, temperate deciduous forest, E162, E178, photos by Doug Sherman, Geo File Photography

E141, photo by Mike Smith

E120, photo courtesy of Walter Smith, NASA and David Sandwell, Scripps Institution of Oceanography

E179, E185, image courtesy of Smithsonian Institution

E186, photo courtesy of Smithsonian Institution

E176 Smilodon Californicus and Diplodocus, photos courtesy of Smithsonian Institution

E73, photo by Susan Tereby, Extrasolar Research Group, NASA, and National Space Science Data Center

E100 Fig. 2, E122 Fig. 3, E158 polar ice, photos by Mark Twickler, Institute for the Study of Earth, Oceans and Space, University of New Hampshire

E65 Fig. 2, photo by Dave Westpfahl, New Mexico Tech University, and Dave Finely, National Radio Astronomy Observatory

E23, photo by Jerome Wycoff

E75 Fig. 3, photo by Hui Yang, University of Illinois and NASA

E60, table modified with permission from "Scaling the Spectrum," courtesy of Donna Young, Tufts University

E123, photo by Barbara Zahm

Principal Investigator

Michael Smith is Director of Education at the American Geological Institute in Alexandria, Virginia. Dr. Smith worked as an exploration geologist and hydrogeologist. He began his Earth Science teaching career with Shady Side Academy in Pittsburgh, PA in 1988 and most recently taught Earth Science at the Charter School of Wilmington, DE. He earned a doctorate from the University of Pittsburgh's Cognitive Studies in Education Program and joined the faculty of the University of Delaware School of Education in 1995. Dr. Smith received the Outstanding Earth Science Teacher Award for Pennsylvania from the National Association of Geoscience Teachers in 1991, served as Secretary of the National Earth Science Teachers Association, and is a reviewer for Science Education and The Journal of Research in Science Teaching. He worked on the Delaware Teacher Standards, Delaware Science Assessment, National Board of Teacher Certification, and AAAS Project 2061 Curriculum Evaluation programs.

Senior Writer

Dr. Southard received his undergraduate degree from the Massachusetts Institute of Technology in 1960 and his doctorate in geology from Harvard University in 1966. After a National Science Foundation postdoctoral fellowship at the California Institute of Technology, he joined the faculty at the Massachusetts Institute of Technology, where he is currently Professor of Geology. He was awarded the MIT School of Science teaching prize in 1989 and was one of the first cohorts of first MacVicar Fellows at MIT, in recognition of excellence in undergraduate teaching. He has taught numerous undergraduate courses in introductory geology, sedimentary geology, field geology, and environmental Earth Science both at MIT and in Harvard's adult education program. He was editor of the Journal of Sedimentary Petrology from 1992 to 1996, and he continues to do technical editing of scientific books and papers for SEPM, a professional society for sedimentary geology. Dr. Southard received the 2001 Neil Miner Award from the National Association of Geoscience Teachers.

Safety Reviewer Dr. Edward Robeck, Salisbury University, MD

PRIMARY AND CONTRIBUTING AUTHORS

Earth's Dynamic Geosphere

Daniel J. Bisaccio
Souhegan High School
Amherst, NH

Steve Carlson
Middle School, OR

Warren Fish
Paul Revere School
Los Angeles, CA

Miriam Fuhrman
Carlsbad, CA

Steve Mattox
Grand Valley State University

Keith McKain
Milford Senior High School
Milford, DE

Mary McMillan
Niwot High School
Niwot, CO

Bill Romey
Orleans, MA

Michael Smith
American Geological Institute

Tom Vandewater
Colton, NY

Understanding Your Environment

Geoffrey A. Briggs
Batavia Senior High School
Batavia, NY

Cathey Donald
Auburn High School
Auburn, AL

Richard Duschl
Kings College
London, UK

Fran Hess
Cooperstown High School
Cooperstown, NY

Laurie Martin-Vermilyea
American Geological Institute

Molly Miller
Vanderbilt University

Mary-Russell Roberson
Durham, NC

Charles Savrda
Auburn University

Michael Smith
American Geological Institute

Earth's Fluid Spheres

Chet Bolay
Cape Coral High School
Cape Coral, FL

Steven Dutch
University of Wisconsin

Virginia Jones
Bonneville High School
Idaho Falls, ID

Laurie Martin-Vermilyea
American Geological Institute

Joseph Moran
University of Wisconsin

Mary-Russell Roberson
Durham, NC

Bruce G. Smith
Appleton North High School
Appleton, WI

Michael Smith
American Geological Institute

Earth's Natural Resources

Chuck Bell
Deer Valley High School
Glendale, AZ

Jay Hackett
Colorado Springs, CO

John Kemeny
University of Arizona

John Kounas
Westwood High School
Sloan, IA

Laurie Martin-Vermilyea
American Geological Institute

Mary Poulton
University of Arizona

David Shah
Deer Valley High School
Glendale, AZ

Janine Shigihara
Shelley Junior High School
Shelley, ID

Michael Smith
American Geological Institute

Earth System Evolution

Julie Bartley
University of West Georgia

Lori Borroni-Engle
Taft High School
San Antonio, TX

Richard M. Busch
West Chester University
West Chester, PA

Kathleen Cochrane
Our Lady of Ransom School
Niles, IL

Cathey Donald
Auburn High School, AL

Robert Gasataldo
Colby College

William Leonard
Clemson University

Tim Lutz
West Chester University

Carolyn Collins Petersen
C. Collins Petersen Productions
Groton, MA

Michael Smith
American Geological Institute

Content Reviewers

Gary Beck
BP Exploration

Phil Bennett
University of Texas, Austin

Steve Bergman
Southern Methodist University

Samuel Berkheiser
Pennsylvania Geologic Survey

Arthur Bloom
Cornell University

Craig Bohren
Penn State University

Bruce Bolt
University of California, Berkeley

John Callahan
Appalachian State University

Sandip Chattopadhyay
R.S. Kerr Environmental Research
Center

Beth Ellen Clark
Cornell University

Jimmy Diehl
Michigan Technological University

Sue Beske-Diehl
Michigan Technological University

Neil M. Dubrovsky
United States Geological Survey

Frank Ethridge
Colorado State University

Catherine Finley
University of Northern Colorado

Ronald Greeley
Arizona State University

Michelle Hall-Wallace
University of Arizona

Judy Hannah
Colorado State University

Blaine Hanson
Dept. of Land, Air, and Water
Resources

James W. Head III
Brown University

Patricia Heiser
Ohio University

John R. Hill
Indiana Geological Survey

Travis Hudson
American Geological Institute

Jackie Huntoon
Michigan Tech. University

Teresa Jordan
Cornell University

Allan Juhas
Lakewood, Colorado

Robert Kay
Cornell University

Chris Keane
American Geological Institute

Bill Kirby
United States Geological Survey

Mark Kirschbaum
United States Geological Survey

Dave Kirtland
United States Geological Survey

Jessica Elzea Kogel
Thiele Kaolin Company

Melinda Laituri
Colorado State University

Martha Leake
Valdosta State University

Donald Lewis
Happy Valley, CA

Steven Losh
Cornell University

Jerry McManus
Woods Hole Oceanographic
Institution

Marcus Milling
American Geological Institute

Alexandra Moore
Cornell University

Jack Oliver
Cornell University

Don Pair
University of Dayton

Mauri Pelto
Nicolas College

Bruce Pivetz
ManTech Environmental Research
Services Corp.

Stephen Pompea
Pompea & Associates

Peter Ray
Florida State University

William Rose
Michigan Technological Univ.

Lou Solebello
Macon, Gerogia

Robert Stewart
Texas A&M University

Ellen Stofan
NASA

Barbara Sullivan
University of Rhode Island

Carol Tang
Arizona State University

Bob Tilling
United States Geological Survey

Stanley Totten
Hanover College

Scott Tyler
University of Nevada, Reno

Michael Velbel
Michigan State University

Ellen Wohl
Colorado State University

David Wunsch
State Geologist of New Hampshire

Pilot Test Evaluator
Larry Enochs
Oregon State University

Pilot Test Teachers
Rhonda Artho
Dumas High School
Dumas, TX

Mary Jane Bell
Lyons-Decatur Northeast
Lyons, NE

Rebecca Brewster
Plant City High School
Plant City, FL

Terry Clifton
Jackson High School
Jackson, MI

Virginia Cooter
North Greene High School
Greeneville, TN

Monica Davis
North Little Rock High School
North Little Rock, AR

Joseph Drahuschak
Troxell Jr. High School
Allentown, PA

Ron Fabick
Brunswick High School
Brunswick, OH

Virginia Jones
Bonneville High School
Idaho Falls, ID

Troy Lilly
Snyder High School
Snyder, TX

Sherman Lundy
Burlington High School
Burlington, IA

Norma Martof
Fairmont Heights High School
Capitol Heights, MD

Keith McKain
Milford Senior High School
Milford, DE

Mary McMillan
Niwot High School
Niwot, CO

Kristin Michalski
Mukwonago High School
Mukwonago, WI

Dianne Mollica
Bishop Denis J. O'Connell
High School
Arlington, VA

Arden Rauch
Schenectady High School
Schenectady, NY

Laura Reysz
Lawrence Central High School
Indianapolis, IN

Floyd Rogers
Palatine High School
Palatine, IL

Ed Ruszczyk
New Canaan High School
New Canaan, CT

Jane Skinner
Farragut High School
Knoxville, TN

Shelley Snyder
Mount Abraham High School
Bristol, VT

Joy Tanigawa
El Rancho High School
Pico Rivera, CA

Dennis Wilcox
Milwaukee School of Languages
Milwaukee, WI

Kim Willoughby
SE Raleigh High School
Raleigh, NC

Field Test Workshop Staff
Don W. Byerly
University of Tennessee

Derek Geise
University of Nebraska

Michael A. Gibson
University of Tennessee

David C. Gosselin
University of Nebraska

Robert Hartshorn
University of Tennessee

William Kean
University of Wisconsin

Ellen Metzger
San Jose State University

Tracy Posnanski
University of Wisconsin

J. Preston Prather
University of Tennessee

Ed Robeck
Salisbury University

Richard Sedlock
San Jose State University

Bridget Wyatt
San Jose State University

Field Test Evaluators
Bob Bernoff
Dresher, PA

Do Yong Park
University of Iowa

Field Test Teachers
Kerry Adams
Alamosa High School
Alamosa, CO

Jason Ahlberg
Lincoln High
Lincoln, NE

Gregory Bailey
Fulton High School
Knoxville, TN

Mary Jane Bell
Lyons-Decatur Northeast
Lyons, NE

Rod Benson
Helena High
Helena, MT

Sandra Bethel
Greenfield High School
Greenfield, TN

John Cary
Malibu High School
Malibu, CA

Elke Christoffersen
Poland Regional High School
Poland, ME

Tom Clark
Benicia High School
Benicia, CA

Julie Cook
Jefferson City High School
Jefferson City, MO

Virginia Cooter
North Greene High School
Greeneville, TN

Mary Cummane
Perspectives Charter
Chicago, IL

Sharon D'Agosta
Creighton Preparatory
Omaha, NE

Mark Daniels
Kettle Morraine High School
Milwaukee, WI

Beth Droughton
Bloomfield High School
Bloomfield, NJ

Steve Ferris
Lincoln High
Lincoln, NE

Bob Feurer
North Bend Central Public
North Bend, NE

Sue Frack
Lincoln Northeast High
Lincoln, NE

Rebecca Fredrickson
Greendale High School
Greendale, WI

Sally Ghilarducci
Hamilton High School
Milwaukee, WI

Kerin Goedert
Lincoln High School
Ypsilanti, MI

Martin Goldsmith
Menominee Falls High School
Menominee Falls, WI

Randall Hall
Arlington High School
St. Paul, MN

Theresa Harrison
Wichita West High
Wichita, KS

Gilbert Highlander
Red Bank High School
Chattanooga, TN

Jim Hunt
Chattanooga School of Arts
& Sciences
Chattanooga, TN

Patricia Jarzynski
Watertown High School
Watertown, WI

Pam Kasprowicz
Bartlett High School
Bartlett, IL

Caren Kershner
Moffat Consolidated
Moffat, CO

Mary Jane Kirkham
Fulton High School

Ted Koehn
Lincoln East High
Lincoln, NE

Philip Lacey
East Liverpool High School
East Liverpool, OH

Joan Lahm
Scotus Central Catholic
Columbus, NE

Erica Larson
Tipton Community

Michael Laura
Banning High School
Wilmington, CA

Fawn LeMay
Plattsmouth High
Plattsmouth, NE

Christine Lightner
Smethport Area High School
Smethport, PA

Nick Mason
Normandy High School
St. Louis, MO

James Matson
Wichita West High
Wichita, KS

Jeffrey Messer
Western High School
Parma, MI

Dave Miller
Parkview High
Springfield, MO

Rick Nettesheim
Waukesha South
Waukesha, WI

John Niemoth
Niobrara Public
Niobrara, NE

Margaret Olsen
Woodward Academy
College Park, GA

Ronald Ozuna
Roosevelt High School
Los Angeles, CA

Paul Parra
Omaha North High
Omaha, NE

D. Keith Patton
West High
Denver, CO

Phyllis Peck
Fairfield High School
Fairfield, CA

Randy Pelton
Jackson High School
Massillon, OH

Reggie Pettitt
Holderness High School
Holderness, NH

June Rasmussen
Brighton High School
South Brighton, TN

Russ Reese
Kalama High School
Kalama, WA

Janet Ricker
South Greene High School
Greeneville, TN

Wendy Saber
Washington Park High School
Racine, WI

Garry Sampson
Wauwatosa West High School
Tosa, WI

Daniel Sauls
Chuckey-Doak High School
Afton, TN

Todd Shattuck
L.A. Center for Enriched Studies
Los Angeles, CA

Heather Shedd
Tennyson High School
Hayward, CA

Lynn Sironen
North Kingstown High School
North Kingstown, RI

Jane Skinner
Farragut High School
Knoxville, TN

Sarah Smith
Garringer High School
Charlotte, NC

Aaron Spurr
Malcolm Price Laboratory
Cedar Falls, IA

Karen Tiffany
Watertown High School
Watertown, WI

Tom Tyler
Bishop O'Dowd High School
Oakland, CA

Valerie Walter
Freedom High School
Bethlehem, PA

Christopher J. Akin Williams
Milford Mill Academy
Baltimore, MD

Roseanne Williby
Skutt Catholic High School
Omaha, NE

Carmen Woodhall
Canton South High School
Canton, OH

Field Test Coordinator
William Houston
American Geological Institute

Advisory Board
Jane Crowder
Bellevue, WA

Arthur Eisenkraft
Bedford (NY) Public Schools

Tom Ervin
LeClaire, IA

Mary Kay Hemenway
University of Texas at Austin

Bill Leonard
Clemson University

Don Lewis
Lafayette, CA

Wendell Mohling
National Science Teachers Association

Harold Pratt
Littleton, CO

Barb Tewksbury
Hamilton College

Laure Wallace
USGS

AGI Foundation
Jan van Sant
Executive Director

The American Geological Institute and EarthComm

The American Geological Institute and EarthComm Imagine more than 500,000 Earth scientists worldwide sharing a common voice, and you've just imagined the mission of the American Geological Institute. Our mission is to raise public awareness of the Earth sciences and the role that they play in mankind's use of natural resources, mitigation of natural hazards, and stewardship of the environment. For more than 50 years, AGI has served the scientists and teachers of its Member Societies and hundreds of associated colleges, universities, and corporations by producing Earth science educational materials, *Geotimes*–a geoscience news magazine, GeoRef–a reference database, and government affairs and public awareness programs.

So many important decisions made every day that affect our lives depend upon an understanding of how our Earth works. That's why AGI created *EarthComm*. In your *EarthComm* classroom, you'll discover the wonder and importance of Earth science by studying it where it counts—in your community. As you use the rock record to investigate climate change, do field work in nearby beaches, parks, or streams, explore the evolution and extinction of life, understand where your energy resources come from, or find out how to forecast severe weather, you'll gain a better understanding of how to use your knowledge of Earth science to make wise personal decisions.

We would like to thank the AGI Foundation Members that have been supportive in bringing Earth science to students. These AGI Foundation Members include: Anadarko Petroleum Corp., The Anschutz Foundation, Baker Hughes Foundation, Barrett Resources Corp., Elizabeth and Stephen Bechtel, Jr. Foundation, BPAmoco Foundation, Burlington Resources Foundation, CGG Americas, Inc., ChevronTexaco Corp., Conoco Inc., Consolidated Natural Gas Foundation, Diamond Offshore Co., Dominion Exploration & Production, Inc., EEX Corp., ExxonMobil Foundation, Global Marine Drilling Co., Halliburton Foundation, Inc., Kerr McGee Foundation, Maxus Energy Corp., Noble Drilling Corp., Occidental Petroleum Charitable Foundation, Parker Drilling Co., Phillips Petroleum Co., Santa Fe Snyder Corp., Schlumberger Foundation, Shell Oil Company Foundation, Southwestern Energy Co., Texas Crude Energy, Inc., Unocal Corp. USX Foundation (Marathon Oil Co.).

We at AGI wish you success in your exploration of the Earth System and your Community.

Michael J. Smith
Director of Education, AGI

Marcus E. Milling
Executive Director, AGI

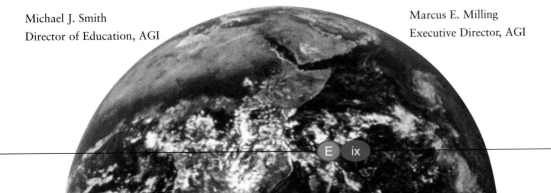

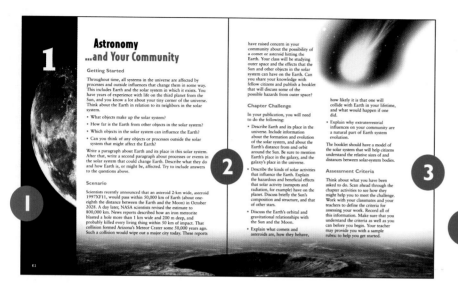

1. Scenario
Each chapter begins with an event or situation in the Earth system that has happened or could actually take place.

2. Challenge
This feature challenges you to solve a problem based in your community. You will need to use the Earth science knowledge you gain from working through the chapter.

3. Assessment Criteria
Before you begin, you and your classmates, along with your teacher, will explore exactly how you will be graded. You will review the criteria and expectations for solving the challenge, and make decisions about how your work should be evaluated.

4. Goals
At the beginning of each activity you are provided with a list of goals that you should be able to achieve by completing your science inquiry.

5. Think about It
What do you already know? Before you start each activity you will be asked one or two questions to consider. You will have a chance to discuss your ideas with your group and your class. You are not expected to come up with the "right" answer, but to share your current understanding and reasoning.

6. Investigate
In EarthComm you learn by doing science. In your small groups, or as a class, you will take part in scientific inquiry by doing hands-on experiments, participating in fieldwork, or searching for answers using the Internet and reference materials.

7. Reflecting on the Activity and the Challenge
Each activity will help you meet the chapter challenge. This feature gives you a brief summary of the activity. It will help you relate the activity that you just completed to the "Big Picture."

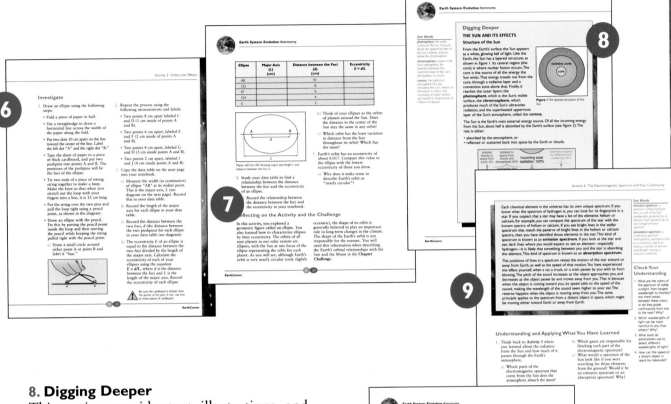

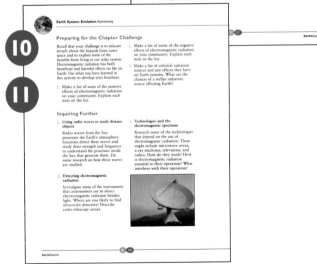

8. Digging Deeper

This section provides text, illustrations, and photographs that will give you a greater insight into the concepts you explored in the activity. Words that may be new or unfamiliar to you are defined and explained. "Check Your Understanding" questions are included to guide you in your reading. Key terms are highlighted as "Geo Words."

9. Understanding and Applying What You Have Learned

Questions in this feature ask you to use the key principles and concepts introduced in the activity. You may also be presented with new situations in which you will be asked to apply what you have learned.

10. Preparing for the Chapter Challenge

This feature suggests ways in which you can organize your work and get ready for the challenge. It prompts you to combine the results of your inquiry as you work through the chapter.

11. Inquiring Further

This feature provides lots of suggestions for deepening your understanding of the concepts and skills developed in the activity. It also gives you an opportunity to relate what you have learned to the Earth system.

EARTH SYSTEMS

The **atmosphere** is the gaseous envelope that surrounds the Earth and consists of a mixture of gases composed primarily of nitrogen, oxygen, carbon dioxide, argon, and water vapor.

The **biosphere** is the life zone of the Earth and includes all living organisms, including humans, and all organic matter that has not yet decomposed.

The **cryosphere** is the portion of the climatic system consisting of the world's ice masses and snow deposits. This includes ice sheets, ice shelves, ice caps and other glaciers, sea ice, seasonal snow cover, lake and river ice, and seasonally frozen ground and permafrost.

The **geosphere** is the solid Earth that includes the continental and oceanic crust as well as the various layers of the Earth's interior.

The **hydrosphere** includes the water of the Earth, including surface lakes, streams, oceans, underground water, and water in the atmosphere.

1

Astronomy
...and Your Community

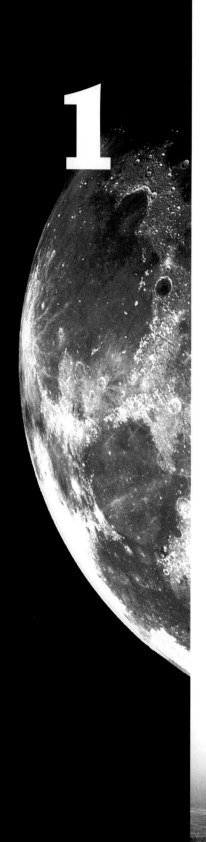

Astronomy
...and Your Community

Getting Started

Throughout time, all systems in the universe are affected by processes and outside influences that change them in some way. This includes Earth and the solar system in which it exists. You have years of experience with life on the third planet from the Sun, and you know a lot about your tiny corner of the universe. Think about the Earth in relation to its neighbors in the solar system.

• What objects make up the solar system?

• How far is the Earth from other objects in the solar system?

• Which objects in the solar system can influence the Earth?

• Can you think of any objects or processes outside the solar system that might affect the Earth?

Write a paragraph about Earth and its place in this solar system. After that, write a second paragraph about processes or events in the solar system that could change Earth. Describe what they do and how Earth is, or might be, affected. Try to include answers to the questions above.

Scenario

Scientists recently announced that an asteroid 2-km wide, asteroid 1997XF11, would pass within 50,000 km of Earth (about one-eighth the distance between the Earth and the Moon) in October 2028. A day later, NASA scientists revised the estimate to 800,000 km. News reports described how an iron meteorite blasted a hole more than 1 km wide and 200 m deep, and probably killed every living thing within 50 km of impact. That collision formed Arizona's Meteor Crater some 50,000 years ago. Such a collision would wipe out a major city today. These reports have raised concern in your community about the possibility of a comet or asteroid hitting the Earth. Your class will be studying outer space and the effects that the Sun and other objects in the solar system can have on the Earth. Can you share your knowledge with fellow citizens and publish a booklet that will discuss some of the possible hazards from outer space?

Chapter Challenge

In your publication, you will need to do the following:

- Describe Earth and its place in the universe. Include information about the formation and evolution of the solar system, and about the Earth's distance from and orbit around the Sun. Be sure to mention Earth's place in the galaxy, and the galaxy's place in the universe.

- Describe the kinds of solar activities that influence the Earth. Explain the hazardous and beneficial effects that solar activity (sunspots and radiation, for example) have on the planet. Discuss briefly the Sun's composition and structure, and that of other stars.

- Discuss the Earth's orbital and gravitational relationships with the Sun and the Moon.

- Explain what comets and asteroids are, how they behave, how likely it is that one will collide with Earth in your lifetime, and what would happen if one did.

- Explain why extraterrestrial influences on your community are a natural part of Earth system evolution.

The booklet should have a model of the solar system that will help citizens understand the relative sizes of and distances between solar-system bodies.

Assessment Criteria

Think about what you have been asked to do. Scan ahead through the chapter activities to see how they might help you to meet the challenge. Work with your classmates and your teachers to define the criteria for assessing your work. Record all of this information. Make sure that you understand the criteria as well as you can before you begin. Your teacher may provide you with a sample rubric to help you get started.

Activity 1

The History and Scale of the Solar System

Goals

In this activity you will:

- Produce a scale model of the solar system.

- Identify some strengths and limitations of scale models.

- Calculate distances to objects in the solar system in astronomical units (AU), light years, and parsecs.

- Explain, in your own words, the nebular theory of the formation of the solar system.

- Explain the formation of the universe.

Think about It

Earth is part of a large number of objects that orbit around a star called the Sun.

- What objects make up the solar system? Where are they located in relation to Earth?

What do you think? Record your ideas in the form of a diagram of the solar system in your *EarthComm* notebook. Without looking ahead in this book, draw the Sun and the planets, and the distances from the Sun to the planets, as nearly to scale as you can. Be prepared to discuss your diagram with your small group and the class.

Investigate

1. Use the data in *Table 1* to make a scale model of the solar system. Try using the scale 1 m = 150,000,000 km.

   a) Divide all the distances in the first column by 150,000,000 (one hundred and fifty million). Write your scaled-down distances in your notebook, in meters.

   b) Divide all the diameters in the second column by 150,000,000. Write your scaled-down diameters in your notebook, in meters.

   c) Looking at your numbers, what major drawback is there to using the scale 1 m = 150,000,000 km?

Table I Diameters of the Sun and Planets, and Distances from the Sun		
Object	**Distance from Sun (km)**	**Diameter (km)**
Sun	0	1,391,400
Mercury	57,900,000	4878
Venus	108,209,000	12,104
Earth	149,598,770	12,756
Mars	227,900,000	6794
Jupiter	778,200,000	142,984
Saturn	1,429,200,000	120,536
Uranus	2,875,000,000	51,118
Neptune	4,504,400,000	49,528
Pluto	5,915,800,000	2302

2. Now try another scale: 1 m = 3,000,000 km (three million kilometers).

   a) Divide all the distances in the first column by 3,000,000. Write your scaled-down distances in your notebook in meters.

   b) Divide all the diameters in the second column by 3,000,000. Write your scaled-down diameters in your notebook in meters.

   c) Looking at your numbers, what major drawback is there to using the scale 1 m = 3,000,000 km?

3. Using what you have learned about scaling distances and diameters in the solar system, make models of the Sun and the planets. Each of the planets can be drawn on a different sheet of paper using a ruler to lay out the correct sizes for the different planets and the Sun.

4. To represent the distances from the Sun to the planets you will need to use a tape measure. You may want to measure the size of your stride and use this as a simple measuring tool.

To do this, stand behind a line and take five steps in as normal a way as possible and note where your last step ended. Now measure the distance from where you started to the end. Divide by five to determine how far you walk with each step. Knowing the length of your stride is an easy way to determine distances.

a) Explain the scale(s) you decided to use and your reasons for your choices.

b) Is it possible to make a model of the solar system on your school campus in which both the distances between bodies and the diameters of the bodies are to the same scale? Why or why not?

Reflecting on the Activity and the Challenge

In this activity you used ratios to make a scale model of the solar system. You found out that scale models help you appreciate the vastness of distances in the solar system. You also found out that there are some drawbacks to the use of scale models. Think about how you might use the model you made as part of your **Chapter Challenge**.

Geo Words

astronomical unit: a unit of measurement equal to the average distance between the Sun and Earth, i.e., about 149,600,000 (1.496×10^8) km.

light year: a unit of measurement equal to the distance light travels in one year, i.e., 9.46×10^{12} km.

Digging Deeper

OUR PLACE IN THE UNIVERSE

Distances in the Universe

Astronomers often study objects far from Earth. It is cumbersome to use units like kilometers (or even a million kilometers) to describe the distances to the stars and planets. For example, the star nearest to the Sun is called Proxima Centauri. It is 39,826,600,000,000 km away. (How would you say this distance?)

Astronomers get around the problem by using larger units to measure distances. When discussing distances inside the solar system, they often use the **astronomical unit** (abbreviated as AU). One AU is the average distance of the Earth from the Sun. It is equal to 149,598,770 km (about 93 million miles).

Stars are so far away that using astronomical units quickly becomes difficult, too! For example, Proxima Centauri is 266,221 AU away. This number is easier to use than kilometers, but it is still too cumbersome for most purposes. For distances to stars and galaxies, astronomers use a unit called a **light-year**. A light-year sounds as though it is a unit of time, because a year is a unit of time, but it is really the distance that light travels in a year. Because light travels extremely fast, a light-year is a very large distance. For example, the Sun is only 8 light *minutes* away from Earth, and the nearest stars are several light-years away. Light travels at a speed of 300,000 km/s. This makes a light year 9.46×10^{12} (9,460,000,000,000) km. Light from Proxima Centauri takes 4.21 years to reach Earth, so this star is 4.21 light years from Earth.

Astronomers also use a unit called the **parsec** (symbol pc) to describe large distances. One parsec equals 3.26 light years. Thus, Proxima Centauri is 1.29 pc away. The kiloparsec (1000 pc) and megaparsec (1,000,000 pc) are used for objects that are extremely far away. The nearest spiral galaxy to the Milky Way galaxy is the Andromeda galaxy. It is about 2.5 million light years, or about 767 kpc (kiloparsecs), away.

The Nebular Theory

As you created a scale model of the solar system, you probably noticed how large the Sun is in comparison to most of the planets. In fact, the Sun contains over 99% of all of the mass of the solar system. Where did all this mass come from? According to current thinking, the birthplace of our solar system was a **nebula**. A nebula is a cloud of gas and dust probably cast off from other stars that used to live in this region of our galaxy. More than 4.5 billion years ago this nebula started down the long road to the formation of a star and planets. The idea that the solar system evolved from such a swirling cloud of dust is called the nebular theory.

You can see one such nebula in the winter **constellation** Orion (see *Figure 1*), just below the three stars that make up the Belt of Orion. Through a pair of binoculars or a small, backyard-type telescope, the Orion Nebula looks like a faint green, hazy patch of light. If you were able to view this starbirth region through a much higher-power telescope, you would be able to see amazing details in the gas and dust clouds. The Orion Nebula is very much like the one that formed our star, the Sun. There are many star nurseries like this one scattered around our galaxy. On a dark night, with binoculars or a small telescope, you can see many gas clouds that are forming stars.

Figure I Orion is a prominent constellation in the night sky.

Geo Words

parsec: a unit used in astronomy to describe large distances. One parsec equals 3.26 light-years.

nebula: general term used for any "fuzzy" patch on the sky, either light or dark; a cloud of interstellar gas and dust.

constellation: a grouping of stars in the night sky into a recognizable pattern. Most of the constellations get their name from the Latin translation of one of the ancient Greek star patterns that lies within it. In more recent times, more modern astronomers introduced a number of additional groups, and there are now 88 standard configurations recognized.

Figure 2 The Keyhole Nebula. Imaged by the Hubble Space Telescope.

In the nebula that gave birth to our solar system, gravity caused the gases and dust to be drawn together into a denser cloud. At the same time, the rate of rotation (swirling) of the entire nebula gradually increased. The effect is the same as when a rotating ice skater draws his or her arms in, causing the rate of rotation to speed up. As the nebular cloud began to collapse and spin faster, it flattened out to resemble a disk, with most of the mass collapsing into the center. Matter in the rest of the disk clumped together into small masses called **planetesimals**, which then gradually collided together to form larger bodies called **protoplanetary bodies**.

At the center of the developing solar system, material kept collapsing under gravitational force. As the moving gases became more concentrated, the temperature and pressure of the center of the cloud started to rise. The same kind of thing happens when you pump up a bicycle tire with a tire pump: the pump gets warmer as the air is compressed. When you let the air out of a tire, the opposite occurs and the air gets colder as it expands rapidly. When the temperature in the center of the gas cloud reached about 15 million degrees Celsius, hydrogen atoms in the gas combined or fused to create helium atoms. This process, called **nuclear fusion**, is the source of the energy from the Sun. A star—the Sun—was born!

Fusion reactions inside the Sun create very high pressure, and like a bomb, threaten to blow the Sun apart. The Sun doesn't fly apart under all this outward pressure, however. The Sun is in a state of equilibrium. The gravity of the Sun is pulling on each part of it and keeps the Sun together as it radiates energy out in all directions, providing solar energy to the Earth community.

The Birth of the Planets

The rest of the solar system formed in the swirling disk of material surrounding the newborn Sun. Nine planets, 67 satellites (with new ones still being discovered!), and a large number of comets and asteroids formed. The larger objects were formed mostly in the flat disk surrounding where the Sun was forming.

Geo Words

planetesimal: one of the small bodies (usually micrometers to kilometers in diameter) that formed from the solar nebula and eventually grew into protoplanets.

protoplanetary body: a clump of material, formed in the early stages of solar system formation, which was the forerunner of the planets we see today.

nuclear fusion: a nuclear process that releases energy when lightweight nuclei combine to form heavier nuclei.

Four of these planets, shown in *Figure 3*—Mercury, Venus, Earth, and Mars—are called the **terrestrial** ("Earth-like") **planets**. They formed in the inner part of our solar system, where temperatures in the original nebula were high. They are relatively small, rocky bodies. Some have molten centers, with a layer of rock called a mantle outside their centers, and a surface called a crust. The Earth's crust is its outer layer. Even the deepest oil wells do not penetrate the crust.

The larger planets shown in *Figure 3*—Jupiter, Saturn, Uranus, and Neptune—consist mostly of dense fluids like liquid hydrogen. These **gas giants** formed in the colder, outer parts of the early solar nebula. They have solid rocky cores about the size of Earth, covered with layers of hydrogen in both gas and liquid form. They lie far from the Sun and their surfaces are extremely cold.

Pluto is the most distant planet from the Sun. Some astronomers do not even classify Pluto as a planet. Instead, they put it in the category of smaller icy bodies that are found in the outer solar system. Pluto is very different from the terrestrial or the gaseous planets. If anything, it resembles the icy moons of the gas giants. Some scientists think that it may not have been part of the original solar system but instead was captured later by the Sun's gravity, or that it is a moon of an outer planet thrown into a unique tilted orbit around the Sun. Currently, there is a controversy among planetary scientists about whether to include Pluto among the "official" planets! If Pluto were discovered today (instead of in 1930), it probably would not be classified as a planet.

Figure 3 Composite image of the planets in the solar system, plus the Moon.

Geo Words

terrestrial planets: any of the planets Mercury, Venus, Earth, or Mars, or a planet similar in size, composition, and density to the Earth. A planet that consists mainly of rocky material.

gas giant planets: the outer solar system planets: Jupiter, Saturn, Uranus, and Neptune, composed mostly of hydrogen, helium, and methane, and having a density of less than 2 gm/cm^2.

EarthComm

Geo Words

comet: a chunk of frozen gases, ice, and rocky debris that orbits the Sun.

asteroid: a small planetary body in orbit around the Sun, larger than a meteoroid (a particle in space less than a few meters in diameter) but smaller than a planet. Many asteroids can be found in a belt between the orbits of Mars and Jupiter.

There are trillions of **comets** and **asteroids** scattered throughout the solar system. Earth and other solar-system bodies are scarred by impact craters formed when comets and asteroids collided with them. On Earth, erosion has removed obvious signs of many of these craters. Astronomers see these comets and asteroids as the leftovers from the formation of the solar system. Asteroids are dark, rocky bodies that orbit the Sun at different distances. Many are found between the orbits of Mars and Jupiter, making up what is called the asteroid belt. Many others have orbits outside of the asteroid belt. Comets are mixtures of ice and dust grains. They exist mainly in the outer solar system, but when their looping orbits bring them close to the Sun, their ices begin to melt. That is when you can see tails streaming out from them in the direction away from the Sun. Some comets come unexpectedly into the inner solar system. Others have orbits that bring them close to the Sun at regular intervals. For example, the orbit of Halley's comet brings it into the inner solar system every 76 years.

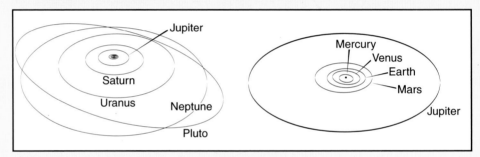

Figure 4 Two diagrams are required to show the orbits of the planets to scale.

Where is the Solar System in Our Galaxy?

Have you ever seen the Milky Way? It is a swath of light, formed by the glow of billions of stars, which stretches across the dark night sky. From Earth, this band of celestial light is best seen from dark-sky viewing sites. Binoculars and backyard-type telescopes magnify the view and reveal individual stars and nebulae. Unfortunately, for those who like to view the night sky, light pollution in densely populated areas makes it impossible to see the Milky Way even on nights when the atmosphere is clear and cloudless.

Galaxies are classified according to their shape: elliptical, spiral, or irregular. Our home galaxy is a flat spiral, a pinwheel-shaped collection of stars held together by their mutual gravitational attraction. Our galaxy shown in *Figure 5* is called the Milky Way Galaxy, or just the galaxy. Our solar system is located in one of the spiral arms about two-thirds of the way out from the center of the galaxy. What is called the Milky Way is the view along the flat part of our galaxy. When you look at the Milky Way, you are looking out through the galaxy parallel to the

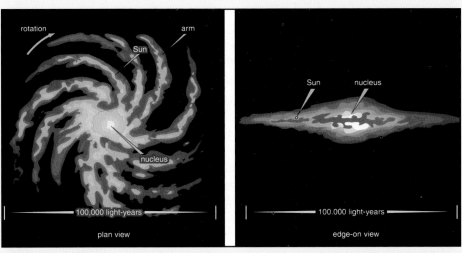

rotation   arm

Sun

nucleus

100,000 light-years

plan view

Sun   nucleus

100.000 light-years

edge-on view

Figure 5 The Milky Way Galaxy. Our solar system is located in a spiral band about two-thirds of the way from the nucleus of the galaxy.

Geo Words

cosmologist: a scientist who studies the origin and dynamics of the universe.

plane of its disk. The individual stars you see dotting the night sky are just the ones nearest to Earth in the galaxy. When you view the Milky Way, you are "looking through" those nearest stars to see the more distant parts of the galaxy. In a sense, you are looking at our galaxy from the inside. In other directions, you look through the nearest stars to see out into intergalactic space!

Our Milky Way Galaxy formed about 10 billion years ago and is one of billions of galaxies in the universe. The universe itself formed somewhere between 12 to 14 billion years ago in an event called the Big Bang. This sounds like the universe began in an explosion, but it did not. In the beginning, at what a scientist would call "time zero," the universe consisted almost entirely of energy, concentrated into a volume smaller than a grain of sand. The temperatures were unimaginably high. Then the universe expanded, extremely rapidly, and as it expanded the temperature dropped and matter was formed from some of the original energy. **Cosmologists** (scientists who study the origin and dynamics of the universe) think that most of the matter in the universe was formed within minutes of time zero! The expansion and cooling that started with the Big Bang continues to this day.

The galaxies and stars are the visible evidence of the Big Bang, but there is other, unseen evidence that it happened. It's called the cosmic background radiation, which is radiation that is left over from the initial moments of the Big Bang. Astronomers using special instruments sensitive to low-energy radio waves have detected it coming in from all directions from the universe. The existence of the cosmic background radiation is generally considered to be solid evidence of how the Big Bang happened.

Check Your Understanding

1. What are the distances represented by a light-year, an astronomical unit, and a parsec?

2. Which of the units in Question 1 would you use to describe each of the following? Justify your choice.

   a) Distances to various stars (but not our Sun)?

   b) Distances to various planets within our solar system?

   c) Widths of galaxies?

3. In your own words, explain the nebular theory for the beginning of our solar system.

4. Briefly describe the origin of the universe.

Understanding and Applying What You Have Learned

1. Using the second scale (1 m = 3,000,000 km) you used for distance in your model of the solar system:

   a) How far away would Proxima Centauri be from Earth?
   b) How far away would the Andromeda galaxy be on your scale, given that Andromeda is 767 kiloparsecs or 2.5 million light years away?

2. The Moon is 384,000 km from Earth and has a diameter of 3476 km. Calculate the diameter of the Moon and its distance from the Earth using the scale of the model you developed in the **Investigate** section.

3. Refer again to *Table 1*. If the Space Shuttle could travel at 100,000 km/hr, how long would it take to go from Earth to each of the following objects? Assume that each object is as close to the Earth as it can be in its orbit.

   a) The Moon?
   b) Mars?
   c) Pluto?

4. What is the largest distance possible between any two planets in the solar system?

5. Use your understanding of a light-year and the distances from the Sun shown in *Table 1*. Calculate how many minutes it takes for sunlight to reach each of the nine planets in the solar system. Then use the unit "light-minutes" (how far light travels in one minute) to describe the *distances* to each object.

6. Write down your school address in the following ways:

   a) As you would normally address an envelope.
   b) To receive a letter from another country.
   c) To receive a letter from a friend who lives at the center of our galaxy.
   d) To receive a letter from a friend who lives in a distant galaxy.

Preparing for the Chapter Challenge

Begin to develop your brochure for the **Chapter Challenge**. In your own words, explain your community's position relative to the Earth, Sun, the other planets in our solar system, and the entire universe. Include a few paragraphs explaining what your scale model represents and how you chose the scale or scales you used.

Inquiring Further

1. **Solar-system walk**

   Create a "solar-system walk" on your school grounds or your neighborhood. Draw the Sun and the planets to scale on the sidewalk in chalk. Pace off the distances between the Sun and the nine planets at a scale that is appropriate for the site.

2. **Scaling the nearest stars**

   Look up the distances to the five stars nearest to the Sun. Where would they be in your scale model? To show their location, would you need a map of your state? Country? Continent? The world?

3. **Nuclear fusion**

   Find out more about the process of nuclear fusion. Explain how and why energy is released in the process by which hydrogen atoms are converted into helium atoms within the Sun. Be sure to include Albert Einstein's famous equation, $E = mc^2$, in your explanation, and explain what it means.

4. **Star formation**

   Write a newspaper story about star formation. Visit the *EarthComm* web site to find information available on the web sites of the Hubble Space Telescope and the European Southern Observatory to find examples of star-forming nebulae in the galaxy. How are they similar? How are they different? What instruments do astronomers use to study these nebulae?

Activity 2   The Earth—Moon System

Goals

In this activity you will:

• Investigate lunar phases using a model and observations in your community.

• Investigate the general idea of tidal forces.

• Understand the role of the Earth, the Moon, and the Sun in creating tides on Earth.

• Understand the Earth–Moon system and the Moon's likely origin.

• Compare the appearance of the Moon to other solar-system bodies.

Think about It

Think about the last time that you gazed at a full Moon.

• What happened to make the Moon look the way it does?
• What is the origin of the Moon?
• How does the Moon affect the Earth?

What do you think? Record your ideas about these questions in your *EarthComm* notebook. Be prepared to discuss your responses with your small group and the class.

Investigate

Part A: Lunar Phases

1. Attach a pencil to a white Styrofoam® ball (at least 5 cm in diameter) by pushing the pencil into the foam. Set up a light source on one side of the room. Use a lamp with a bright bulb (150-W) without a lampshade or have a partner hold a flashlight pointed in your direction. Close the shades and turn off the overhead lights.

2. Stand approximately 2 m in front of the light source. Hold the pencil and ball at arm's length away with your arm extended towards the light source. The ball represents the Moon. The light source is the Sun. You are standing in the place of Earth.

   a) How much of the illuminated Moon surface is visible from Earth? Draw a sketch of you, the light source, and the foam ball to explain this.

3. Keeping the ball straight in front of you, turn 45° to your left but stay standing in one place.

   a) How much of the illuminated Moon surface is visible from Earth?

   b) Has the amount of light illuminating the Moon changed?

   c) Which side of the Moon is illuminated? Which side of the Moon is still dark? Draw another diagram in your notebook of the foam ball, you, and the light source in order to explain what you see.

4. Continue rotating counterclockwise away from the light source while holding the ball directly in front of you. Observe how the illuminated portion of the Moon changes shape as you turn 45° each time.

a) After you pass the full Moon phase, which side of the Moon is illuminated? Which side of the Moon is dark?

b) How would the Moon phases appear from Earth if the Moon rotated in the opposite direction?

 Be careful not to poke the sharp end of the pencil into your skin while pushing the pencil into the foam. Use caution around the light source. It is hot. Do not touch the Styrofoam to the light.

Part B: Observing the Moon

1. Observe the Moon for a period of at least four weeks. During this time you will notice that the apparent shape of the Moon changes.

   a) Construct a calendar chart to record what you see and when you see it. Sketch the Moon, along with any obvious surface features that you can see with the naked eye or binoculars.

   b) Do you always see the Moon in the night sky?

   c) How many days does it take to go through a cycle of changes?

   d) What kinds of surface features do you see on the Moon?

   e) Label each phase of the Moon correctly and explain briefly the positions of the Sun, the Earth, and the Moon during each phase.

 Tell an adult before you go outside to observe the Moon.

Part C: Tides and Lunar Phases

1. Investigate the relationship between tides and phases of the Moon.

   a) On a sheet of graph paper, plot the high tides for each city and each day in January shown in *Table 1*. To prepare the graph, look at the data to find the range of values. This will help you plan the scales for the vertical axis (tide height) and horizontal axis (date).

   b) On the same graph, plot the Moon phase using a bold line. Moon phases were assigned values that range from zero (new Moon) to four (full Moon).

2. Repeat this process for low tides.

3. Answer the following questions in your *EarthComm* notebook:

   a) What relationships exist between high tides and phases of the Moon?

   b) What relationships exist between low tides and phases of the Moon?

   c) Summarize your ideas about how the Moon affects the tides. Record your ideas in your *EarthComm* notebook.

Table 1 Heights of High and Low Tides in Five Coastal Locations during January 2001 (All heights are in feet.)												
			Breakwater, Delaware		Savannah, Georgia		Portland, Maine		Cape Hatteras, North Carolina		New London, Connecticut	
Date	Moon Phase	Moon Phase	High	Low	High	Low	High	Low	High	Low	High	Low
1/3/01	First Quarter	2	3.6	0.2	7.3	0.5	8.5	1	2.6	0.2	2.4	0.3
1/6/01	Waxing Gibbous	3	4.5	0	8.2	0.5	9.7	0.1	3.4	−0.4	3	−0.2
1/10/01	Full Moon	4	5.6	−0.9	9.4	−1.5	11.6	−1.9	4.2	−0.8	3.5	−0.7
1/13/01	Waning Gibbous	3	5.1	−0.7	8.8	−0.9	11	−1.4	3.7	−0.6	3	−0.5
1/16/01	Last Quarter	2	4.1	−0.1	7.9	−0.2	9.7	0.1	3	−0.2	2.7	0
1/20/01	Waning Crescent	1	4.3	0.1	7.3	0.2	9.4	0.2	3.2	0	2.8	0
1/24/01	New Moon	0	4.6	0	8.1	−0.1	9.7	−0.1	3.3	−0.1	2.8	−0.1
1/30/01	Waxing Crescent	1	3.7	0.1	7.4	0.1	8.7	0.6	2.6	0	2.4	0.2

4. *Table 1* shows data from the month of January 2001. At the *EarthComm* web site, you can obtain tidal data during the same period that you are doing your Moon observations. Select several cities nearest your community.

a) Record the highest high tide and the lowest low tide data for each city. Choose at least eight different days to compare. Correlate these records to the appearance of the Moon during your observation period. Make a table like *Table 1* showing high and low tides for each location.

b) What do you notice about the correlation between high and low tides and the appearance of the Moon?

Part D: Tidal Forces and the Earth System
1. Use the data in *Table 2*.

a) Plot this data on graph paper.

Label the vertical axis "Number of Days in a Year" and the horizontal axis "Years before Present." Give your graph a title.

b) Calculate the rate of decrease in the number of days per 100 million years (that is, calculate the slope of the line).

2. Answer the following questions:

a) How many fewer days are there every 10 million years? every million years?

b) Calculate the rate of decrease per year.

c) Do you think that changes in the number of days in a year reflect changes in the time it takes the Earth to orbit the Sun, or changes in the time it takes the Earth to rotate on its axis? In other words, is a year getting shorter, or are days getting longer? How would you test your idea?

Table 2 Change in Rotation of Earth Due to Tidal Forces		
Period	**Date (millions of years ago)**	**Length of Year (days)**
Precambrian	600	424
Cambrian	500	412
Ordovician	425	404
Silurian	405	402
Devonian	345	396
Mississippian	310	393
Pennsylvanian	280	390
Permian	230	385
Triassic	180	381
Jurassic	135	377
Cretaceous	65	371
Present	0	365.25

Reflecting on the Activity and the Challenge

In this activity you used a simple model and observations of the Moon to explore lunar phases and surface characteristics of the Moon. You also explored the relationship between tides and the phases of the Moon. The tides also have an effect that decreases the number of days in a year over time. That's because tides slow the rotation of the Earth, making each day longer. You now understand that tides slow the rotation of the Earth, and how this has affected the Earth. This will be useful when describing the Earth's gravitational relationships with the Moon for the **Chapter Challenge**.

Geo Words

accretion: the process whereby dust and gas accumulated into larger bodies like stars and planets.

Digging Deeper

THE EVOLUTION OF THE EARTH–MOON SYSTEM

The Formation of the Earth and Moon

Figure 1 The Moon is the only natural satellite of Earth.

You learned in the previous activity that during the formation of the solar system, small fragments of rocky material called planetesimals stuck together in a process called **accretion**. Larger and larger pieces then came together to form the terrestrial planets. The leftovers became the raw materials for the asteroids and comets. Eventually, much of this material was "swept up" by the newborn inner planets. Collisions between the planets and the leftover planetesimals were common. This was how the Earth was born and lived its early life, but how was the Moon formed?

Scientists theorize that an object the size of Mars collided with and probably shattered the early Earth. The remnants of this titanic collision formed a ring of debris around what was left of our planet. Eventually this material accreted into a giant satellite, which became the Moon. Creating an Earth–Moon system from such a collision is not easy. In computer simulations, the Moon sometimes gets thrown off as a separate planet or collides with the Earth and is destroyed. However, scientists have created accurate models that predict the orbit and composition of both the Earth and Moon from a collision with a Mars-sized object. The Moon's orbit (its distance from the Earth, and its speed of movement) became adjusted so that the gravitational pull of the Earth is just offset by the centrifugal force that tends to make the Moon move off in a straight line rather than circle the Earth. After the Earth–Moon system became stabilized, incoming planetesimals continued to bombard the two bodies, causing impact craters. The Earth's surface has evolved since then. Because the Earth is geologically an active place, very few craters remain. The Moon, however, is geologically inactive. *Figure 2* shows the Moon's pockmarked face that has preserved its early history of collisions.

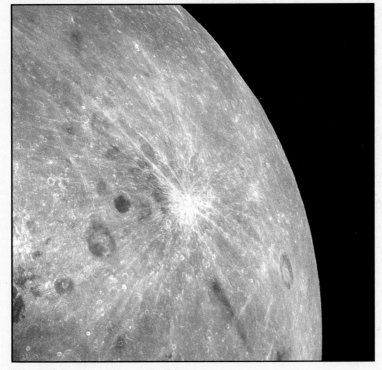

Figure 2 Impact craters on the Moon.

When the Earth was first formed, its day probably lasted only about six hours. Over time, Earth days have been getting longer and longer. In other words, the Earth takes longer to make one full rotation on its axis. On the other hand, scientists have no reason to think that the time it takes for the Earth to make one complete revolution around the Sun has changed through geologic time. The result is that there are fewer and fewer days in a year, as you saw in the **Investigate** section. Why is the Earth's rotation slowing down? It has to do with the gravitational forces between the Earth, the Moon, and the Sun, which create ocean tides.

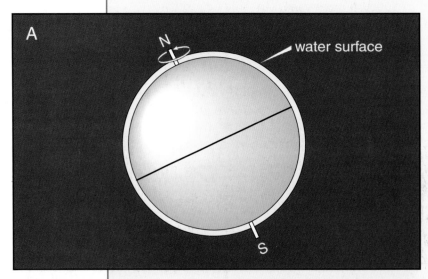

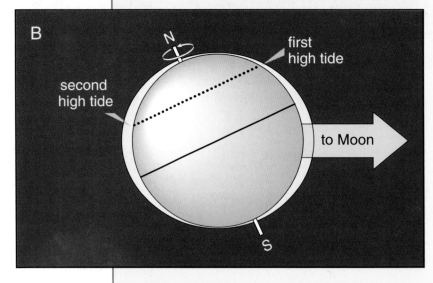

Tides

The gravitational pull between the Earth and the Moon is strong. This force actually stretches the solid Earth about 20 cm along the Earth–Moon line. This stretching is called the Earth tide. The water in the oceans is stretched in the same way. The stretching effect in the oceans is greater than in the solid Earth, because water flows more easily than the rock in the Earth's interior. These bulges in the oceans, called the ocean tide, are what create the high and low tides (see *Figure 3*). It probably will seem strange

Figure 3 Schematic diagram of tides. Diagram A illustrates how the ocean surface would behave without the Moon and the Sun (no tides). Diagram B illustrates, that in the presence of the Moon and the Sun, shorelines away from the poles experience two high tides and two low tides per day.

Geo Words

spring tide: the tides of increased range occurring semimonthly near the times of full Moon and new Moon.

to you that there are two bulges, one pointing toward the Moon and the other away from the Moon. If the tides are caused by the pull of the Moon, why is there not just one bulge pointing toward the Moon? The explanation is not simple. If you are curious, you can pursue it further in the **Inquiring Further** section of this activity.

As the Earth rotates through a 24-h day, shorelines experience two high tides—one when the tidal bulge that points toward the Moon passes by, and once when the tidal bulge that points away from the Moon passes by. The tidal cycle is not exactly 24 h. By the time the Earth has completed one rotation (in 24 h), the Moon is in a slightly different place because it has traveled along about 1/30 of the way in its orbit around the Earth in that 24-h period. That's why the Moon rises and sets about 50 min. later each day, and why high and low tides are about 50 min. later each day. Because there are two high tides each day, each high tide is about 25 min. later than the previous one.

The gravitational pull of the Sun also affects tides. Even though it has much greater mass than the Moon, its tidal effect is not as great, because it is so much farther away from the Earth. The Moon is only 386,400 km away from the Earth, whereas the Sun is nearly 150,000,000 km away. The Moon exerts 2.4 times more tide-producing force on the Earth than the Sun does. The changing relative positions of the Sun, the Moon, and the Earth cause variations in high and low tides.

The lunar phase that occurs when the Sun and the Moon are both on the same side of the Earth is called the new Moon. At a new Moon, the Moon is in the same direction as the Sun and the Sun and Moon rise together in the sky. The tidal pull of the Sun and the Moon are adding together, and high tides are even higher than usual, and low tides are even lower than usual. These tides are called **spring tides** (see *Figure 4*). Don't be confused by this use of the word "spring." The spring tides have nothing to do with the spring season of the year! Spring tides happen when the Sun and Moon are in general alignment and raising larger tides. This also happens at another lunar phase: the full Moon. At full Moon, the Moon and Sun are on opposite sides of the Earth. When the Sun is setting, the full Moon is rising. When the Sun is rising, the full Moon is setting. Spring tides also occur during a full Moon, when the Sun and the Moon are on opposite sides of the Earth. Therefore, spring tides occur twice a month at both the new-Moon and full-Moon phases.

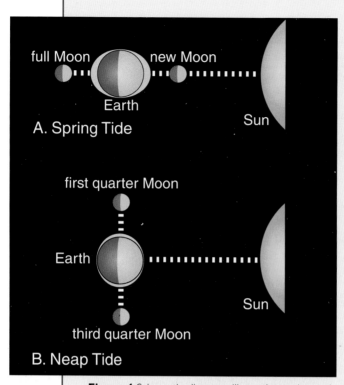

full Moon   new Moon

Earth

A. Spring Tide   Sun

first quarter Moon

Earth   Sun

third quarter Moon

B. Neap Tide

Figure 4 Schematic diagrams illustrating spring and neap tides.

When the line between the Earth and Sun makes a right angle with the line from the Earth to the Moon, as shown in *Figure 4*, their tidal effects tend to counteract one another. At those times, high tides are lower than usual and low tides are higher than usual. These tides are called **neap tides**. They occur during first quarter and third-quarter Moons. As with spring tides, neap tides occur twice a month.

The tide is like a kind of ocean wave. The high and low tides travel around the Earth once every tidal cycle, that is, twice per day. This wave lags behind the Earth's rotation, because it is forced by the Moon to travel faster than it would if it were free to move on its own. That's why the time of high tide generally does not coincide with the time that the Moon is directly overhead. The friction of this lag gradually slows the Earth's rotation.

Another way to look at tides is that the tidal bulges are always located on the sides of the Earth that point toward and away from the Moon, while the Earth with its landmasses is rotating below the bulges. Each time land on the spinning Earth encounters a tidal bulge there is a high tide at that location. The mass of water in the tidal bulge acts a little like a giant brake shoe encircling the Earth. Each time the bulge of water hits a landmass, energy is lost by friction. The water heats up slightly. (This is in addition to the energy lost by waves hitting the shore, which also heats the water by a small fraction of a degree.) Over long periods of time, the tidal bulge has the effect of slowing down the rotation of the Earth, and actually causing the Moon to move away from the Earth. The current rate of motion of the Moon away from the Earth is a few centimeters a year. This has been established by bouncing laser beams off of reflectors on the Moon to measure its distance. Although the Moon's orbit is not circular and is complex in its shape, measurements over many years have established that the

Geo Words

neap tide: the tides of decreased range occurring semimonthly near the times of the first and last quarter of the Moon.

Moon is indeed moving away from the Earth. Special super-accurate clocks have also established that the day is gradually becoming slightly longer as well, because of this same phenomenon, called "tidal friction." The day (one rotation of the Earth on its axis) has gradually become longer over geologic time. As the Earth system evolves, cycles change as well.

In this activity you limited the factors that cause and control the tides to the astronomical forces. These factors play only one part. The continents and their different shapes and ocean basins also play a large role in shaping the nature of the tides. Although many places on Earth have two high tides and two low tides every day (a semidiurnal tide), some places experience only one high tide and one low tide every day (a diurnal tide). There are still other places that have some combination of diurnal and semidiurnal tides (mixed tides). In these places (like along the west coast of the United States) there are two high tides and two low tides per day, but the heights of the successive highs and lows are considerably different from one another.

Figure 5 How do tides affect coastal communities?

Check Your Understanding

1. How did the Moon likely form?

2. Describe the relative positions of the Earth, the Moon, and the Sun for a spring tide and for a neap tide.

3. What effect have tides had on the length of a day? Explain.

Understanding and Applying What You Have Learned

1. Refer back to the graph of the changing length of the day that you produced in the investigation. Think about the causes of tidal friction and the eventual outcome of tidal friction. Predict how long you think the day will eventually be. Explain the reasoning for your prediction.

2. Think about the roles that the Sun and Moon play in causing the ocean tides.

   a) If the Earth had no Moon, how would ocean tides be different? Explain your answer.
   b) How would the ocean tides be different if the Moon were twice as close to the Earth as it is now?
   c) What differences would there be in the ocean tides if the Moon orbited the Earth half as fast as it does now?

3. Look at Figure 3B on page E20. Pretend that you are standing on a shoreline at the position of the dotted line. You stand there for 24 h and 50 min, observing the tides as they go up and down.

   a) What differences would do you notice, if any, between the two high tides that day?
   b) Redraw the diagram from *Figure 3B*, only this time, make the arrow to the moon parallel to the equator. Make sure you adjust the tidal bulge to reflect this new position of the moon relative to the Earth. What differences would you now see between the two high tides that day (assuming that you are still at the same place)?
   c) Every month, the moon goes through a cycle in which its orbit migrates from being directly overhead south of the equator to being directly overhead north of the equator and back again. To complicate things, the maximum latitude at which the moon is directly overhead varies between about 28.5° north and south, to about 18.5° north and south (this variation is on a 16.8 year cycle). How do you think the monthly cycle relates to the relative heights of successive high tides (or successive low tides)?

4. Return to the tide tables for the ocean shoreline that is nearest to your community (your teacher may provide a copy of these to you).

   a) When is the next high tide going to occur? Find a calendar to determine the phase of the Moon. Figure out how to combine these two pieces of information to determine whether this next high tide is the bulge toward the Moon or away from the Moon.
   b) The tide tables also provide the predicted height of the tides. Look down the table to see how much variation there is in the tide heights. Recalling that the Sun also exerts tidal force on the ocean water, try to draw a picture of the positions of the Earth, Moon, and Sun for:
   i)   The highest high tide you see on the tidal chart.
   ii) The lowest high tide you see on the tidal chart.
   iii) The lowest low tide you see on the tidal chart.

5. The questions below refer to your investigation of lunar phases.

   a) Explain why the moon looks different in the sky during different times of the month.

b) What advantage is there to knowing the phases of the Moon? Who benefits from this knowledge?

c) It takes 27.32166 days for the Moon to complete one orbit around the Earth. The Moon also takes 27.32166 days to complete the rotation about its axis. How does this explain why we see the same face of the Moon all the time?

Preparing for the Chapter Challenge

Write several paragraphs explaining the evolution of the Earth–Moon system, how mutual gravitational attraction can affect a community through the tides, and how the changing length of the day could someday affect the Earth system. Be sure to support your positions with evidence.

Inquiring Further

1. **Tidal bulge**

   Use your school library or the library of a nearby college or university, or the Internet, to investigate the reason why the tidal bulge extends in the direction away from the Moon as well as in the direction toward the Moon. Why does the Earth have two tidal bulges instead of just one, on the side closest to the Moon?

2. **Tidal forces throughout the solar system**

   Tidal forces are at work throughout the solar system. Investigate how Jupiter's tidal forces affect Jupiter's Moons Europa, Io, Ganymede, and Callisto. Are tidal forces involved with Saturn's rings? Write a short report explaining how tidal friction is affecting these solar-system bodies.

3. **Impact craters**

   Search for examples of impact craters throughout the solar system. Do all the objects in the solar system show evidence of impacts: the planets, the moons, and the asteroids? Are there any impact craters on the Earth, besides the Meteor Crater in Arizona?

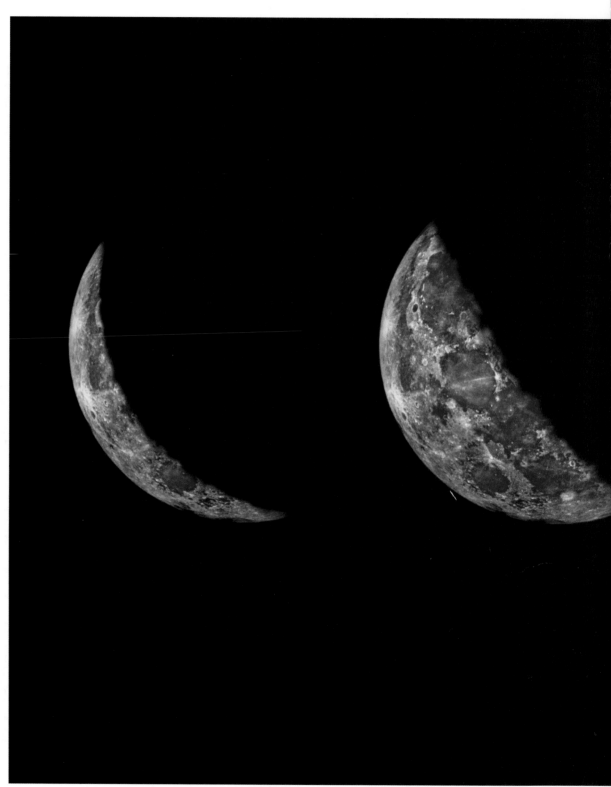

Activity 3　　Orbits and Effects

Goals

In this activity you will:

- Measure the major axis and distance between the foci of an ellipse.

- Understand the relationship between the distance between the foci and eccentricity of an ellipse.

- Calculate the eccentricity of the Earth's orbit.

- Draw the Earth's changing orbit in relation to the Sun.

- Explain how the Earth's changing orbit and its rotation rate could affect its climate.

- Draw the orbits of a comet and an asteroid in relation to the Earth and the Sun.

Think about It

The Earth rotates on its axis as it revolves around the Sun, some 150,000,000 km away. The axis of rotation is now tilted about 23.5°.

- What is the shape of the Earth's orbit around the Sun?
- How might a change in the shape of the Earth's orbit or its axis of rotation affect weather and climate?

What do you think? In your *EarthComm* notebook, draw a picture of the Earth's orbit around the Sun, as seen from above the solar system. Record your ideas about how this shape affects weather and climate. Be prepared to discuss your responses with your small group and the class.

Investigate

1. Draw an ellipse using the following steps:

   • Fold a piece of paper in half.

   • Use a straightedge to draw a horizontal line across the width of the paper along the fold.

   • Put two dots 10 cm apart on the line toward the center of the line. Label the left dot "A" and the right dot "B."

   • Tape the sheet of paper to a piece of thick cardboard, and put two pushpins into points A and B. The positions of the pushpins will be the foci of the ellipse.

   • Tie two ends of a piece of strong string together to make a loop. Make the knot so that when you stretch out the loop with your fingers into a line, it is 12 cm long.

   • Put the string over the two pins and pull the loop tight using a pencil point, as shown in the diagram.

   • Draw an ellipse with the pencil. Do this by putting the pencil point inside the loop and then moving the pencil while keeping the string pulled tight with the pencil point.

   a) Draw a small circle around either point A or point B and label it "Sun."

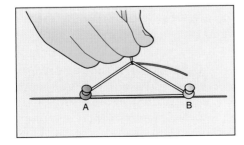

2. Repeat the process using the following measurements and labels:

   • Two points 8 cm apart labeled C and D (1 cm inside of points A and B).

   • Two points 6 cm apart, labeled E and F (2 cm inside of points A and B).

   • Two points 4 cm apart, labeled G and H (3 cm inside points A and B).

   • Two points 2 cm apart, labeled I and J (4 cm inside points A and B).

3. Copy the data table on the next page into your notebook.

   a) Measure the width (in centimeters) of ellipse "AB" at its widest point. This is the major axis, L (see diagram on the next page). Record this in your data table.

   b) Record the length of the major axis for each ellipse in your data table.

   c) Record the distance between the two foci, d (the distance between the two pushpins) for each ellipse in your data table (see diagram).

   d) The eccentricity E of an ellipse is equal to the distance between the two foci divided by the length of the major axis. Calculate the eccentricity of each of your ellipses using the equation $E = d/L$, where d is the distance between the foci and L is the length of the major axis. Record the eccentricity of each ellipse.

 Be sure the cardboard is thicker than the points of the pins. If not, use two or more pieces of cardboard.

Ellipse	Major Axis (L) (cm)	Distance between the Foci (d) (cm)	Eccentricity E = d/L
AB		10	
CD		8	
EF		6	
GH		4	
IJ		2	

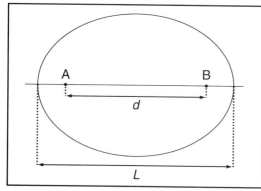

Ellipse with foci AB showing major axis length L and distance between the foci d.

4. Study your data table to find a relationship between the distance between the foci and the eccentricity of an ellipse.

   a) Record the relationship between the distance between the foci and the eccentricity in your notebook.

b) Think of your ellipses as the orbits of planets around the Sun. Does the distance to the center of the Sun stay the same in any orbit?

c) Which orbit has the least variation in distance from the Sun throughout its orbit? Which has the most?

5. Earth's orbit has an eccentricity of about 0.017. Compare this value to the ellipse with the lowest eccentricity of those you drew.

a) Why does it make sense to describe Earth's orbit as "nearly circular"?

Reflecting on the Activity and the Challenge

In this activity, you explored a geometric figure called an ellipse. You also learned how to characterize ellipses by their eccentricity. The orbits of all nine planets in our solar system are ellipses, with the Sun at one focus of the ellipse representing the orbit for each planet. As you will see, although Earth's orbit is very nearly circular (only slightly eccentric), the shape of its orbit is generally believed to play an important role in long-term changes in the climate. The shape of the Earth's orbit is not responsible for the seasons. You will need this information when describing the Earth's orbital relationships with the Sun and the Moon in the **Chapter Challenge**.

Digging Deeper

ECCENTRICITY, AXIAL TILT, PRECESSION, AND INCLINATION

Eccentricity

Geo Words

eccentricity: the ratio of the distance between the foci and the length of the major axis of an ellipse.

After many years of analyzing observational data on the motions of the planets, the astronomer Johannes Kepler (1571–1630) developed three laws of planetary motion that govern orbits. The first law states that the orbit of each planet around the Sun is an ellipse with the Sun at one focus. The second law, as shown in *Figure 1*, explains that as a planet moves around the Sun in its orbit, it covers equal areas in equal times. The third law states that the time a planet takes to complete one orbit is related to its average distance from the Sun.

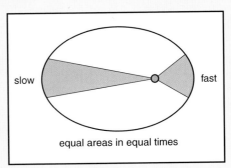

Figure 1 Kepler's Second Law states that a line joining a planet and the Sun sweeps out equal areas in equal intervals of time.

As you saw in the **Investigate** section, the shape of an ellipse can vary from a circle to a very highly elongated shape, and even to a straight line. The more flattened the ellipse is, the greater its eccentricity. Values of **eccentricity** range from zero for a circle, to one, for a straight line. (A mathematician would say that the circle and the line are "special cases" of an ellipse.) The two planets in the solar system with the most elliptical orbits are Mercury, the closest planet, and Pluto, the farthest one. Both have eccentricities greater than 0.2. The orbit of Mars is also fairly elliptical, with an eccentricity of 0.09. In comparison, the Earth's orbit is an ellipse with an eccentricity of 0.017. (This is a much lower value than even the eccentricity of ellipse IJ in the investigation, which looked much like a circle.) If you were to draw an ellipse with an eccentricity of 0.017 on a large sheet of paper, most people would call it a circle. It's eccentric enough, however, to make the Earth's distance from the Sun vary between 153,000,000 km and 147,000,000 km. To make things more complicated, the eccentricity of the Earth's orbit changes over time, because of complicated effects having to do with the weak gravitational pull of other planets in the solar system. Over the course of about 100,000 years, the Earth's orbit ranges from nearly circular (very close to zero eccentricity) to more elliptical (with an eccentricity of about 0.05).

Planetary scientists have found that some solar-system objects have highly elliptical orbits. Comets are a well-known example. As they move closer

Figure 2 The comet's head or coma is the fuzzy haze that surrounds the comet's true nucleus.

to the Sun, the icy mix that makes up a comet's nucleus begins to turn into gas and stream away. The result is a ghostly looking tail and a fuzzy "shroud," that you can see in *Figure 2*. It is called a **coma**, and it forms around the nucleus. When a comet gets far enough away from the Sun, the ices are no longer turned to gas and the icy nucleus continues on its way.

Another good example is the distant, icy world Pluto. Throughout much of its year (which lasts 248 Earth years) this little outpost of the solar system has no measurable atmosphere. It does have a highly eccentric orbit, and its distance from the Sun varies from 29.5 to 49.5 AU. The strength of solar heating varies by a factor of almost four during Pluto's orbit around the Sun. As Pluto gets closest to the Sun, Pluto receives just enough solar heating to vaporize some of its ices. This creates a thin, measurable atmosphere. Then, as the planet moves farther out in its orbit, this atmosphere freezes out and falls to the surface as a frosty covering. Some scientists predict that when Pluto is only 20 years past its point of being closest to the Sun, its atmosphere will collapse as the temperature decreases.

Axial Tilt (Obliquity)

The Earth's axis of rotation is now tilted at an angle of 23.5° to the plane of the Earth's orbit around the Sun, as seen in *Figure 3*. Over a cycle lasting about 41,000 years, the axial tilt varies from 22.1° to 24.5°. The greater the angle of tilt, the greater the difference in solar energy, and therefore temperature, between summer and winter. This small change, combined with other long-term changes in the Earth's orbit, is thought to be responsible for the Earth's ice ages.

Precession

The Earth also has a slight wobble, the same as the slow wobble of a spinning top. This wobble is called the **precession** of the Earth's axis. It is caused by differences in the gravitational pull of the Moon and the Sun on the Earth. It takes about 25,725 years for this wobble to complete a cycle. As the axis wobbles, the timing of the seasons changes. Winter occurs when a hemisphere, northern or southern, is tilted away from the Sun. Nowadays, the Earth is slightly closer to the Sun during winter (January 5) in the Northern Hemisphere. Don't let anybody tell you that winter happens because the Earth is farthest from the Sun! The Earth's orbit is nearly circular! Also, even if a particular hemisphere of the Earth is tilted towards the Sun, it is not significantly closer to the Sun than the other hemisphere, which is tilted away.

Geo Words

coma: a spherical cloud of material surrounding the head of a comet. This material is mostly gas that the Sun has caused to boil off the comet's icy nucleus. A cometary coma can extend up to a million miles from the nucleus.

precession: slow motion of the axis of the Earth around a cone, one cycle in about 26,000 years, due to gravitational tugs by the Sun, Moon, and major planets.

The precession of the Earth's axis is one part of the precession cycle. Another part is the precession of the Earth's orbit. As the Earth moves around the Sun in its elliptical orbit, the major axis of the Earth's orbital ellipse is rotating about the Sun. In other words, the orbit itself rotates around the Sun! These two precessions (the axial and orbital precessions) combine to affect how far the Earth

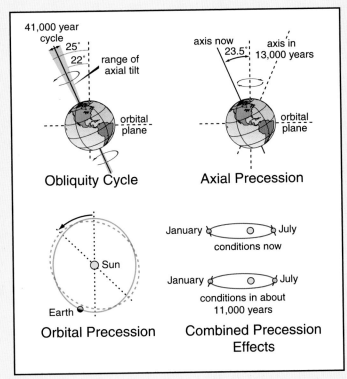

Obliquity Cycle

Axial Precession

Orbital Precession

Combined Precession Effects

Figure 3 The tilt of the Earth's axis and its orbital path about the Sun go through several cycles of change.

Geo Words

orbital plane: (also called the ecliptic or plane of the ecliptic). A plane formed by the path of the Earth around the Sun.

inclination: the angle between the orbital plane of the solar system and the actual orbit of an object around the Sun.

is from the Sun during the different seasons. This combined effect is called precession of the equinoxes, and this change goes through one complete cycle about every 22,000 years. Ten thousand years from now, about halfway through the precession cycle, winter will be from June to September, when the Earth will be farthest from the Sun during the Northern Hemisphere winter. That will make winters there even colder, on average.

Inclination

When you study a diagram of the solar system, you notice that the orbits of all the planets except Pluto stay within a narrow range called the **orbital plane** of the solar system. If you were making a model of the orbits of the planets in the solar system you could put many of the orbits on a tabletop. However, Pluto's orbit, as shown in *Figure 4*, could not be drawn or placed on a tabletop (a plane, as it is called in geometry). Pluto's path around the Sun is inclined 17.1° from the plane described by the Earth's motion around the Sun. This 17.1° tilt is called its orbital **inclination**.

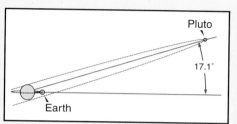

Figure 4 Pluto's orbit is inclined 17.1° to the orbital plane of the rest of the solar system.

What are the orbital planes of asteroids and comets? Both are found mainly in the part of the solar system beyond the Earth. Although some asteroids can be found in the inner solar system, many are found between the orbits of Mars and Jupiter. The common movie portrayal of the "asteroid belt" as a densely populated part of space through which one must dodge asteroids is wrong. The asteroids occupy very little space. Another misconception is that asteroids are the remains of a planet that exploded.

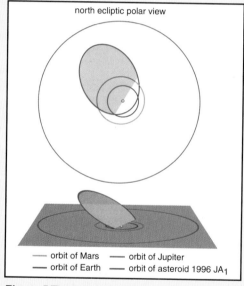

north ecliptic polar view

— orbit of Mars — orbit of Jupiter
— orbit of Earth — orbit of asteroid 1996 JA₁

Figure 5 The orbit of the Earth-approaching asteroid 1996 JA, in relation to the Earth.

The orbits of asteroids are more eccentric than the orbits of the planets, and they are often slightly inclined from the orbital plane. As the Earth orbits the Sun, it can cross the orbital paths of objects called Earth-approaching asteroids. There is a great deal of interest in finding Earth-approaching or Earth-crossing asteroids. A collision with an object a few miles across could be devastating, because of its very high velocity relative to the Earth. Astronomers search the skies for asteroids and map their orbits. In this way they hope to learn what's coming toward Earth long before it poses a danger to your community.

Comets are "loners" that periodically visit the inner solar system. They usually originate in the outer solar system. As shown in *Figure 5*, they have very high-inclination orbits—some as much as 30° from the plane of the solar system. In addition, their orbits are often highly eccentric. Astronomers also search the skies for comets. Once a comet is discovered, its orbit is calculated and the comet is observed as it moves closer to the Sun and changes. A collision of a comet's nucleus with the Earth would be serious, but a collision with a comet's tail is much more likely. A collision with the tail would have little, if any, effect on the Earth, because the tail consists mainly of glowing gas with very little mass.

Check Your Understanding

1. In your own words, explain what is meant by the eccentricity of an ellipse.

2. For an ellipse with a major axis of 25 cm, which one is more eccentric; the one with a distance between the foci of 15 cm or with a distance between the foci of 20 cm? Explain.

3. How does the precession of the Earth's axis of rotation affect the seasons? Justify your answer.

4. Why is there a danger that a large asteroid might strike the Earth at some time in the future?

Understanding and Applying What You Have Learned

1. The major axis of the Earth's orbit is 299,200,000 km, and the distance between the foci is 4,999,632 km. Calculate the eccentricity of the Earth's orbit. How does this value compare to the value noted in the **Digging Deeper** reading section?

2. On the GH line on the ellipse that you created for your **Investigate** activity, draw the Earth at its closest position to the Sun and the farthest position away from the Sun.

3. Refer to the table that shows the eccentricities of the planets to answer the following questions:

   a) Which planet would show the greatest percentage variation in its average distance from the Sun during its year? Explain.

   b) Which planet would show the least percentage variation in its average distance from the Sun throughout its year? Explain.

   c) Is there any relationship between the distance from the Sun and the eccentricity of a planet's orbit? Refer to *Table 1* on page E5.

   d) Why might Neptune be farther away from the Sun at times than Pluto is?

   e) Look up the orbital inclinations of the planets and add them to a copy of the table.

Eccentricities of the Planets	
Planet	**Eccentricity**
Mercury	0.206
Venus	0.007
Earth	0.017
Mars	0.093
Jupiter	0.048
Saturn	0.054
Uranus	0.047
Neptune	0.009
Pluto	0.249

4. Draw a scale model to show changes in the Earth's orbit of about the same magnitude as in nature (a cycle of 100,000 years).

   a) Draw the orbit of the Earth with a perfectly circular orbit at 150,000,000 km from the Sun. Use a scale of 1 cm = 20,000,000 km. Make sure that your pencil is sharp, and draw the thinnest line possible.

   b) Make another drawing of the actual shape of the Earth orbit—an ellipse. This ellipse has 153,000,000 km as the farthest distance and 147,000,000 km as the closest point to the Sun.

   c) Does the difference in distance from the Sun look significant enough to cause much difference in temperature? Explain.

5. Draw the solar system as viewed from the plane of the ecliptic (orbital plane).

a) How will Pluto's orbit look with its 17° inclination?

b) How will the orbits of the other planets look?

c) Draw in the orbits of Earth-crossing asteroids with inclinations of 20° and 30° to the orbital plane.

d) Draw in the orbits of several comets with high inclinations. Some typical high-inclination comets are Comet Halley (162.22°) and Ikeya-Seki (141.86°).

6. Now that you know that the Earth's orbit is elliptical (and the Moon's is too), you can think about a third astronomical factor that controls the nature of tides. Tidal forces are stronger when the Moon is closer to the Earth, and when the Earth is closer to the Sun.

a) Draw a diagram to show the positions of the Moon, Earth, and Sun that would generate the highest tidal ranges (difference in height between high and low tides) of the year.

b) Draw a diagram to show the positions of the Moon, Earth, and Sun that would generate the lowest tidal ranges (difference in height between high and low tides) of the year.

Preparing for the Chapter Challenge

1. In your own words, explain the changes in the Earth's orbital eccentricity, and how it might have affected your community in the past. What effect might it have in the future?

2. Describe the orbits of comets and asteroids and how they are different from those of the planets. What effect could comets and asteroids have on your community if their orbits intersected the Earth's orbit and the Earth and the comet or asteroid were both at that same place in their orbits?

Inquiring Further

1. **The gravitational "slingshot" effect on spacecraft**

   The gravitational tug of the Sun and the planets plays a role in shaping the orbits of solar-system bodies. NASA has used the gravitational pull of Jupiter and Saturn to influence the paths of spacecraft like Pioneer and Voyager. Investigate how this gravitational "slingshot" effect works and its role in moving small bodies from one orbit to another.

2. **Investigate the orbits of comets and asteroids**

   Look up the orbital information for some typical comets and asteroids. Try to include some with high inclinations and orbital eccentricities.

Activity 4

Impact Events and the Earth System

Goals

In this activity you will:

- Investigate the mechanics of an impact event and make scale drawings of an impact crater.

- Calculate the energy (in joules) released when an asteroid collides with Earth.

- Compare natural and man-made disasters to the impact of an asteroid.

- Understand the consequences to your community should an impact event occur.

- Investigate the chances for an asteroid or comet collision.

Think about It

Meteor Crater in Arizona is one of the best-preserved meteor craters on Earth. It is 1.25 km across and about 4 km in circumference. Twenty football games could be played simultaneously on its floor, while more than two million spectators observed from its sloping sides.

- How large (in diameter) do you think the meteor was that formed Meteor Crater?
- How would the impact of the meteor have affected living things near the crater?

What do you think? Record your ideas about these questions in your *EarthComm* notebook. Be prepared to discuss your responses with your small group and the class.

Investigate

1. Given the following information, calculate the energy released when an asteroid collides with Earth:

   - The spherical, iron–nickel asteroid has a density of 7800 kg/m^3.

   - It is 40 m in diameter.

   - It has a velocity of 20,000 m/s relative to the Earth.

     Note: It is very important to keep track of your units during these calculations. You will be expressing energy with a unit called a "joule." A joule is 1 kg m^2/s^2.

   a) Find the volume of the asteroid in cubic meters. The equation for the volume of a sphere is as follows:

   $$V = \frac{4}{3}\pi r^3$$

   where V is volume of the sphere, and r is the radius of the sphere.

   b) Multiply the volume by the density to find the total mass of the asteroid.

   c) Calculate the energy of the asteroid. Because the asteroid is moving, you will use the equation for kinetic energy, as follows:

   $$KE = \frac{1}{2}mv^2$$

   where KE is kinetic energy, m is the mass, and v is the velocity.

   Express your answer in joules. To do this express mass in kilograms, and velocity in meters per second.

   For some perspective, a teenager uses over 10,000 kJ (kilojoules) of energy each day. (There are 1000 J (joules) in a kilojoule.)

2. The combination of calculations that you just performed can be summarized as:

   $$\text{Energy} = \frac{2}{3}\pi\rho r^3 v^2$$

   where r is the radius, ρ is the density, and v is the velocity of the object.

   a) Suppose an object makes an impact with the Earth at 10 times the velocity of another identical object. By what factor will the energy of the object increase?

   b) Suppose an object makes an impact with the Earth, and it has 10 times the radius of another object traveling at the same speed. By what factor will the energy of the object increase?

   c) How do these relationships help to explain how small, fast-moving objects can release a tremendous amount of energy as well as larger yet slower-moving objects?

3. The asteroid described in **Step 1** above was the one responsible for Meteor Crater in Arizona.

   a) Copy the following table into your notebook. Enter your calculation for Meteor Crater.

   b) Calculate the energy released by the impacts shown in the table.

Object	Radius (m)	Density (kg/m³)	Impact Velocity (m/s)	Energy (joules)	Richter Scale Magnitude Equivalent
Asclepius	100	3000	30,000		
Comet Swift-Tuttle	1000	5000	60,000		
Chicxulub impactor	5000	3000	32,000		
SL9 Fragment Q	2150	1000	60,000		
Meteor Crater	20	7800	20,000		

Note:

- Asclepius is an asteroid that passed within 690,000 km of Earth in 1989.

- Comet Swift-Tuttle is a future threat to the Earth–Moon system, having passed Earth in 1992 and being scheduled for return in 2126.

- SL9 Fragment Q is a fragment of Comet Shoemaker-Levy that impacted Jupiter in 1994.

- Chicxulub impactor is the name of the asteroid that triggered the extinction of the dinosaurs 65 million years ago.

4. Use the table below to compare the energy from all these events to known phenomena.

   a) In your notebook, explain how the energies of these four impact events compare to some other known phenomena.

Phenomena	Kinetic Energy (joules)
Annual output of the Sun	10^{34}
Severe earthquake	10^{18}
100-megaton hydrogen bomb	10^{17}
Atomic bomb	10^{13}

5. Make a scale drawing of the Chicxulub impactor compared with Earth. The diameter of the Earth is 12,756 km.

   a) If you made the diameter of the Chicxulub impactor 1 mm, what would the diameter of the Earth be?

   b) If you made the diameter of the Chicxulub impactor 0.5 mm, which is probably about as small as you can draw, what would the diameter of the Earth be?

6. How do these impact events compare with the energy released in an earthquake? If you have a calculator capable of handling logarithms, answer the following questions:

   a) Calculate the Richter scale equivalent of the energy released by the four impact events. Use the following equation:

   $$M = 0.67 \log_{10} E - 5.87$$

   where M is the equivalent magnitude on the Richter scale, and E is the energy of the impact, in joules.

   b) How do your results compare with the table below, which shows the five greatest earthquakes in the world between 1900 and 1998? Which impacts exceed the world's greatest earthquakes?

Location	Year	Magnitude
Chile	1960	9.5
Prince William Sound, Alaska	1964	9.2
Andreanof Islands, Aleutian Islands	1957	9.1
Kamchatka	1952	9.0
Off the Coast of Ecuador	1906	8.8

Reflecting on the Activity and the Challenge

You have calculated the energy released when asteroids of different sizes hit the Earth's surface, and you have compared these to other energy-releasing events. This comparison will be helpful as you explain the hazards associated with an impact in your **Chapter Challenge** brochure.

Digging Deeper

ASTEROIDS AND COMETS

Asteroids

Asteroids are rocky bodies smaller than planets. They are leftovers from the formation of the solar system. In fact, the early history of the solar system was a period of frequent impacts. The many scars (impact craters) seen on the Moon, Mercury, Mars, and the moons of the outer planets are the evidence for this bombardment. Asteroids orbit the Sun in very elliptical orbits with inclinations up to 30°. Most asteroids are in the region between Jupiter and Mars called the asteroid belt. There are probably at least 100,000 asteroids 1 km in diameter and larger. The largest, called Ceres, is about 1000 km across. Some of the asteroids have very eccentric orbits that cross Earth's orbit. Of these, perhaps a few dozen are larger than one kilometer in diameter. As you learned in the activity, the energy of an asteroid impact event increases with the cube of the radius. Thus, the larger asteroids are the ones astronomers worry about when they consider the danger of collision with Earth.

The closest recent approach of an asteroid to Earth was Asteroid 1994 XM 11. On December 9, 1994, the asteroid approached within 115,000 km of Earth. On March 22, 1989 the asteroid 4581 Asclepius came within 1.8 lunar distances, which is close to 690,000 km. Astronomers think that asteroids at least 1 km in diameter hit Earth every few hundred million years. They base this upon the number of impact craters that have been found and dated on Earth. A list of asteroids that have approached within

Figure 1 Image of the asteroid Ida, which is 58 km long and 23 km wide.

two lunar distances of Earth (the average distance between Earth and the Moon) is provided in *Table 1* on the following page. Only close-approach distances less than 0.01 AU for asteroids are included in this table.

Table 1 Asteroids with Close-Approach Distances to Earth			
Name or Designation	**Date of Close Earth Approach**	**Distance**	
		(AU)	**(LD)**
1994 XM1	1994–Dec–09	0.0007	0.3
1993 KA2	1993–May–20	0.001	0.4
1994 ES1	1994–Mar–15	0.0011	0.4
1991 BA	1991–Jan–18	0.0011	0.4
1996 JA1	1996–May–19	0.003	1.2
1991 VG	1991–Dec–05	0.0031	1.2
1999 VP11	1982–Oct–21	0.0039	1.5
1995 FF	1995–Apr–03	0.0045	1.8
1998 DV9	1975–Jan–31	0.0045	1.8
4581 Asclepius	1989–Mar–22	0.0046	1.8
1994 WR12	1994–Nov–24	0.0048	1.9
1991 TU	1991–Oct–08	0.0048	1.9
1995 UB	1995–Oct–17	0.005	1.9
1937 UB (Hermes)	1937–Oct–30	0.005	1.9
1998 KY26	1998–Jun–08	0.0054	2.1

(AU) – Astronomical distance Unit: 1.0 AU is roughly the average distance between the Earth and the Sun.
(LD) – Lunar Distance unit: 1.0 LD is the average distance from the Earth to the Moon (about 0.00257 AU).

Most (but not all) scientists believe that the extinction of the dinosaurs 65 million years ago was caused by the impact of an asteroid or comet 10 km in diameter. Such a large impact would have sent up enough dust to cloud the entire Earth's atmosphere for many months. This would have blocked out sunlight and killed off many plants, and eventually, the animals that fed on those plants. Not only the dinosaurs died out. About 75% of all plants and animals became extinct. One of the strong pieces of evidence supporting this hypothesis is a 1-cm-thick layer of iridium-rich sediment about 65 million years old that has been found worldwide. Iridium is rare on Earth but is common in asteroids.

Our planet has undergone at least a dozen mass-extinction events during its history, during which a large percentage of all plant and animal species became extinct in an extremely short interval of geologic time. It is likely that at least some of these were related to impacts. It is also likely that Earth will suffer another collision sometime in the future. NASA is currently forming plans to discover and monitor asteroids that are at least 1 km in size and with orbits that cross the Earth's orbit. Asteroid experts take the threat from asteroids very seriously, and they strongly suggest that a program of systematic observation be put into operation to predict and, hopefully avoid an impact.

Comets

Comets are masses of frozen gases (ices) and rocky dust particles. Like asteroids, they are leftovers from the formation of the solar system. There are many comets in orbit around the Sun. Their orbits are usually very eccentric with large inclinations. The orbits of many comets are very large, with distances from the Sun of greater than 20,000 astronomical units (AU). The icy head of a comet (the nucleus) is usually a few kilometers in diameter, but it appears much larger as it gets closer to the Sun. That's because the Sun's heat vaporizes the ice, forming a cloud called a coma. Radiation pressure and the action of the **solar wind** (the stream of fast-moving charged particles coming from the Sun) blow the gases and dust in the coma in a direction away from the Sun. This produces a tail that points away from the Sun even as the comet moves around the Sun. Halley's Comet, shown in *Figure 2*, is the best known of these icy visitors. It rounds the Sun about every 76 years, and it last passed by Earth in 1986.

Figure 2 Halley's Comet last appeared in the night sky in 1986.

Geo Words

solar wind: a flow of hot charged particles leaving the Sun.

Comets have collided with the Earth since its earliest formation. It is thought that the ices from comet impacts melted to help form Earth's oceans. In 1908 something hit the Earth at Tunguska, in Siberian Russia. It flattened trees for hundreds of miles, and researchers believe that the object might have been a comet. Had such an event occurred in more recent history in a more populated area, the damage and loss of life would have been enormous. A list of comets that have approached within less than 0.11 AU of Earth is provided in *Table 2* on the following page.

EarthComm

Geo Words

meteoroid: a small rock in space.

meteor: the luminous phenomenon seen when a meteoroid enters the atmosphere (commonly known as a shooting star).

meteorite: a part of a meteoroid that survives through the Earth's atmosphere.

Table 2 Close Approaches of Comets				
Name	**Designation**	**Date of Close Earth Approach**	**Distance**	
			(AU)	**(LD)**
Comet of 1491	C/1491 B1	1491–Feb–20	0.0094	3.7*
Lexell	D/1770 L1	1770–Jul–01	0.0151	5.9
Tempel-Tuttle	55P/1366 U1	1366–Oct–26	0.0229	8.9
IRAS-Araki-Alcock	C/1983 H1	1983–May–11	0.0313	12.2
Halley	1P/ 837 F1	837–Apr–10	0.0334	13
Biela	3D/1805 V1	1805–Dec–09	0.0366	14.2
Comet of 1743	C/1743 C1	1743–Feb–08	0.039	15.2
Pons-Winnecke	7P/	1927–Jun–26	0.0394	15.3
Comet of 1014	C/1014 C1	1014–Feb–24	0.0407	15.8*
Comet of 1702	C/1702 H1	1702–Apr–20	0.0437	17
Comet of 1132	C/1132 T1	1132–Oct–07	0.0447	17.4*
Comet of 1351	C/1351 W1	1351–Nov–29	0.0479	18.6*
Comet of 1345	C/1345 O1	1345–Jul–31	0.0485	18.9*
Comet of 1499	C/1499 Q1	1499–Aug–17	0.0588	22.9*
Schwassmann-Wachmann 3	73P/1930 J1	1930–May–31	0.0617	24

* Distance uncertain because comet's orbit is relatively poorly determined.
(AU) – Astronomical distance Unit: 1.0 AU is roughly the average distance between the Earth and the Sun.
(LD) – Lunar Distance unit: 1.0 LD is the average distance from the Earth to the Moon (about 0.00257 AU).

Meteoroids, Meteors, and Meteorites

Meteoroids are tiny particles in space, like leftover dust from a comet's tail or fragments of asteroids. Meteoroids are called **meteors** when they enter Earth's atmosphere, and **meteorites** when they reach the Earth's surface. About 1000 tons of material is added to the Earth each year by meteorites, much of it through dust-sized particles that settle slowly through the atmosphere. There are several types of meteorites. About 80% that hit Earth are stony in nature and are difficult to tell apart from Earth rocks. About 15% of meteorites consist of the metals iron and nickel and are very dense. The rest are either a mixture of iron–nickel and stony material, or are made of a very different material. These very different ones are called chondrites, and they may represent material that was never part of a larger body like a Moon, a planet, or an asteroid. They are probably original solar-system materials.

Figure 3 Lunar meteorite.

Check Your Understanding

1. Where are asteroids most abundant in the solar system?

2. How might a major asteroid impact have caused a mass extinction of the Earth's plant and animal species at certain times in the geologic past?

3. Why do comets have tails? Why do the tails point away from the Sun?

4. What are the compositions of the major kinds of meteorites?

Understanding and Applying What You Have Learned

1. Look at the table of impact events shown in the **Investigate** section. Compare the densities of the object that formed Meteor Crater and SL9 Fragment Q from the Shoemaker-Levy Comet. Use what you have learned in this activity to explain the large difference in densities between the two objects.

2. If an asteroid or comet were on a collision course for Earth, what factors would determine how dangerous the collision might be for your community?

3. How would an asteroid on a collision course endanger our Earth community?

4. Comets are composed largely of ice and mineral grains. Assume a density of 1.1 g/cm^3:

   a) How would the energy released in a comet impact compare to the asteroid impact you calculated in the **Investigate** section? (Assume that the comet has the same diameter and velocity as the asteroid.)

   b) Based upon your calculation, are comets dangerous if they make impact with the Earth? Explain your response.

5. From the information in the **Digging Deeper** reading section, and what you know about the eccentricities and inclinations of asteroid orbits, how likely do you think it is that an asteroid with a diameter of 1 km or greater will hit the Earth in your lifetime? Explain your reasoning. Can you apply the same reasoning to comets?

6. Add the asteroid belt to the model of the solar system you made in the first activity. You will need to think about how best to represent the vast number of asteroids and their wide range of sizes. Don't forget to add in some samples of Earth-approaching asteroids and the orbit of one or two comets.

Preparing for the Chapter Challenge

Assume that scientists learn several months before impact that a large asteroid will hit near your community. Assume that you live 300 km from the impact site. What plans can your family make to survive this disaster? What are some of the potential larger-scale effects of an asteroid impact? Work with your group to make a survival plan. Present your group's plan to the entire class. Be sure to record suggestions made by other groups. This information will prove useful in completing the **Chapter Challenge.**

Inquiring Further

1. **Impact craters on objects other than the Earth**

   In an earlier activity you studied impact sites on the Moon. Look at Mercury, Mars, and the moons of Saturn, Uranus, and Neptune to see other examples of impact craters in the solar system. How are these craters similar to Meteor Crater? How are they different?

2. **Modeling impact craters**

   Simulate an asteroid or comet hitting the Earth. Fill a shoebox partway with plaster of Paris. When the plaster is almost dry, drop two rocks of different sizes into it from the same height. Carefully retrieve the rocks and drop them again in a different place, this time from higher distance. Let the plaster fully harden, then examine, and measure the craters. Measure the depth and diameter and calculate the diameter-to-depth ratio. Which is largest? Which is deepest? Did the results surprise you?

3. **Earth-approaching asteroids**

   Do some research into current efforts by scientists to map the orbits of Earth-approaching asteroids? Visit the *EarthComm* web site to help you get started with your research. How are orbits determined? What is the current thinking among scientists about how to prevent impacts from large comets or asteroids?

4. **Barringer Crater**

   Research the Barringer Crater (Meteor Crater). The crater has been named for Daniel Moreau Barringer, who owned the property that contains the crater. Explain how scientists used Barringer Crater to understand how craters form. Study the work of Dr. Eugene Shoemaker, who was one of the foremost experts on the mechanics of impact cratering.

 Wear goggles while modeling impact craters. Work with adult supervision to complete the activity.

Activity 5

The Sun and Its Effects on Your Community

Goals

In this activity you will:

- Explore the structure of the Sun and describe the flow of solar energy in terms of reflection, absorption, and scattering.

- Understand that the Sun emits charged particles called the solar wind, and how this wind affects "space weather."

- Explain the effect of solar wind on people and communities.

- Understand sunspots, solar flares, and other kinds of solar activities and their effects on Earth.

- Learn to estimate the chances for solar activity to affect your community.

Think about It

Every day of your life you are subjected to radiation from the Sun. Fortunately, the Earth's atmosphere and magnetic field provides protection against many of the Sun's strong outbursts.

- In what ways does solar radiation benefit you?
- In what ways can solar radiation be harmful or disruptive?

What do you think? Record your ideas about these questions in your *EarthComm* notebook. Be prepared to discuss your response with your small group and the class.

Investigate

1. Use the data in *Table 1* to construct a graph of sunspot activity by year.

   a) Plot time on the horizontal axis and number of sunspots on the vertical axis.

   b) Connect the points you have plotted.

   c) Look at your graph. Describe any pattern you find in the sunspot activity.

Table 1 Sunspot Activity 1899 to 1998							
Year	Number of Sunspots	Year	Number of Sunspots	Year	Number of Sunspots	Year	Number of Sunspots
1899	12.1	1924	16.7	1949	134.7	1974	34.5
1900	9.5	1925	44.3	1950	83.9	1975	15.5
1901	2.7	1926	63.9	1951	69.4	1976	12.6
1902	5.0	1927	69.0	1952	31.5	1977	27.5
1903	24.4	1928	77.8	1953	13.9	1978	92.5
1904	42.0	1929	64.9	1954	4.4	1979	155.4
1905	63.5	1930	35.7	1955	38.0	1980	154.6
1906	53.8	1931	21.2	1956	141.7	1981	140.4
1907	62.0	1932	11.1	1957	190.2	1982	115.9
1908	48.5	1933	5.7	1958	184.8	1983	66.6
1909	43.9	1934	8.7	1959	159.0	1984	45.9
1910	18.6	1935	36.1	1960	112.3	1985	17.9
1911	5.7	1936	79.7	1961	53.9	1986	13.4
1912	3.6	1937	114.4	1962	37.6	1987	29.4
1913	1.4	1938	109.6	1963	27.9	1988	100.2
1914	9.6	1939	88.8	1964	10.2	1989	157.6
1915	47.4	1940	67.8	1965	15.1	1990	142.6
1916	57.1	1941	47.5	1966	47.0	1991	145.7
1917	103.9	1942	30.6	1967	93.8	1992	94.3
1918	80.6	1943	16.3	1968	105.9	1993	54.6
1919	63.6	1944	9.6	1969	105.5	1994	29.9
1920	37.6	1945	33.2	1970	104.5	1995	17.5
1921	26.1	1946	92.6	1971	66.6	1996	8.6
1922	14.2	1947	151.6	1972	68.9	1997	21.5
1923	5.8	1948	136.3	1973	38.0	1998	64.3

The number of sunspots on the visible solar surface is counted by many solar observatories and is averaged into a single standardized quantity called the sunspot number. This explains the fractional values in the table.

2. *Table 2* contains a list of solar flares that were strong enough to disrupt terrestrial communications and power systems.

   a) Plot the data from *Table 2* onto a histogram.

   b) What pattern do you see in the activity of solar flares?

3. Compare the two graphs you have produced.

   a) What pattern do you see that connects the two?

   b) How would you explain the pattern?

Table 2 Strongest Solar Flare Events 1978–2001			
Date of Activity Onset	**Strength**	**Date of Activity Onset**	**Strength**
August 16, 1989	X20.0	December 17, 1982	X10.1
March 06, 1989	X15.0	May 20, 1984	X10.1
July 07, 1978	X15.0	January 25, 1991	X10.0
April 24, 1984	X13.0	June 09, 1991	X10.0
October 19, 1989	X13.0	July 09, 1982	X 9.8
December 12, 1982	X12.9	September 29, 1989	X9.8
June 06, 1982	X12.0	March 22, 1991	X9.4
June 01, 1991	X12.0	November 6, 1997	X9.4
June 04, 1991	X12.0	May 24, 1990	X9.3
June 06, 1991	X12.0	November 6, 1980	X9.0
June 11, 1991	X12.0	November 2, 1992	X9.0
June 15, 1991	X12.0		

The X before the number is a designation of the strongest flares.
Source: IPS Solar Flares & Space Service in Australia.

Reflecting on the Activity and the Challenge

In this activity you used data tables to plot the number of sunspots in a given year and to correlate strong solar-flare activity with larger numbers of sunspots. You found out that the number of sunspots varies from year to year in a regular cycle and that strong solar flares occur in greater numbers during high-sunspot years. In your **Chapter Challenge,** you will need to explain sunspots and solar flares, their cycles, and the effects of these cycles on your community.

Geo Words

photosphere: the visible surface of the Sun, lying just above the uppermost layer of the Sun's interior, and just below the chromosphere.

chromosphere: a layer in the Sun's atmosphere, the transition between the outermost layer of the Sun's atmosphere, or corona.

corona: the outermost atmosphere of a star (including the Sun), millions of kilometers in extent, and consisting of highly rarefied gas heated to temperatures of millions of degrees.

Digging Deeper

THE SUN AND ITS EFFECTS

Structure of the Sun

From the Earth's surface the Sun appears as a white, glowing ball of light. Like the Earth, the Sun has a layered structure, as shown in *Figure 1*. Its central region (the core) is where nuclear fusion occurs. The core is the source of all the energy the Sun emits. That energy travels out from the core, through a radiative layer and a convection zone above that. Finally, it reaches the outer layers: the **photosphere**, which is the Sun's visible surface, the **chromosphere**, which produces much of the Sun's ultraviolet radiation, and the superheated uppermost layer of the Sun's atmosphere, called the **corona**.

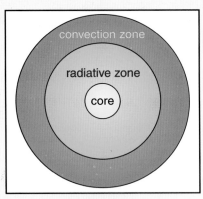

Figure 1 The layered structure of the Sun.

The Sun is the Earth's main external energy source. Of all the incoming energy from the Sun, about half is absorbed by the Earth's surface (see *Figure 2*). The rest is either:

• absorbed by the atmosphere, or
• reflected or scattered back into space by the Earth or clouds.

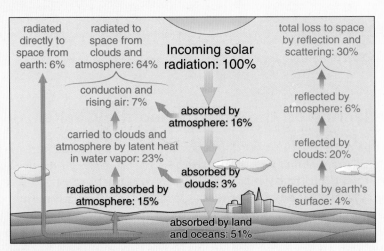

Figure 2 Schematic of Earth's solar energy budget.

Molecules of dust and gas in the atmosphere interfere with some of the incoming solar radiation by changing its direction. This is called scattering, and it explains the blue color of the sky. The atmosphere scatters shorter visible wavelengths of visible light, in the blue range, more strongly than longer visible wavelengths, in the red and orange range. The blue sky you see on a clear day is the blue light that has been scattered from atmospheric particles that are located away from the line of sight to the Sun. When the Sun is low on the horizon, its light has to travel through a much greater thickness of atmosphere, and even more of the blue part of the spectrum of sunlight is scattered out of your line of sight. The red and orange part of the spectrum remains, so the light you see coming directly from the Sun is of that color. The effect is greatest when there is dust and smoke in the atmosphere, because that increases the scattering. The scattered light that makes the sky appear blue is what makes it possible for you to see in a shaded area.

Figure 3 Dust and smoke in the atmosphere enhance the beauty of sunsets.

Most of the sunlight that passes through the atmosphere reaches the Earth's surface without being absorbed. The Sun heats the atmosphere not directly, but rather by warming the Earth's surface. The Earth's surface in turn warms the air near the ground. As the Earth's surface absorbs solar radiation, it re-radiates the heat energy back out to space as infrared radiation. The wavelength of this infrared radiation is much longer than that of visible light, so you can't see the energy that's re-radiated. You can feel it, however, by standing next to a rock surface or the wall of a building that has been heated by the Sun.

The reflectivity of a surface is referred to as its **albedo**. Albedo is expressed as a percentage of radiation that is reflected. The average albedo of the Earth, including its atmosphere, as would be seen from space, is about 0.3. That means that 30% of the light is reflected. Most of this 30% is due to the high reflectivity of clouds, although the air itself scatters about 6% and the Earth's surface (mainly deserts and oceans) reflects another 4%. (See *Figure 2* on page E50.) The albedo of particular surfaces on Earth varies. Thick clouds have albedo of about 0.8, and freshly fallen snow has an even higher albedo. The albedo of a dark soil, on the other hand, is as low as 0.1, meaning that only 10% of the light is reflected. You know from your own experience that light-colored clothing stays much cooler in the Sun than dark-colored clothing. You can think of your clothing as having an albedo, too!

The Earth's Energy Budget

The amount of energy received by the Earth and delivered back into space is the Earth's energy budget. Like a monetary budget, the energy resides in various kinds of places, and moves from place to place in various ways and by various amounts. The energy budget for a given location changes from day to day and from season to season. It can even change on geologic time scales. Daily changes in solar energy are the most familiar. It is usually cooler in the morning, warmer at midday, and cooler again at night. Visible light follows the same cycle, as day moves from dawn to dusk and back to dawn again. But overall, the system is in balance. The Earth gains energy from the Sun and loses energy to space, but the amount of energy entering the Earth system is equal to the amount of energy flowing out, on a long-term average. This flow of energy is the source of energy for almost all forms of life on Earth. Plants capture solar energy by photosynthesis, to build plant tissue. Animals feed on the plants (or on one another). Solar energy creates the weather, drives the movement of the oceans, and powers the water cycle. All of Earth's systems depend on the input of energy from the Sun. The Sun also supplies most of the energy for human civilization, either directly, as with solar power and wind power, or indirectly, in the form of fossil fuels.

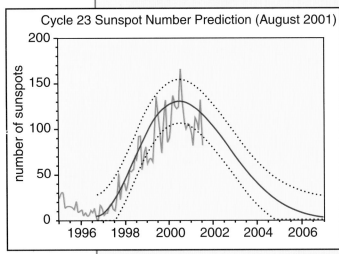

Cycle 23 Sunspot Number Prediction (August 2001)

Figure 4 The jagged line represents the actual number of sunspots; the smooth dark line is the predicted number of sunspots.

Harmful Solar Radiation

Just as there are benefits to receiving energy from the Sun, there are dangers. The ill effects of sunlight are caused by ultraviolet (UV) radiation, which causes skin damage. The gas called ozone (a molecule made up of three oxygen atoms) found in the upper atmosphere shields the Earth from much of the Sun's harmful UV rays. The source of the ozone in the upper atmosphere is different from the ozone that is produced (often by cars) in polluted cities. The latter is a health hazard and in no way protects you. Scientists have recently noted decreasing levels of ozone in the upper atmosphere. Less ozone means that more UV radiation reaches Earth, increasing the danger of Sun damage. There is general agreement about the cause of the ozone depletion. Scientists agree that future levels of ozone will depend upon a combination of natural and man-made factors, including the phase-out, now under way, of chlorofluorocarbons and other ozone-depleting chemicals.

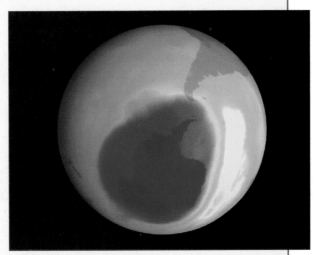

Figure 5 Depletion in the ozone layer over Antarctica. Rather than actually being a hole, the ozone hole is a large area of the stratosphere with extremely low concentrations of ozone.

Sunspots and Solar Flares

Sunspots are small dark areas on the Sun's visible surface. They can be as small as the Earth or as large as Uranus or Neptune. They are formed when magnetic field lines just below the Sun's surface are twisted and poke through the solar photosphere. They look dark because they are about 1500 K cooler than the surrounding surface of the Sun. Sunspots are highly magnetic. This magnetism may cause the cooler temperatures by suppressing the circulation of heat in the region of the sunspot.

Sunspots last for a few hours to a few months. They appear to move across the surface of the Sun over a period of days. Actually, the sunspots move because the Sun is rotating. The number of sunspots varies from year to year and tends to peak in 11-year cycles along with the number of dangerously strong solar flares. Both can affect systems here on Earth. During a solar

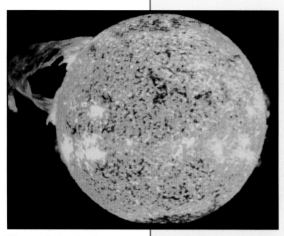

Figure 6 A solar flare.

Geo Words

plasma: a state of matter wherein all atoms are ionized; a mixture of free electrons and free atomic nuclei.

ionosphere: the part of the Earth's atmosphere above about 50 km where the atoms are significantly ionized and affect the propagation of radio waves.

ion: an atom with one or more electrons removed (or added), giving it a positive (or negative) charge.

flare like the one shown in *Figure 6*, enormous quantities of ultraviolet, x-ray, and radio waves blast out from the Sun. In addition, protons and electrons stream from flares at 800 km/hr. These high-radiation events can be devastating to Earth-orbiting satellites and astronauts, as well as systems on the ground. In 1989 a major solar flare created electric currents that caused a surge of power that knocked out a power grid in Canada, leaving hundreds of thousands of people without power. More recently, in 1997, radiation from a flare affected an Earth-orbiting satellite that carried telecommunications traffic. For at least a day people whose beeper messages went through that satellite had no service.

The flow of charged particles (also called a **plasma**) from the Sun is called the solar wind. It flows out from the solar corona in all directions and is responsible for "space weather"—the environment outside our planet. Like severe storms in our atmosphere, space weather can cause problems for Earth systems. Strong outbursts in this ongoing stream of charged particles can disrupt radio signals by disturbing the upper layers of the atmosphere. The sounds of your favorite short-wave radio station or the signals sent by a ham radio operator travel as radio waves (a form of electromagnetic radiation). These signals travel around the Earth by bouncing off the **ionosphere**, a layer of the atmosphere 80 to 400 km above the Earth's surface. The ionosphere forms when incoming solar radiation blasts electrons out of the upper-atmosphere gases, leaving a layer of electrons and of charged atoms, called **ions**. The ionosphere acts like a mirror, reflecting a part of the radio waves (AM radio waves in the 1000 kHz range) back to Earth.

Solar flares intensify the solar wind, which makes the ionosphere thicken and strengthen. When this happens, radio signals from Earth are trapped inside the ionosphere. This causes a lot of interference. As discussed above, solar activity can also be a problem for satellite operations. Astronauts orbiting the Earth and people aboard high-flying aircraft—particularly those who fly polar routes, where exposure to radiation may be greatest—also have cause to worry about space weather. To provide up-to-date information about current solar activity, the United States government operates a Space Environment Center Web site called "Space Weather Now."

At least one effect of space weather is quite wonderful. When the solar wind encounters the Earth's magnetic field, it excites gases in the Earth's atmosphere, causing them to glow. The charged particles from the solar wind end up in an oval-shaped area around the Earth's magnetic poles. The result is a beautiful display called an **aurora**, seen in *Figure 7*. People who live in northern areas see auroras more often than those who live near the Equator do. During periods of heavy solar activity, however, an aurora can be seen as far south as Texas and New Mexico. Auroras are often called the northern lights (aurora borealis) or southern lights (aurora australis). From the ground, they often appear as green or red glows, or shimmering curtains of white, red, and green lights in the sky.

Figure 7 The aurora borealis or northern lights light up the sky in the Northern Hemisphere.

Collecting Data about the Sun

How do astronomers collect data about the Sun? From the ground, they use solar telescopes—instruments outfitted with special sensors to detect the different kinds of solar activity. There are dozens of solar telescope sites around the world. They include the Sacramento Peak Solar Observatory in New Mexico, the McMath Solar telescope in Arizona, and the Mount Wilson solar observatory in California. From space, they study the Sun using orbiting spacecraft like the Yohkoh satellite (*Yohkoh* is the Japanese word for "sunbeam"). Other missions include the Transition Region and Coronal Explorer (TRACE), the Ulysses Solar-Polar mission, the Solar and Heliospheric Observatory, the GOES satellites, and many others. These spacecraft are equipped with detectors sensitive to x-rays, radio waves, and other wavelengths of radiation coming from the Sun. In this way, scientists keep very close track of solar activity and use that information to keep the public informed of any upcoming dangers.

Some scientists theorize that sunspot cycles affect weather on Earth. They think that during times of high sunspot activity, the climate is warmer. During times of no or low sunspot activity, the climate is colder. A sharp decrease in sunspots occurred from 1645 to 1715. This period of lower solar activity, first noted by G. Sporer and later studied by E. W. Maunder, is called the Maunder Minimum. It coincided with cooler temperatures on Earth, part of a period now known as the "Little Ice Age." Similar solar minimums occurred between 1420–1530, 1280–1340, and 1010-1050 (the Oort minimum). These periods preceded the discovery of sunspots, so no correlation between sunspots and temperature is available. Solar astronomers number the solar cycles from one minimum to the next starting with number one, the 1755–1766 cycle. Cycle 23 peaked (was at a maximum) in the year 2000. (See *Figure 4* on page E52.) There is still much debate about the connection between sunspot cycles and climate.

Geo Words

aurora: the bright emission of atoms and molecules near the Earth's poles caused by charged particles entering the upper atmosphere.

Check Your Understanding

1. How do solar flares interfere with communication and power systems?

2. In your own words, explain what is meant by the term "solar wind." How does the Sun contribute to "space weather?"

3. Describe the Earth's energy budget.

Understanding and Applying What You Have Learned

1. Study the graph that you made showing sunspot activity. You have already determined that sunspot activity occurs in cycles. Using graph paper, construct a new graph that predicts a continuation of the cycle from 2001 to 2015. Indicate which years you think would see increased solar-flare activity and more dangerous "space weather."

2. The latest sunspot maximum occurred in 2001. Using the data from your sunspot-activity data table, predict the next sunspot minimum.

3. Make lists of the possible consequences of solar flares to the following members of your community: an air traffic controller, a radio station manager,

and the captain of a ship at sea. Can you think of other members of your community that would be affected by solar activity?

4. You have read that Earth's albedo is about 0.30.

   a) In your own words, describe what this means.
   b) Is the Earth's albedo constant? Why or why not?
   c) How does changing a planet's albedo change a planet's temperature? Why does this occur?
   d) If Earth's albedo was higher, but Earth was farther from the Sun, could the Earth have the same temperature? Why or why not?

Preparing for the Chapter Challenge

You have been asked to help people in your community to understand how events from outside the Earth affect their daily lives. Write a short paper in which you address the following questions:

1. How has the Sun affected your community in the past?

2. How has the Sun affected you personally?

3. How might the Sun affect your community in the future?

4. What are some of the benefits attained from a study of the Sun?

5. What are some of the problems caused by sunspots and solar flares?

6. Explain how auroras are caused. Explain also why they can or cannot be viewed in your community.

7. Compare the chances of dangerous effects from the Sun with the chances of an impact event affecting the Earth.

Inquiring Further

1. Viewing sunspots

If you have a telescope, you can view sunspots by projecting an image of the Sun onto white cardboard. Never look directly at the Sun, with or without a telescope. Stand with your back to the Sun, and set up a telescope so that the large (front) end is pointing toward the Sun and the other end is pointing toward a piece of white cardboard. You should see a projection of the Sun on the cardboard, including sunspots. If you map the positions of the sunspots daily, you should be able to observe the rotation of the Sun over a couple of weeks. Use the *EarthComm* web site to locate good science sites on the Internet that show daily images of solar activity. Search them out and compare your observations of sunspots to what you see from the large observatories.

 Work with an adult during this activity. Do not look at the bright image for long periods of time.

2. Aurorae

Have people in your community ever seen the northern lights? Even if your community is not very far north, do some research to see if the auroras have ever been spotted from your community.

3. Solar radiation and airplanes

Periods of sunspot maximum increase the dosage of radiation that astronauts and people traveling in airplanes receive. Do some research on how much radiation astronauts receive during sunspot minima and maxima. How much radiation do airplane passengers receive? How do the amounts compare to the solar radiation you receive at the Earth's surface? How do scientists balance safety with the issue of the extra weight that would be added to aircraft, spacecraft, or space suits to provide protection?

4. The hole in the ozone layer

People who live near the South Pole of the Earth are at risk for increased ultraviolet exposure from the Sun. This is due to a thinning in the atmosphere called the ozone hole. Research this ozone hole. Is there a northern ozone hole? Could these ozone holes grow? If so, could your community be endangered in the future?

5. History of science

Research the life of British physicist Edward Victor Appleton, who was awarded the Nobel Prize in physics in 1947 for his work on the ionosphere. Other important figures in the discovery of the properties of the upper atmosphere include Oliver Heaviside, Arthur Edwin Kennelly, F. Sherwood Rowland, Paul Crutzen, and Mario Molina.

Activity 6   The Electromagnetic Spectrum and Your Community

Goals

In this activity you will:

- Explain electromagnetic radiation and the electromagnetic spectrum in terms of wavelength, speed, and energy.

- Investigate the different instruments astronomers use to detect different wavelengths in the electromagnetic spectrum.

- Understand that the atoms of each of the chemical elements have a unique spectral fingerprint.

- Explain how electromagnetic radiation reveals the temperature and chemical makeup of objects like stars.

- Understand that some forms of electromagnetic radiation are essential and beneficial to us on Earth, and others are harmful.

Think about It

Look at the spectrum as your teacher displays it on the overhead projector. Record in your *EarthComm* notebook the colors in the order in which they appear. Draw a picture to accompany your notes.

- What does a prism reveal about visible light?
- The Sun produces light energy that allows you to see. What other kinds of energy come from the Sun? Can you see them? Why or why not?

What do you think? Record your ideas in your *EarthComm* notebook. Be prepared to discuss your responses with your small group and the class.

Investigate

Part A: Observing Part of the Electromagnetic Spectrum

1. Obtain a spectroscope, similar to the one shown in the illustration. Hold the end with the diffraction grating to your eye. Direct it toward a part of the sky away from the Sun. (**CAUTION:** never look directly at the Sun; doing so even briefly can damage your eyes permanently.) Look for a spectrum along the side of the spectroscope. Rotate the spectroscope until you see the colors going from left to right rather than up and down.

   a) In your notebook, write down the order of the colors you observed.

   b) Move the spectroscope to the right and left. Record your observations.

2. Look through the spectroscope at a fluorescent light.

   a) In your notebook, write down the order of the colors you observed.

3. Look through the spectroscope at an incandescent bulb.

   a) In your notebook, write down the order of the colors you observed.

   ⚠ Do not look directly at a light with the unaided eye. Use the spectroscope as instructed.

4. Use your observations to answer the following questions:

   a) How did the colors and the order of the colors differ between reflected sunlight, fluorescent light, and the incandescent light? Describe any differences that you noticed.

   b) What if you could use your spectroscope to look at the light from other stars? What do you think it would look like?

Part B: Scaling the Electromagnetic Spectrum

1. Tape four sheets of photocopy paper end to end to make one sheet 112 cm long. Turn the taped sheets over so that the tape is on the bottom.

2. Draw a vertical line 2 cm from the left edge of the paper. Draw two horizontal lines from that line, one about 8 cm from the top of the page, and one about 10 cm below the first line.

3. On the top line, plot the frequencies of the electromagnetic spectrum on a logarithmic scale. To do this, mark off 24 1-cm intervals starting at the left vertical line. Label the marks from 1 to 24 (each number represents increasing powers of 10, from 10^1 to 10^{24}).

4. Use the information from the table of frequency ranges ($\log_{10}$) to divide your scale into the individual bands of electromagnetic radiation. For the visible band, use the entire band, not the individual colors.

Frequency Range Table			
EMR Bands	**Frequency Range (hertz)**	**Log_{10} Frequency Range (hertz)**	**10^{14} Conversions**
Radio and Microwave	Near 0 to 3.0×10^{12}	0 to 12.47	.
Infrared	3.0×10^{12} to 4.6×10^{14}	12.47 to 14.66	.
Visible	4.6×10^{14} to 7.5×10^{14}	14.66 to 14.88	4.6×10^{14} to 7.5×10^{14}
Red	4.6×10^{14} to 5.1×10^{14}	14.66 to 14.71	4.6×10^{14} to 5.1×10^{14}
Orange	5.1×10^{14} to 5.6×10^{14}	14.71 to 14.75	5.1×10^{14} to 5.6×10^{14}
Yellow	5.6×10^{14} to 6.1×10^{14}	14.75 to 14.79	5.6×10^{14} to 6.1×10^{14}
Green	6.1×10^{14} to 6.5×10^{14}	14.79 to 14.81	6.1×10^{14} to 6.5×10^{14}
Blue	6.5×10^{14} to 7.0×10^{14}	14.81 to 14.85	6.5×10^{14} to 7.0×10^{14}
Violet	7.0×10^{14} to 7.5×10^{14}	14.85 to 14.88	7.0×10^{14} to 7.5×10^{14}
Ultraviolet	7.5×10^{14} to 6.0×10^{16}	14.88 to 16.78	.
X-ray	6.0×10^{16} to 1.0×10^{20}	16.78 to 20	.
Gamma Ray	1.0×10^{20} to...	20 to ...	.

5. To construct a linear scale, you will need to convert the range of frequencies that each band of radiation covers for the logarithmic scale. This will allow you to compare the width of the bands of radiation relative to each other. Convert the frequency numbers for all bands (except visible) to 10^{14} and record them in the table.

Example: 10^{17} is 1000 times greater than 10^{14}, so $2.5 \times 10^{17} = 2500 \times 10^{14}$.

6. On the lower horizontal line, mark off ten 10-cm intervals from the vertical line. Starting with the first interval, label each mark with a whole number times 10^{14}, from 1×10^{14} to 10×10^{14}. Label the bottom of your model "Frequency in hertz." Plot some of the 10^{14} frequencies you calculated on the bottom line of your constructed model. Plot the individual colors of the visible spectrum and color them.

a) Compare the logarithmic and linear scales. Describe the differences.

7. Look at the range of ultraviolet radiation.

a) How high do the ultraviolet frequencies extend (in hertz)?

b) Using the same linear scale that you constructed in **Step 6** (10 cm = 1×10^{14} Hz), calculate the width (in centimeters) of the ultraviolet electromagnetic radiation band.

c) Using this same scale what do you think you would need to measure the distance from the beginning of the ultraviolet band of the electromagnetic radiation to the end of the ultraviolet band of the electromagnetic radiation?

d) Using your calculations above and the linear scale you created in **Steps 5** and **6**, how much wider is the ultraviolet band than the entire visible band? How does this compare to the relative widths of these two bands on the log scale you created in **Steps 1-4?**

8. X-rays are the next band of radiation.

   a) Using the same linear scale (10 cm = 1×10^{14} Hz) calculate the distance from the end of the ultraviolet band to the end of the x-ray band. Obtain a map from the Internet or use a local or state highway map to plot the distance.

   b) Based on your results for the width of the x-ray band, what would be your estimate for the width of the gamma-ray band of radiation? What would you need to measure the distance?

Part C: Using Electromagnetic Radiation in Astronomy

1. Astronomers use electromagnetic radiation to study objects and events within our solar system and beyond to distant galaxies. In this part of the activity, you will be asked to research a space science mission and find out how astronomers are using the electromagnetic spectrum in the mission and then report to the rest of the class. The *EarthComm* web site will direct you to links for missions that are either in development, currently operating, or operated in the past. A small sampling is provided in the table on the next page. Many missions contain multiple instruments (it is very expensive to send

instruments into space, so scientists combine several or more studies into one mission), so you should focus upon one instrument and aspect of the mission and get to know it well. The **Digging Deeper** reading section of this activity might help you begin your work.

Questions that you should try to answer in your research include:

- What is the purpose or key question of the mission?

- How does the mission contribute to our understanding of the origin and evolution of the universe or the nature of planets within our solar system?

- Who and/or how many scientists and countries are involved in the mission?

- What instrument within the mission have you selected?

- What wavelength range of electromagnetic radiation does the instrument work at?

- What is the detector and how does it work?

- What does the instrument look like?

- How are the data processed and rendered? Images? Graphs?

- Any other questions that you and your teacher agree upon.

2. When you have completed your research, provide a brief report to the class.

Descriptions of Selected Missions	
Mission/Instrument	**Description**
Hubble – NICMOS Instrument	Hubble's Near Infrared Camera and Multi-Object Spectrometer (NICMOS) can see objects in deepest space—objects whose light takes billions of years to reach Earth. Many secrets about the birth of stars, solar systems, and galaxies are revealed in infrared light, which can penetrate the interstellar gas and dust that block visible light.
Cassini Huygens Mission to Saturn and Titan	The Ultraviolet Imaging Spectrograph (UVIS) is a set of detectors designed to measure ultraviolet light reflected or emitted from atmospheres, rings, and surfaces over wavelengths from 55.8 to 190 nm (nanometers) to determine their compositions, distribution, aerosol content, and temperatures.
SIRTF	The Space InfraRed Telescope Facility (SIRTF) is a space-borne, cryogenically cooled infrared observatory capable of studying objects ranging from our solar system to the distant reaches of the Universe. SIRTF is the final element in NASA's Great Observatories Program, and an important scientific and technical cornerstone of the new Astronomical Search for Origins Program.
HETE-2 High Energy Transient Explorer	The High Energy Transient Explorer is a small scientific satellite designed to detect and localize gamma-ray bursts (GRB's). The primary goals of the HETE mission are the multi-wavelength observation of gamma-ray bursts and the prompt distribution of precise GRB coordinates to the astronomical community for immediate follow-up observations. The HETE science payload consists of one gamma-ray and two x-ray detectors.
Chandra X-Ray Observatory	NASA's Chandra X-ray Observatory, which was launched and deployed by Space Shuttle Columbia in July of 1999, is the most sophisticated x-ray observatory built to date. Chandra is designed to observe x-rays from high-energy regions of the universe, such as the remnants of exploded stars.

Reflecting on the Activity and the Challenge

The spectroscope helped you to see that visible light is made up of different color components. Visible light is only one of the components of radiation you receive from the Sun. In the second part of the activity, you explored models for describing the range of frequencies of energy within electromagnetic radiation.

Finally, you researched a space mission to learn how astronomers are using electromagnetic radiation to understand the evolution of the Earth system. Radiation from the Sun and other objects in the universe is something you will need to explain to your fellow citizens in your **Chapter Challenge** brochure.

Digging Deeper

ELECTROMAGNETIC RADIATION

The Nature of Electromagnetic Radiation

In 1666, Isaac Newton found that he could split light into a spectrum of colors. As he passed a beam of sunlight through a glass prism, a spectrum of colors appeared from red to violet. Newton deduced that visible light was in fact a mixture of different kinds of light. About 10 years later, Christiaan Huygens proposed the idea that light travels in the form of tiny waves. It's known that light with shorter wavelengths is bent (refracted) more than light with longer wavelengths when it passes through a boundary between two different substances. Violet light is refracted the most, because it has the shortest wavelength of the entire range of visible light. This work marked the beginning of **spectroscopy**—the science of studying the properties of light. As you will learn, many years of research in spectroscopy has answered many questions about matter, energy, time, and space.

In your study of the Sun you learned that the Sun radiates energy over a very wide range of wavelengths. Earth's atmosphere shields you from some of the most dangerous forms of electromagnetic radiation. You are familiar with the wavelengths of light that do get through and harm you—mostly in the form of sunburn-causing ultraviolet radiation. Now you can take what you learned and apply the principles of spectroscopy to other objects in the universe.

In the **Investigate** section, you used a **spectroscope** to study the Sun's light by separating it into its various colors. Each color has a characteristic wavelength. This range of colors, from red to violet, is called the **visible spectrum**. The visible spectrum is a small part of the entire spectrum of **electromagnetic radiation** given off by the Sun, other stars, and galaxies.

Electromagnetic radiation is in the form of electromagnetic waves that transfer energy as they travel through space. Electromagnetic waves (like ripples that expand after you toss a stone into a pond) travel at the speed of light (300,000 m/s). That's eight laps around the Earth in one second. Although it's not easy to appreciate from everyday life, it turns out that electromagnetic radiation has properties of both particles and waves. The colors of the visible spectrum are best described as waves, but the same energy that produces an electric current in a solar cell is best described as a particle.

Geo Words

spectroscopy: the science that studies the way light interacts with matter.

spectroscope: an instrument consisting of, at a minimum, a slit and grating (or prism) which produces a spectrum for visual observation.

visible spectrum: part of the electromagnetic spectrum that is detectable by human eyes. The wavelengths range from 350 to 780 nm (a nanometer is a billionth of a meter).

electromagnetic radiation: the energy propagated through space by oscillating electric and magnetic fields. It travels at 3×10^8 m/s in a vacuum and includes (in order of increasing energy) radio, infrared, visible light (optical), ultraviolet, x-rays, and gamma rays.

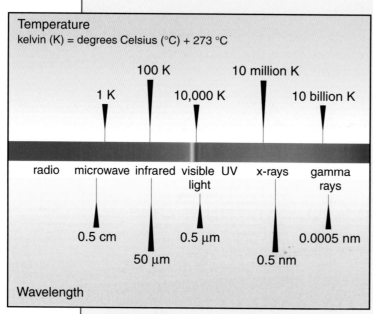

Temperature
kelvin (K) = degrees Celsius (°C) + 273 °C

100 K   10 million K

1 K   10,000 K   10 billion K

radio microwave infrared visible UV   x-rays   gamma
                            light   rays

0.5 cm   0.5 μm   0.0005 nm

50 μm   0.5 nm

Wavelength

Figure I The electromagnetic spectrum. Wavelengths decrease from left to right, and energy increases from left to right. The diagram shows that a relationship exists between the temperature of an object and the peak wavelength of electromagnetic radiation it emits.

Figure I summarizes the spectrum of energy that travels throughout the universe. Scientists divide the spectrum into regions by the wavelength of the waves. Long radio waves have wavelengths from several centimeters to thousands of kilometers, whereas gamma rays are shorter than the width of an atom.

Humans can see only wavelengths between 0.4 and 0.7 μm, which is where the visible spectrum falls. A micrometer (μm) is a millionth of a meter. This means that much of the electromagnetic radiation emitted by the Sun is invisible to human eyes. You are probably familiar, however, with some of the kinds of radiation besides visible light. For example, **ultraviolet** radiation gives you sunburn. **Infrared** radiation you detect as heat. Doctors use x-rays to help diagnose broken bones or other physical problems. Law-enforcement officers use radar to measure the speed of a motor vehicle, and at home you may use microwaves to cook food.

Astronomy and the Electromagnetic Spectrum

Humans have traveled to the Moon and sent probes deeper into our solar system, but how do they learn about distant objects in the universe? They use a variety of instruments to collect electromagnetic radiation from these distant objects. Each tool is designed for a specific part of the spectrum. Visible light reveals the temperature of stars. Visible light is what you see when you look at the stars through telescopes, binoculars, or your unaided eyes. All other forms of light are invisible to the human eye, but they can be detected.

Radio telescopes like the Very Large Array (VLA) and Very Large Baseline Array (VLBA) in New Mexico are sensitive to wavelengths in the radio range. Radio telescopes produce images of celestial bodies by recording the different amounts of radio emission coming from an area of the sky

Geo Words

ultraviolet: electromagnetic radiation at wavelengths shorter than the violet end of visible light; with wavelengths ranging from 5 to 400 nm.

infrared: electromagnetic radiation with wavelengths between about 0.7 to 1000 μm. Infrared waves are not visible to the human eye.

radio telescope: an instrument used to observe longer wavelengths of radiation (radio waves), with large dishes to collect and concentrate the radiation onto antennae.

observed. Astronomers process the information with computers to produce an image. The VLBA has 27 large dish antennas that work together as a single instrument. By using recorders and precise atomic clocks installed at each antenna, the signals from all antennas are combined after the observation is completed.

Geo Words

x-ray telescope: an instrument used to detect stellar and interstellar x-ray emission. Because the Earth's atmosphere absorbs x-rays, x-ray telescopes are placed high above the Earth's surface.

The galaxy M81 is a spiral galaxy about 11 million light years from Earth and is about 50,000 light years across. The spiral structure is clearly shown in *Figure 2*, which shows the relative intensity of emission from neutral atomic hydrogen gas. In this pseudocolor image, red indicates strong radio emission and blue weaker emission.

Figure 2 The galaxy M81.

The orbiting Chandra **x-ray telescope** routinely detects the highly energetic radiation streaming from objects like supernova explosions, active galaxies, and black holes. The Hubble Space Telescope is outfitted with a special infrared instrument sensitive to radiation being produced by star-forming nebulae and cool stars. It also has detectors sensitive to ultraviolet light being emitted by hot young stars and supernova explosions.

A wide array of solar telescopes both on Earth and in space study every wavelength of radiation from our nearest star in minute detail. The tools of astronomy expand scientists' vision into realms that human eyes can never see, to help them understand the ongoing processes and evolution of the universe.

Figure 3 Astronauts working on the Hubble Space Telescope high above the Earth's atmosphere.

Geo Words

peak wavelength: the
wavelength of electromagnetic
radiation with the most
electromagnetic energy
emitted by any object.

Using Electromagnetic Radiation to Understand Celestial Objects

The wavelength of light with the most energy produced by any object, including the Sun, is called its **peak wavelength**. Objects that are hot and are radiating visible light usually look the color of their peak wavelength. People are not hot enough to emit visible light, but they do emit infrared radiation that can be detected with infrared cameras. The Sun has its peak wavelength in the yellow region of the visible spectrum. Hotter objects produce their peaks toward the blue direction. Very hot objects can have their peaks in the ultraviolet, x-ray, or even gamma-ray range of wavelength. A gas under high pressure radiates as well as a hot solid object. Star colors thus reflect temperature. Reddish stars are a "cool" 3000 to 4000 K (kelvins are celsius degrees above absolute zero, which is at minus 273°C). Bluish stars are hot (over 20,000 K).

One of the most important tools in astronomy is the spectrum—a chart of the entire range of wavelengths of light from an object. Astronomers often refer to this chart as the spectrum of the star. These spectra come in two forms: one resembles a bar code with bright and dark lines (see *Figure 4*), and the other is a graph with horizontal and vertical axes (see *Figure 5*). Think of these spectra as "fingerprints" that reveal many kinds of things about an object: its chemical composition, its temperature and pressure, and its motion toward or away from us.

Figure 4 One of the forms of the spectrum of a star. The data encoded here tell astronomers that this star is bright in some elements and dim in others.

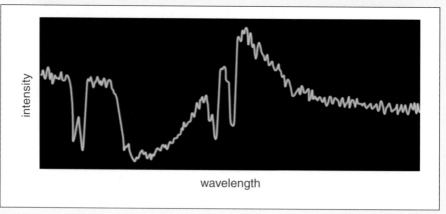

Figure 5 The spectrum of a star can also be represented as a graph with horizontal and vertical axes.

Each chemical element in the universe has its own unique spectrum. If you know what the spectrum of hydrogen is, you can look for its fingerprint in a star. If you suspect that a star may have a lot of the elements helium or calcium, for example, you can compare the spectrum of the star with the known spectra of helium or calcium. If you see bright lines in the stellar spectrum that match the patterns of bright lines in the helium or calcium spectra, then you have identified those elements in the star. This kind of spectrum is known as an **emission spectrum**. If you look at the star and see dark lines where you would expect to see an element—especially hydrogen—it is likely that something between you and the star is absorbing the element. This kind of spectrum is known as an **absorption spectrum**.

The positions of lines in a spectrum reveal the motion of the star toward or away from Earth, as well as the speed of that motion. You have experienced the effect yourself, when a car, a truck, or a train passes by you with its horn blowing. The pitch of the sound increases as the object approaches you, and decreases as the object passes by and moves away from you. That is because when the object is coming toward you, its speed adds to the speed of the sound, making the wavelength of the sound seem higher to your ear. The reverse happens when the object is moving away from you. The same principle applies to the spectrum from a distant object in space, which might be moving either toward Earth or away from Earth.

Geo Words

emission spectrum: a spectrum containing bright lines or a set of discrete wavelengths produced by an element. Each element has its own unique emission spectrum.

absorption spectrum: a continuous spectrum interrupted by absorption lines or a continuous spectrum having a number of discrete wavelengths missing or reduced in intensity.

Check Your Understanding

1. What are the colors of the spectrum of visible sunlight, from longest wavelength to shortest? Are there breaks between these colors, or do they grade continuously from one to the next? Why?

2. Which wavelengths of light can be more harmful to you than others? Why?

3. What tools do astronomers use to detect different wavelengths of light?

4. How can the speed of a distant object in space be measured?

Understanding and Applying What You Have Learned

1. Imagine that you are on a distant planet. Name two parts of the electromagnetic spectrum that you would use to investigate Earth. Explain the reasoning for your choices.

2. Refer to Figure 1 to answer the questions below.

   a) Describe the relationship between wavelength and energy in the electromagnetic spectrum.

   b) Based upon this relationship, why do astronomers use x-ray telescopes to study super nova explosions and black holes?

3. The Sun looks yellow, can warm the surface of your skin, and can also give you a bad sunburn. Explain these three everyday phenomena in terms of the electromagnetic spectrum and peak wavelength.

Preparing for the Chapter Challenge

Recall that your challenge is to educate people about the hazards from outer space and to explain some of the benefits from living in our solar system. Electromagnetic radiation has both beneficial and harmful effects on life on Earth. Use what you have learned in this activity to develop your brochure.

1. Make a list of some of the positive effects of electromagnetic radiation on your community. Explain each item on the list.

2. Make a list of some of the negative effects of electromagnetic radiation on your community. Explain each item on the list.

3. Make a list of celestial radiation sources and any effects they have on Earth systems. What are the chances of a stellar radiation source affecting Earth?

Inquiring Further

1. **Using radio waves to study distant objects**

   Radio waves from the Sun penetrate the Earth's atmosphere. Scientists detect these waves and study their strength and frequency to understand the processes inside the Sun that generate them. Do some research on how these waves are studied.

2. **Detecting electromagnetic radiation**

   Investigate some of the instruments that astronomers use to detect electromagnetic radiation besides light. Where are you likely to find ultraviolet detectors? Describe radio telescope arrays.

3. **Technologies and the electromagnetic spectrum**

   Research some of the technologies that depend on the use of electromagnetic radiation. These might include microwave ovens, x-ray machines, televisions, and radios. How do they work? How is electromagnetic radiation essential to their operation? What interferes with their operation?

Activity 7

Our Community's Place Among the Stars

Goals

In this activity you will:

- Understand the place of our solar system in the Milky Way galaxy.

- Study stellar structure and the stellar evolution (the life histories of stars).

- Understand the relationship between the brightness of an object (its luminosity) and its magnitude.

- Estimate the chances of another star affecting the Earth in some way.

Think about It

When you look at the nighttime sky, you are looking across vast distances of space.

- As you stargaze, what do you notice about the stars?
- Do some stars appear brighter than others? Larger or smaller? What about their colors?

What do you think? Record your impressions and sketch some of the stars in your *EarthComm* notebook. Be prepared to discuss your thoughts with your small group and the class.

Investigate

Part A: Brightness versus Distance from the Source

1. Set a series of lamps with 40-, 60-, and 100-W bulbs (of the same size and all with frosted glass envelopes) up at one end of a room (at least 10 m away). Use the other end of the room for your observing site. Turn all the lamps on. Close all of the shades in the room.

   a) Can you tell the differences in brightness between the lamps?

2. Move the lamp with the 40-W bulb forward 5 m toward you.

   a) Does the light look brighter than the 60-W lamp?

   b) Does it look brighter than the 100-W lamp?

3. Shift the positions of the lamps so that the 40-W lamp and the 100-W lamp are in the back of the room and the 60-W lamp is halfway between you and the other lamps.

   a) How do the brightnesses compare?

4. Using a light meter, test one bulb at a time. If you do not have a light meter, you will have to construct a qualitative scale for brightness.

   a) Record the brightness of each bulb at different distances.

5. Graph the brightness versus the distance from the source for each bulb (wattage).

   a) Plot distance on the horizontal axis of the graph and brightness on the vertical axis. Leave room on the graph so that you can extrapolate the graph beyond the data you have collected. Plot the data for each bulb and connect the points with lines.

   b) Extrapolate the data by extending the lines on the graph using dashes.

6. Use your graph to answer the following questions:

   a) Explain the general relationship between wattage and brightness (as measured by your light meter).

   b) What is the general relationship between distance and brightness?

   c) Do all bulbs follow the same pattern? Why or why not?

   d) Draw a light horizontal line across your graph so that it crosses several of the lines you have graphed.

   e) Does a low-wattage bulb ever have the same brightness as a high-wattage bulb? Describe one or two such cases in your data.

   f) The easiest way to determine the absolute brightness of objects of different brightness and distance is to move all objects to the same distance. How do you think astronomers handle this problem when trying to determine the brightness and distances to stars?

7. When you have completed this activity, spend some time outside stargazing. Think about the relationship between brightness and distance as it applies to stars.

   a) Write your thoughts down in your *EarthComm* notebook.

 Do not stare at the light bulbs for extended periods of time.

Part B: Luminosity and Temperature of Stars

1. An important synthesis of understanding in the study of stars is the Hertzsprung-Russell (HR) diagram. Obtain a copy of the figure below. Examine the figure and answer the following questions:

   a) What does the vertical axis represent?

   b) What does the horizontal axis represent?

   c) The yellow dot on the figure is the Sun. What is its temperature and luminosity?

   d) Put four more dots on the diagram labeled A through D to show the locations of stars that are:

      A. hot and bright
      B. hot and dim
      C. cool and dim
      D. cool and bright

2. Obtain a copy of the *Table 1* and the HR diagram that shows the locations of main sequence stars, supergiants, red giants, and white dwarfs.

   a) Using the luminosity of the stars, and their surface temperatures, plot the locations of stars shown in *Table 1* on a second HR diagram.

3. Classify each of the stars into one of the following four categories, and record the name in your copy of the table:

   — Main sequence
   — Red giants
   — Supergiants
   — White dwarfs

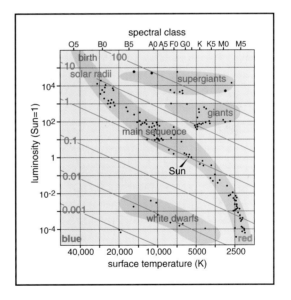

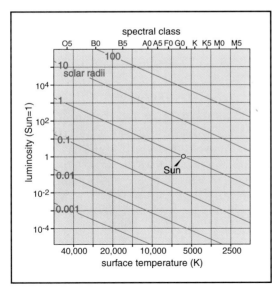

Table 1 Selected Properties of Fourteen Stars							
Star	Surface Temperature (K)	Luminosity (Relative to Sun)	Distance (Light Years)	Mass (Solar Masses)	Diameter (Solar Diameters)	Color	Type of Star
Sirius A	9100	22.6	8.6	2.3	2.03	Blue	
Arcturus	4300	115	36.7	4.5	31.5	Red	
Vega	10300	50.8	25.3	3.07	3.1	Blue	
Capella	5300	75.8	42.2	3	10.8	Red	
Rigel	11000	38,679	733	20	62	Blue	
Procyon A	6500	7.5	11.4	1.78	1.4	Yellow	
Betelgeuse	2300	4520–14,968 (variable)	427	20	662	Red	
Altair	7800	11.3	65.1	2	1.6	Yellow	
Aldebaran	4300	156–171 (variable)	65	25	51.5	Red	
Spica	25300	2121	262	10.9	7.3	Blue	
Pollux	4500	31	33	4	8	Red	
Deneb	10500	66,500	1600	25	116	Yellow	
Procyon B	8700	0.0006	11.2	0.65	0.02	White	
Sirius B	24000	0.00255	13.2	0.98	0.022	Blue-white	

Note: Mass, diameter, and luminosity are given in solar units. For example, Sirius A has 2.3 solar masses, has a diameter 2.03 that of the Sun, and has luminosity 22.6 times brighter than the Sun.

1 solar mass = 2×10^{30} kg = 330,000 Earth masses; 1 solar diameter = 700,000 km = 110 Earth diameters.

Reflecting on the Activity and the Challenge

Measuring the apparent differences in brightness of the light bulbs at different distances helps you to see that distance and brightness are important factors in helping you understand the objects in our universe. When you look at the stars at night, you are seeing stars at different distances and brightnesses. In your **Chapter Challenge** you will be telling people about the effects of distant objects on the Earth. When you assess danger from space, it is important to understand that stars in and of themselves don't pose a danger unless they are both relatively nearby and doing something that could affect Earth. The spectral characteristics of stars help you to understand their temperature, size, and other characteristics. In turn, that helps you to understand if a given star is or could be a threat to Earth. The light from distant stars can also be used to understand our own star, and our own solar system's makeup and evolution.

Digging Deeper

EARTH'S STELLAR NEIGHBORS

Classifying Stars

You already know that our solar system is part of the Milky Way galaxy. Our stellar neighborhood is about two-thirds of the way out on a spiral arm that stretches from the core of the galaxy. The galaxy contains hundreds of billions of stars. Astronomers use a magnitude scale to describe the brightness of objects they see in the sky. A star's brightness decreases with the square of the distance. Thus, a star twice as far from the Earth as an identical star would be one-fourth as bright as the closer star. The first magnitude scales were quite simple—the brightest stars were described as first magnitude, the next brightest stars were second magnitude, and so on down to magnitude 6, which described stars barely visible to the naked eye. The smaller the number, the brighter the star; the larger the number, the dimmer the star.

Today, scientists use a more precise system of magnitudes to describe brightness. The brightest star in the sky is called Sirius A, and its magnitude is −1.4. Of course, the Sun is brighter at −27 and the Moon is −12.6! The dimmest naked-eye stars are still sixth magnitude. To see anything dimmer than that, you have to magnify your view with binoculars or telescopes. The best ground-based telescopes can detect objects as faint as 25th magnitude. To get a better view of very faint, very distant objects, you have to get above the Earth's atmosphere. The Hubble Space Telescope, for example can detect things as dim as 30th magnitude!

Figure 1 This NASA Hubble Space Telescope near-infrared image of newborn binary stars reveals a long thin nebula pointing toward a faint companion object which could be the first extrasolar planet to be imaged directly.

Perhaps you have seen a star described as a G-type star or an O-type star. These are stellar classifications that depend on the color and temperature of the stars. They also help astronomers understand where a given star is in its evolutionary history. To get such information, astronomers study stars with spectrographs to determine their temperature and chemical makeup. As you can see in the table below, there are seven main categories of stars:

Stellar Classification	Temperature (kelvins)
O	25,000 K and higher
B	11,000–25,000 K
A	7500–11,000 K
F	6000–7500 K
G	5000–6000 K
K	3500–5000 K
M	less than 3500 K

The Lives of Stars

Astronomers use the term **luminosity** for the total rate at which a star emits radiation energy. Unlike apparent brightness (how bright the star appears to be) luminosity is an intrinsic property. It doesn't depend on how far away the star is. In the early 1900s Ejnar Hertzsprung and Henry Norris Russell independently made the discovery that the luminosity of a star was related to its surface temperature. In the second part of this activity, you worked with a graph that shows this relationship. It is called the Hertzsprung-Russell (HR) diagram in honor of the astronomers who discovered this relationship. The HR diagram alone does not tell you how stars change. By analogy, if you were to plot the IQ versus the weight of everyone in your school, you would probably find a very poor relationship between these two variables. Your graph would resemble a scatter plot more than it would a line. However, if you plotted the height versus weight for the same people, you are more likely to find a strong relationship (data would be distributed along a trend or line). The graph doesn't tell you why this relationship exists — that's up to you to determine. Similarly, the HR diagram shows that stars don't just appear randomly on a plot of luminosity versus temperature, but fall into classes of luminosity (red giants, white dwarfs, and so on).

The life cycle of a star begins with its formation in a cloud of gas and dust called a **molecular cloud**. The material in the cloud begins to clump

Geo Words

luminosity: the total amount of energy radiated by an object every second.

molecular cloud: a large, cold cloud made up mostly of molecular hydrogen and helium, but with some other gases, too, like carbon monoxide. It is in these clouds that new stars are born.

together, mixing and swirling. Eventually the core begins to heat as more material is drawn in by gravitational attraction. When the temperature in the center of the cloud reaches 15 million kelvins, the stellar fusion reaction starts up and a star is born. Such stars are called main-sequence stars. Many stars spend 90% of their lifetimes on the main sequence.

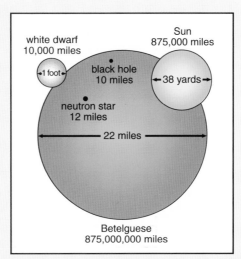

Figure 2 Scaling stars to 10,000 miles to one foot reveals the relative sizes of various stars.

Newborn stars are like baby chickens pecking their way out of a shell. As these infant stars grow, they bathe the cloud surrounding them in strong ultraviolet radiation. This vaporizes the cloud, creating beautiful sculpted shapes in the cloud. In the photograph in *Figure 3*, the Hubble Space Telescope studied a region of starbirth called NGC 603. Notice the cluster of bright white stars in the center "cavern" of the cloud of gas and dust. Their ultraviolet light has carved out a shell of gas and dust around the stellar newborns.

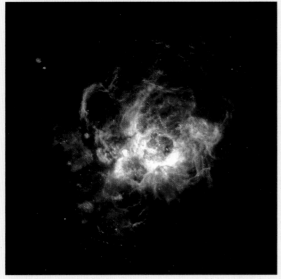

Figure 3 The starforming region NGC 603 in the galaxy M33.

Figure 4 The Orion Nebula is an example of a molecular cloud, from which new stars are born.

How long a star lives depends on its mass (masses of selected stars are shown in *Table 1* in the **Investigate** section of the activity). Stars like our Sun will live about 10 billion years. Smaller, cooler stars might go on twice that long, slowly burning their fuel. Massive supergiant stars consume their mass much more quickly, living a star's life only a few tens of millions of years. Very hot stars also go through their fuel very quickly, existing perhaps only a few hundred thousand years. The time a star spends on the main sequence can be determined using the following formula:

$$\text{Time on main sequence} = \frac{1}{M^{2.5}} \times \textbf{10 billion years}$$

where *M* is the mass of the star in units of solar masses.

Even though high-mass stars have more mass, they burn it much more quickly and end up having very short lives.

In the end, however, stars of all types must die. Throughout its life a star loses mass in the form of a stellar wind. In the case of the Sun this is called the solar wind. As a star ages, it loses more and more mass. Stars about the size of the Sun and smaller end their days as tiny, shrunken remnants of their former selves, surrounded by beautiful shells of gas and dust. These are called planetary nebulae. In about five billion years the Sun will start to resemble one of these ghostly nebulae, ending its days surrounded by the shell of its former self.

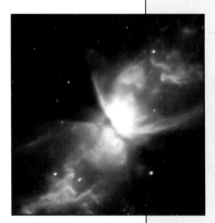
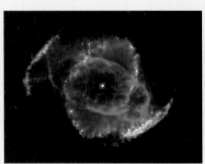
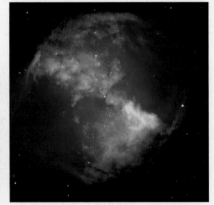

Figure 5A, 5B 5C Three examples of the deaths of stars about the size of the Sun. **A:** The Butterfly Nebula. **B:** The Cat's-Eye Nebula. In both cases at least the dying star lies embedded in a cloud of material exhaled by the star, as it grew older. **C:** The Dumbbell Nebula. European Southern Observatory.

Massive stars (supergiants tens of times more massive than the Sun) also lose mass as they age, but at some point their cores collapse catastrophically. The end of a supergiant's life is a cataclysmic explosion called a **supernova**. In an instant of time, most of the star's mass is hurled out into space, leaving behind a tiny remnant called a **neutron star**. If the star is massive enough, the force of the explosion can be so strong that the remnant is imploded into a **stellar black hole**—a place where the gravity is so strong that not even light can escape.

The material that is shed from dying stars (whether they end their days as slowly fading dwarf stars, or planetary nebulae, or supernovae) makes its way into the space between the stars. There it mixes and waits for a slow gravitational contraction down to a new episode of starbirth and ultimately star death. Because humans evolved on a planet that was born from a recycled cloud of stellar mass, they are very much star "stuff"—part of a long cycle of life, death, and rebirth.

Astronomers search the universe to study the mechanics of star formation. Star nurseries and star graveyards are scattered through all the galaxies. In some cases, starbirth is triggered when one galaxy collides with (actually passes through) another. The clouds of gas and dust get the push they need to start the process.

Scientists also search for examples of planetary nebulae. They want to understand when and how these events occur. Not only are these nebulae interesting, but also they show scientists what the fate of our solar system will be billions of years from now.

What would happen if there were a supernova explosion in our stellar neighborhood sometime in the future? Depending on how close it was, you could be bombarded with strong radiation and shock waves from the explosion. The chances of this happening are extremely small—although some astronomers think that a supernova some five billion years ago may have provided the gravitational kick that started our own proto–solar nebula on the road to stardom and planetary formation.

Figure 6 The Crab Nebula is the remnant of a supernova explosion that took place in the year 1054 AD.

Geo Words

supernova: the death explosion of a massive star whose core has completely burned out. Supernova explosions can temporarily outshine a galaxy.

neutron star: the imploded core of a massive star produced by a supernova explosion.

stellar black hole: the leftover core of a massive single star after a supernova. Black holes exert such large gravitational pull that not even light can escape.

Check Your Understanding

1. How do astronomers classify stars?

2. Write a brief outline of how stars are born.

3. What determines the way a star dies?

Understanding and Applying What You Have Learned

1. Using an astronomy computer program or a guidebook to the stars, make a list of the 10 nearest stars, and their distances, magnitudes, and spectral classes. What do their classes tell you about them?

2. What is mass loss and how does it figure in the death of a star? Is the Sun undergoing mass loss?

3. What happens to the material left over from the death of a star?

4. Two identical stars have different apparent brightnesses. One star is 10 light years away, and the other is 30 light-years away from us. Which star is brighter, and by how much?

5. Refer to *Table 1* to answer the questions below:

   a) Calculate how long the Sun will spend on the main sequence.
   b) Calculate how long Spica will spend on the main sequence.
   c) Relate your results to the statement that the more massive the star, the shorter they live.

6. Explain the relationships between temperature, luminosity, mass, and lifetime of stars.

Preparing for the Chapter Challenge

You are about to complete your **Chapter Challenge**. In the beginning you were directed to learn as much as you could about how extraterrestrial objects and events could affect the Earth and your community. In order to do this you have explored the stars and planets, looking at all the possibilities. By now you have a good idea about how frequently certain kinds of events occur that affect Earth. The Sun is a constant source of energy and radiation.

In this final activity you learned our solar system's place in the galaxy, and you read about how stars are born and die. Because the birth of our solar system led directly to our planet, and the evolution of life here, it's important to know something about stars and how they come into existence.

You now know that the solar system is populated with comets and asteroids, some of which pose a threat to Earth over long periods of time.

The evolution of the Earth's orbit and its gravitational relationship with the Moon make changes to the Earth's climate, length of year, and length of day. The solar system is part of a galaxy of other stars, with the nearest star being only 4.21 light-years away. The Sun itself is going through a ten-billion-year-long period of evolution and will end as a planetary nebula some five billion years in the future. Finally, our Milky Way galaxy is wheeling toward a meeting with another galaxy in the very, very distant future. Your challenge now that you know and understand these things is to explain them to your fellow citizens and help them understand the risks and benefits of life on this planet, in this solar system, and in this galaxy.

Inquiring Further

1. **Evolution of the Milky Way galaxy**

   The Milky Way galaxy formed some 10 billion years ago, when the universe itself was only a fraction of its current age. Research the formation of our galaxy and find out how its ongoing evolution influenced the formation of our solar system.

2. **Starburst knots in other galaxies**

   Other galaxies show signs of star birth and star death. You read about a starbirth region called NGC 603 in the **Digging Deeper** reading section of this activity. Astronomers have found evidence of colliding galaxies elsewhere in the universe. In nearly every case, such collisions have spurred the formation of new stars. In the very distant future the Milky Way will collide with another galaxy, and it's likely that starburst knots will be formed. Look for examples of starbirth nurseries and starburst knots in other galaxies and write a short report on your findings. How do you think such a collision would affect Earth (assuming that anyone is around to experience it)?

Earth Science at Work

ATMOSPHERE: *Astronaut*
There is no atmosphere in space; therefore, astronauts must have pressurized atmosphere in their spacecraft cabins. Protective suits protect them when they perform extra-vehicular activities.

BIOSPHERE: *Exobiologist*
"Did life ever get started on Mars?" By learning more about the ancient biosphere and environments of the early Earth, exobiologists hope that they may be able to answer such questions when space missions return with rocks gathered on Mars.

CRYOSPHERE: *Glaciologist*
Ice is abundant on the Earth's surface, in the planetary system, and in interstellar space. Glaciologists study processes at or near the base of glaciers and ice sheets on Earth and other planets.

GEOSPHERE: *Planetary geologist*
By researching martian volcanism and tectonism, or the geology of the icy satellites of Jupiter, Saturn, and Uranus, planetary geologists hope to develop a better understanding of our place in the universe.

HYDROSPHERE: *Lifeguard*
Surfers and other water-sport enthusiasts rely on lifeguards to inform them of the time of high and low tides. Low tides or high tides can create dangerous situations.

How is each person's work related to the Earth system, and to Astronomy?

2

Climate Change
...and Your Community

CLIMATE CHANGE
...and Your Community

2

Getting Started

The Earth's climate has changed many times over geologic history.

- What kinds of processes or events might cause the Earth's climate to change?

What do you think? Write down your ideas about these questions in your *EarthComm* notebook. Be prepared to discuss your ideas with your small group and the class.

Scenario

Your local newspaper would like to run a series of articles about global warming. However, the newspaper's science reporter is unavailable. The newspaper has come to your class to ask you and your classmates to write the articles. These feature articles and an editorial will be run in the Science and Environment section of the newspaper. The newspaper editor wants to give the readers of the paper a thorough scientific background to understand the idea of global climate change.

Chapter Challenge

Article 1: How Has Global Climate Changed Over Time?

Many people are not aware that the Earth's climate has changed continually over geologic time. This article should contain information about:

- the meaning of "climate," both regional and global;
- examples of different global climates in the geologic past;
- how geologists find out about past climates, and
- a description of your community's present climate and examples of past climates in your part of the country.

Article 2:
Causes of Global Climate Change

Some people might not be aware that human production of greenhouse gases is not the only thing that can cause the Earth's climate to change. There are many different factors that may affect how and when the Earth's climate changes. This article should include information about:

- Milankovitch cycles;
- plate tectonics;
- ocean currents, and
- carbon dioxide levels.

Article 3:
What is "Global Warming" and How Might It Affect Our Community?

Although almost everyone has heard the terms "greenhouse gases" and "global warming," there is a lot of confusion about what these terms actually mean. This article should contain information about:

- greenhouse gases;
- how humans have increased the levels of carbon dioxide in the atmosphere;
- why scientists think increased carbon dioxide might lead to global warming;
- possible effects of global warming, focusing on those that would have the greatest impact on your community, and
- why it is difficult to predict climate change.

Editorial

The final piece is not an article but rather an editorial in which the newspaper expresses its opinion about a particular topic. In the editorial, you should state:

- whether your community should be concerned about global warming and why, and
- what steps, if any, your community should take in response to the possibility of global warming.

Assessment Criteria

Think about what you have been asked to do. Scan ahead through the chapter activities to see how they might help you to meet the challenge. Work with your classmates and your teachers to define the criteria for assessing your work. Record all of this information. Make sure that you understand the criteria as well as you can before you begin. Your teacher may provide you with a sample rubric to help you get started.

Activity 1   Present-Day Climate in Your Community

Goals

In this activity you will:

- Identify factors of the physical environment.

- Use a topographic map to gather data about elevation and latitude, and physical features.

- Interpret data from a climate data table.

- Compare and contrast climate information from two different parts of the United States.

- Understand how physical features can influence the climate of an area.

Think about It

A friend e-mails you from Italy to ask what your environment and climate are like. You plan to e-mail her a reply.

- How would you describe the physical environment of your community?
- How would you describe the climate of your community?

What do you think? Record your ideas about these questions in your *EarthComm* notebook. Be prepared to discuss your responses with your small group and the class.

Investigate

Part A: Physical Features and Climate in Your Community

1. Depending on where your community is located and how large it is, you might wish to expand your definition of "community" to include a larger area, like your county or state. For example, your town does not have to be right on the ocean to have its climate influenced by the ocean.

a) Write a "definition" of the area that you will examine as your "community."

2. Use the climate data tables provided on the following pages and topographic maps of your "community" to describe the climate in your community.

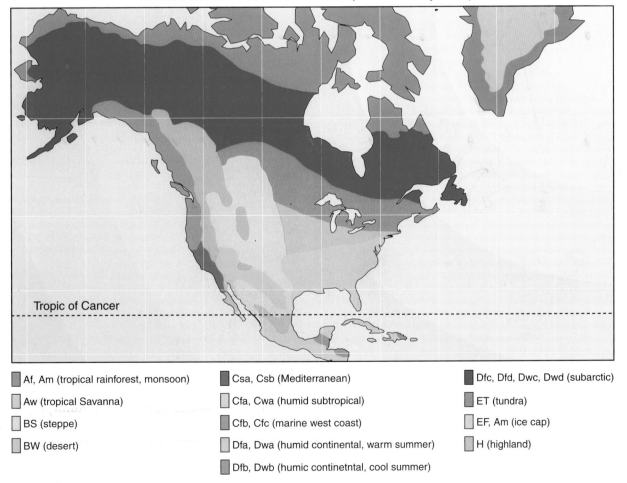

Climatic Zones of North America (Mercator Projection)

Tropic of Cancer

- Af, Am (tropical rainforest, monsoon)
- Aw (tropical Savanna)
- BS (steppe)
- BW (desert)
- Csa, Csb (Mediterranean)
- Cfa, Cwa (humid subtropical)
- Cfb, Cfc (marine west coast)
- Dfa, Dwa (humid continental, warm summer)
- Dfb, Dwb (humic continetntal, cool summer)
- Dfc, Dfd, Dwc, Dwd (subarctic)
- ET (tundra)
- EF, Am (ice cap)
- H (highland)

Abbreviations for climate zones are based upon the Koppen classification system.

Country and Station	Latitude	Longitude	Elevation	Record Length	Temperature										
					Average Daily									Extreme	
					January		April		July		October				
					Max.	Min.	Max.	Min.	Max.	Min.	Max.	Min.		Max.	Min.
United States (Conterminous):	′ ″	′ ″	Feet	Yrs.	°F	°F	°F	°F	°F	°F	°F	°F		°F	°F
Albuquerque, NM	35 03N	106 37W	5311	30	46	24	69	42	91	66	71	45		105	−17
Asheville, NC	35 26N	82 32W	2140	30	48	28	67	42	84	61	68	45		100	−16
Atlanta, GA	33 39N	84 26W	1010	30	52	37	70	50	87	71	72	52		105	− 8
Austin, TX	30 18N	97 42W	597	30	60	41	78	57	95	74	82	60		109	− 2
Birmingham, AL	33 34N	86 45W	620	30	57	36	76	50	93	71	79	52		106	−10
Bismarck, ND	46 46N	100 45W	1647	30	20	0	55	32	86	58	59	34		114	−45
Boise, ID	43 34N	116 13W	2838	30	36	22	63	37	91	59	65	38		112	−28
Brownsville, TX	25 54N	97 26W	16	30	71	52	82	66	93	76	85	67		106	12
Buffalo, NY	42 56N	78 44W	705	30	31	18	53	34	80	59	60	41		99	−21
Cheyenne, WY	41 09N	104 49W	6126	30	37	14	56	30	85	55	63	32		100	−38
Chicago, IL	41 47N	87 45W	607	30	33	19	57	41	84	67	63	47		105	−27
Des Moines, IA	41 32N	93 39W	938	30	29	11	59	38	87	65	66	43		110	−30
Dodge City, KS	37 46N	99 58W	2582	30	42	20	66	41	93	68	71	46		109	−26
El Paso, TX	31 48N	106 24W	3918	30	56	30	78	49	95	69	79	50		112	− 8
Indianapolis, IN	39 44N	86 17W	792	30	37	21	61	40	86	64	67	44		107	−25
Jacksonville, FL	30 25N	81 39W	20	30	67	45	80	58	92	73	80	62		105	7
Kansas City, MO	39 07N	94 36W	742	30	40	23	66	46	92	71	72	49		113	−23
Las Vegas, NV	36 05N	115 10W	2162	30	54	32	78	51	104	76	80	53		117	8
Los Angeles, CA	33 56N	118 23W	97	30	64	45	67	52	76	62	73	57		110	23
Louisville, KY	38 11N	85 44W	477	30	44	27	66	43	89	67	70	46		107	−20
Miami, FL	25 48N	80 16W	7	30	76	58	83	66	89	75	85	71		100	28
Minneapolis, MN	44 53N	93 13W	834	30	22	2	56	33	84	61	61	37		108	−34
Missoula, MT	46 55N	114 05W	3190	30	28	10	57	31	85	49	58	30		105	−33
Nashville, TN	36 07N	86 41W	590	30	49	31	71	48	91	70	76	49		107	−17
New Orleans, LA	29 59N	90 15W	3	30	64	45	78	58	91	73	80	61		102	7
New York, NY	40 47N	73 58W	132	30	40	27	60	43	85	68	66	50		106	−15
Oklahoma City, OK	35 24N	97 36W	1285	30	46	28	71	49	93	72	74	52		113	−17
Phoenix, AZ	33 26N	112 01W	1117	30	64	35	84	50	105	75	87	55		122	16
Pittsburgh, PA	40 27N	80 00W	747	30	40	25	63	42	85	65	65	45		103	−20
Portland, ME	43 39N	70 19W	47	30	32	12	53	32	80	57	60	37		103	−39
Portland, OR	45 36N	122 36W	21	30	44	33	62	42	79	56	63	45		107	− 3
Reno, NV	39 30N	119 47W	4404	30	45	16	65	31	89	46	69	29		106	−19
Salt Lake City, UT	40 46N	111 58W	4220	30	37	18	63	36	94	60	65	38		107	−30
San Francisco, CA	37 37N	122 23W	8	30	55	42	64	47	72	54	71	51		109	20
Sault Ste. Marie, MI	46 28N	84 22W	721	30	23	8	46	30	76	54	55	38		98	−37
Seattle, WA	47 27N	122 18W	400	30	44	33	58	40	76	54	60	44		100	0
Sheridan, WY	44 46N	106 58W	3964	30	34	9	56	31	87	56	62	33		106	−41
Spokane, WA	47 38N	117 32W	2356	30	31	19	59	36	86	55	60	38		108	−30
Washington, DC	38 51N	77 03W	14	30	44	30	66	46	87	69	68	50		104	−18
Wilmington, NC	34 16N	77 55W	28	30	58	37	74	51	89	71	76	55		104	0

Temperatures in the United States

Source: NOAA

Average Precipitation in the United States														
Country and Station	**Average Precipitation**													
United States (Conterminous):	**Record Length**	**Jan.**	**Feb.**	**Mar.**	**Apr.**	**May**	**Jun.**	**Jul.**	**Aug.**	**Sep.**	**Oct.**	**Nov.**	**Dec.**	**Year**
	Years	**In.**	**In.**	**In.**	**In.**	**In.**	**In.**	**In.**	**In.**	**In.**	**In.**	**In.**	**In.**	**In.**
Albuquerque, NM	30	0.4	0.4	0.5	0.5	0.8	0.6	1.2	1.3	1.0	0.8	0.4	0.5	8.4
Asheville, NC	30	4.2	4.0	4.8	4.0	3.7	3.5	5.9	4.9	3.6	3.1	2.8	3.6	48.1
Atlanta, GA	30	4.4	4.5	5.4	4.5	3.2	3.8	4.7	3.6	3.3	2.4	3.0	4.4	47.2
Austin, TX	30	2.4	2.6	2.1	3.6	3.7	3.2	2.2	1.9	3.4	2.8	2.1	2.5	32.5
Birmingham, AL	30	5.0	5.3	6.0	4.5	3.4	4.0	5.2	4.9	3.3	3.0	3.5	5.0	53.1
Bismarck, ND	30	0.4	0.4	0.8	1.2	2.0	3.4	2.2	1.7	1.2	0.9	0.6	0.4	15.2
Boise, ID	30	1.3	1.3	1.3	1.2	1.3	0.9	0.2	0.2	0.4	0.8	1.2	1.3	11.4
Brownsville, TX	30	1.4	1.5	1.0	1.6	2.4	3.0	1.7	2.8	5.0	3.5	1.3	1.7	26.9
Buffalo, NY	30	2.8	2.7	3.2	3.0	3.0	2.5	2.6	3.1	3.1	3.0	3.6	3.0	35.6
Cheyenne, WY	30	0.5	0.6	1.2	1.9	2.5	2.1	1.8	1.4	1.1	0.8	0.6	0.5	15.0
Chicago, IL	30	1.9	1.6	2.7	3.0	3.7	4.1	3.4	3.2	2.7	2.8	2.2	1.9	33.2
Des Moines, IA	30	1.3	1.1	2.1	2.5	4.1	4.7	3.1	3.7	2.9	2.1	1.8	1.1	30.5
Dodge City, KS	30	0.6	0.7	1.2	1.8	3.2	3.0	2.3	2.4	1.5	1.4	0.6	0.5	19.2
El Paso, TX	30	0.5	0.4	0.4	0.3	0.4	0.7	1.3	1.2	1.1	0.9	0.3	0.5	8.0
Indianapolis, IN	30	3.1	2.3	3.4	3.7	4.0	4.6	3.5	3.0	3.2	2.6	3.1	2.7	39.2
Jacksonville, FL	30	2.5	2.9	3.5	3.6	3.5	6.3	7.7	6.9	7.6	5.2	1.7	2.2	53.6
Kansas City, MO	30	1.4	1.2	2.5	3.6	4.4	4.6	3.2	3.8	3.3	2.9	1.8	1.5	34.2
Las Vegas, NV	30	0.5	0.4	0.4	0.2	0.1	*	0.5	0.5	0.3	0.2	0.3	0.4	3.8
Los Angeles, CA	30	2.7	2.9	1.8	1.1	0.1	0.1	*	*	0.2	0.4	1.1	2.4	12.8
Louisville, KY	30	4.1	3.3	4.6	3.8	3.9	4.0	3.4	3.0	2.6	2.3	3.2	3.2	41.4
Miami, FL	30	2.0	1.9	2.3	3.9	6.4	7.4	6.8	7.0	9.5	8.2	2.8	1.7	59.9
Minneapolis, MN	30	0.7	0.8	1.5	1.9	3.2	4.0	3.3	3.2	2.4	1.6	1.4	0.9	24.9
Missoula, MT	30	0.9	0.9	0.7	1.0	1.9	1.9	0.9	0.7	1.0	1.0	0.9	1.1	12.9
Nashville, TN	30	5.5	4.5	5.2	3.7	3.7	3.3	3.7	2.9	2.9	2.3	3.3	4.2	45.2
New Orleans, LA	30	3.8	4.0	5.3	4.6	4.4	4.4	6.7	5.3	5.0	2.8	3.3	4.1	53.7
New York, NY	30	3.3	2.8	4.0	3.4	3.7	3.3	3.7	4.4	3.9	3.1	3.4	3.3	42.3
Oklahoma City, OK	30	1.3	1.4	2.0	3.1	5.2	4.5	2.4	2.5	3.0	2.5	1.6	1.4	30.9
Phoenix, AZ	30	0.7	0.9	0.7	0.3	0.1	0.1	0.8	1.1	0.7	0.5	0.5	0.9	7.3
Pittsburgh, PA	30	2.8	2.3	3.5	3.4	3.8	4.0	3.6	3.5	2.7	2.5	2.3	2.5	36.9
Portland, ME	30	4.4	3.8	4.3	3.7	3.4	3.2	2.9	2.4	3.5	3.2	4.2	3.9	42.9
Portland, OR	30	5.4	4.2	3.8	2.1	2.0	1.7	0.4	0.7	1.6	3.6	5.3	6.4	37.2
Reno, NV	30	1.2	1.0	0.7	0.5	0.5	0.4	0.3	0.2	0.2	0.5	0.6	1.1	7.2
Salt Lake City, UT	30	1.4	1.2	1.6	1.8	1.4	1.0	0.6	0.9	0.5	1.2	1.3	1.2	14.1
San Francisco, CA	30	4.0	3.5	2.7	1.3	0.5	0.1	*	*	0.2	0.7	1.6	4.1	18.7
Sault Ste. Marie, MI	30	2.1	1.5	1.8	2.2	2.8	3.3	2.5	2.9	3.8	2.8	3.3	2.3	31.3
Seattle, WA	30	5.7	4.2	3.8	2.4	1.7	1.6	0.8	1.0	2.1	4.0	5.4	6.3	39.0
Sheridan, WY	30	0.6	0.7	1.4	2.2	2.6	2.6	1.2	0.9	1.2	1.1	0.8	0.6	15.9
Spokane, WA	30	2.4	1.9	1.5	0.9	1.2	1.5	0.4	0.4	0.8	1.6	2.2	2.4	17.2
Washington, DC	30	3.0	2.5	3.2	3.2	4.1	3.2	4.2	4.9	3.8	3.1	2.8	2.8	40.8
Wilmington, NC	30	2.9	3.4	4.0	2.9	3.5	4.3	7.7	6.9	6.3	3.0	3.1	3.4	51.4

Source: NOAA

Average Snowfall in the United States													
Country and Station United States (Conterminous): Data through 1998	**Average Snowfall (includes ice pellets)**												
	Record Length	**Jan.**	**Feb.**	**Mar.**	**Apr.**	**May**	**Jun.**	**Jul.**	**Aug.**	**Sep.**	**Oct.**	**Nov.**	**Dec.**	**Year**
	Years	**In.**	**In.**	**In.**	**In.**	**In.**	**In.**	**In.**	**In.**	**In.**	**In.**	**In.**	**In.**	**In.**
Albuquerque, NM	59	2.5	2.1	1.8	0.6	0	T	T	T	T	0.1	1.2	2.6	10.9
Asheville, NC	34	5	4.3	2.8	0.6	T	T	T	T	0	T	0.7	2	15.4
Atlanta, GA	62	0.9	0.5	0.4	T	0	0	0	0	0	T	0	0.2	2
Austin, TX	57	0.5	0.3	T	T	T	0	0	0	0	0	0.1	T	0.9
Birmingham, AL	55	0.6	0.2	0.3	0.1	T	T	T	0	T	T	T	0.3	1.5
Bismarck, ND	59	7.6	7	8.6	4	0.9	T	T	T	0.2	1.8	7	7	44.1
Boise, ID	59	6.5	3.7	1.6	0.6	0.1	T	T	T	T	0.1	2.3	5.9	20.8
Brownsville, TX	59	T	T	T	0	0	0	0	T	0	0	T	T	T
Buffalo, NY	55	23.7	18	11.9	3.2	0.2	T	T	T	T	0.3	11.2	22.8	91.3
Cheyenne, WY	63	6.6	6.3	11.9	9.2	3.2	0.2	T	T	0.9	3.7	7.1	6.3	55.4
Chicago, IL	39	10.7	8.2	6.6	1.6	0.1	T	T	T	T	0.4	1.9	8.1	37.6
Des Moines, IA	57	8.3	7.2	6	1.8	0	T	T	T	T	0.3	3.1	6.7	33.4
Dodge City, KS	56	4.3	3.9	5	0.8	T	T	T	T	0	0.3	2.1	3.6	20
El Paso, TX	57	1.3	0.8	0.4	0.3	T	T	T	0	T	0	0.9	1.6	5.3
Indianapolis, IN	67	6.6	5.6	3.4	0.5	0	T	0	T	0	0.2	1.9	5.1	23.3
Jacksonville, FL	57	T	0	0	T	0	T	T	0	0	0	0	0	T
Kansas City, MO	64	5.7	4.4	3.4	0.8	T	T	T	0	T	0.1	1.2	4.4	20
Las Vegas, NV	48	0.9	0.1	0	T	0	0	0	T	0	T	0.1	0.1	1.2
Los Angeles, CA	62	T	T	T	0	0	0	0	0	0	0	0	T	T
Louisville, KY	51	5.4	4.6	3.3	0.1	T	T	T	0	0	0.1	1	2.1	16.6
Miami, FL	56	0	0	0	0	T	0	0	0	0	0	0	0	T
Minneapolis, MN	60	10.2	8.2	10.6	2.8	0.1	T	T	T	T	0.5	7.9	9.4	49.7
Missoula, MT	54	12.3	7.3	6	2.1	0.7	T	T	T	T	0.8	6.2	11.3	46.7
Nashville, TN	56	3.7	3	1.5	0	0	T	0	T	0	0	0.4	1.4	10
New Orleans, LA	50	0	0.1	T	T	T	0	0	0	0	0	T	0.1	0.2
New York, NY	130	7.5	8.6	5.1	0.9	T	0	T	0	0	0	0.9	5.4	28.4
Oklahoma City, OK	59	3.1	2.4	1.5	T	T	T	T	T	T	T	0.5	1.8	9.3
Phoenix, AZ	61	T	0	T	T	T	0	0	0	0	T	0	T	T
Pittsburgh, PA	46	11.7	9.2	8.7	1.7	0.1	T	T	T	T	0.4	3.5	8.2	43.5
Portland, ME	58	19.6	16.9	12.9	3	0.2	0	0	0	T	0.2	3.3	14.6	70.7
Portland, OR	55	3.2	1.1	0.4	T	0	T	0	T	T	0	0.4	1.4	6.5
Reno, NV	54	5.8	5.2	4.3	1.2	0.8	0	0	0	0	0.3	2.4	4.3	24.3
Salt Lake City, UT	70	13.8	10	9.4	4.9	0.6	T	T	T	0.1	1.3	6.8	11.7	58.6
San Francisco, CA	69	0	T	T	0	0	0	0	0	0	0	0	0	T
Sault Ste. Marie, MI	55	29	18.4	14.7	5.8	0.5	T	T	T	0.1	2.4	15.8	31.1	117.8
Seattle, WA	48	2.9	0.9	0.6	0	T	0	0	0	0	T	0.7	2.2	7.3
Sheridan, WY	58	11	10.4	12.6	9.9	2	0.1	T	0	1.3	4.6	9.2	10.9	72
Spokane, WA	51	15.6	7.5	3.9	0.6	0.1	T	0	0	T	0.4	6.3	14.6	49
Washington, DC	55	5.5	5.4	2.2	T	T	T	T	T	T	0	0	0.8	2.8	16.7
Wilmington, NC	47	0.4	0.5	0.4	T	T	T	T	T	0	0	0	T	0.6	1.9

Trace (T) is recorded for less than 0.05 inch of snowfall.

Last updated on 5/25/2000 by NRCC.

Source: The National Climatic Data Center/NOAA

City/State	Last Frost Date	First Frost Date	No. of Frost-Free Days per Year
Albany, NY	May 7	September 29	144 days
Albuquerque, NM	April 16	October 29	196 days
Atlanta, GA	March 13	November 12	243 days
Baltimore, MD	March 26	November 13	231 days
Birmingham, AL	March 29	November 6	221 days
Boise, ID	May 8	October 9	153 days
Boston, MA	April 6	November 10	217 days
Charleston, SC	March 11	November 20	253 days
Charlotte, NC	March 21	November 15	239 days
Cheyenne, WY	May 20	September 27	130 days
Chicago, IL	April 14	November 2	201 days
Columbus, OH	April 26	October 17	173 days
Dallas, TX	March 18	November 12	239 days
Denver, CO	May 3	October 8	157 days
Des Moines, IA	April 19	October 17	180 days
Detroit, MI	April 24	October 22	181 days
Duluth, MN	May 21	September 21	122 days
Fargo, ND	May 13	September 27	137 days
Fayetteville, AR	April 21	October 17	179 days
Helena, MT	May 18	September 18	122 days
Houston, TX	February 4	December 10	309 days
Indianapolis, IN	April 22	October 20	180 days
Jackson, MS	March 17	November 9	236 days
Jacksonville, FL	February 14	December 14	303 days
Las Vegas, NV	March 7	November 21	259 days
Lincoln, NB	March 13	November 13	180 days
Los Angeles, CA	None likely	None likely	365 days
Louisville, KY	April 1	November 7	220 days
Memphis, TN	March 23	November 7	228 days
Miami, FL	None	None	365 days
Milwaukee, WI	May 5	October 9	156 days
New Haven, CT	April 15	October 27	195 days
New Orleans, LA	February 20	December 5	288 days
New York, NY	April 1	November 11	233 days
Phoenix, AZ	February 5	December 15	308 days
Pittsburgh, PA	April 16	November 3	201 days
Portland, ME	May 10	September 30	143 days
Portland, OR	April 3	November 7	217 days
Richmond, VA	April 10	October 26	198 days
Salt Lake City, UT	April 12	November 1	203 days
San Francisco, CA	January 8	January 5	362 days
Seattle, WA	March 24	November 11	232 days
St. Louis, MO	April 3	November 6	217 days
Topeka, KS	April 21	October 14	175 days
Tulsa, OK	March 30	November 4	218 days
Washington, D.C.	April 10	October 31	203 days
Wichita, KS	April 13	October 23	193 days

Include the following important climatic factors in your description of the climate in your community:

- Average daily temperatures in the winter and summer.

- Record high and low temperatures in the winter and summer.

- Average monthly precipitation in the winter and summer.

- Average winter snowfall.

- Growing season (number of days between last spring frost and first autumn frost).

3. Inspect a topographic map of your town.

a) What is the latitude of your town?

b) What is the elevation of your school?

c) What is the highest elevation in your town?

d) What is the lowest elevation in your town?

e) Which of the following physical features can be found in or fairly near your community: mountains, rivers, valleys, coasts, lakes, hills, plains, or deserts? Specify where they are in relation to your community.

f) Describe some of the ways that the physical features of your community might influence the climate.

Part B: Physical Features and Climate in a Different Community

1. Select a community that is in a part of the United States that is very different from where you live. For example, if

you live in the mountains, pick a community on the plains. If you live near an ocean, pick a community far from a large body of water.

a) Record the community and the reason you chose that community in your *EarthComm* notebook.

2. Describe the climate in this community.

a) Include information for the same climatic factors that you used to describe your own community.

3. Inspect a topographic map of this community.

a) Describe the same physical features that you did for your community.

4. Compare the physical features and climates of the two communities.

a) In what ways might the physical features influence climate in the two places?

Part C: Heating and Cooling of Land versus Water

1. How does the rate at which rock and soil heat and cool, compared to the rate at which water heats and cools? How might this affect climate in your community?

a) Write down your ideas about these two questions.

b) Develop a hypothesis about the rate at which rock or soil heat and cool compared to the rate at which water heats and cools.

2. Using materials provided by your teacher, design an experiment to investigate the rates of cooling and heating of soil or rock and water. Note the variable that you are

manipulating (the independent variable), the variable that you are measuring (the dependent variable), and the controls within your experiment.

a) Record your design, variables, controls, and any safety concerns in your notebook.

3. When your teacher has approved your design, conduct your experiment.

4. In your *EarthComm* notebook, record your answers to the following questions:

a) Which material heated up faster?

b) Which material cooled more quickly?

c) How did your results compare with your hypothesis?

d) How does this investigation relate to differences in climate between places near a body of water, versus places far from water?

⚠️ Have your teacher approve your design before you begin your experiment. Do not touch any heat source. Report any broken thermometers to your teacher. Clean up any spills immediately.

Reflecting on the Activity and the Challenge

In this activity, you learned about the physical features and climate of your community. You also compared the physical features and climate of your community to that of another community in the United States. This helped you begin to see ways in which physical features influence climate. This will help you explain the meaning of the term "climate" and describe the climate of your community in your newspaper article.

Digging Deeper

WEATHER AND CLIMATE

Factors Affecting Climate

Weather refers to the state of the atmosphere at a place, from day to day and from week to week. The weather on a particular day might be cold or hot, clear or rainy. **Climate** refers to the typical or average weather at a place, on a long-term average. For example, Alaska has a cold climate, but southern Florida has a tropical climate. Minnesota's climate is hot in the summer and cold in the winter. Western Oregon has very rainy winters. Each of these regions has a definite climate, but weather that varies from day to day, often unpredictably.

The climate of a particular place on Earth is influenced by several important factors: latitude, elevation, and nearby geographic features. ➡️

Geo Words

weather: the state of the atmosphere at a specific time and place.

climate: the general pattern of weather conditions for a region over a long period of time (at least 30 years).

Geo Words

latitude: a north-south measurement of position on the Earth. It is defined by the angle measured from the Earth's equatorial plane.

elevation: the height of the land surface relative to sea level.

glacier: a large long-lasting accumulation of snow and ice that develops on land and flows under its own weight.

windward: the upwind side or side directly influenced to the direction that the wind blows from; ~~opposite of leeward~~.

leeward: the downwind side of an elevated area like a mountain; ~~opposite of windward~~.

rain shadow: the reduction of precipitation commonly found on the leeward side of a mountain.

Latitude

Latitude is a measure of the distance of a point on the Earth from the Equator. It is expressed in degrees, from zero degrees at the Equator to 90° at the poles. The amount of solar energy an area receives depends upon its latitude. At low latitudes, near the Equator, the Sun is always nearly overhead in the middle of the day, all year round. Near the poles, the Sun is low in the sky even in summer, and in the winter it is nighttime 24 hours of the day. As a result, regions near the Equator are much warmer than regions near the poles. Assuming a constant elevation, temperatures decrease by an average of about one degree Fahrenheit for every three degrees latitude away from the Equator.

Elevation

Elevation, the height of a point on the Earth's surface above sea level, also affects the physical environment. Places at high elevations are generally cooler than places at low elevations in a given region. On average, temperatures decrease by about 3.6°F for every 1000 ft. (300 m) gain in elevation. In many places at high elevation, **glaciers** form because the summers are not warm enough to melt all of the snow each year. The mountains in Glacier National Park in Montana, which are located at high elevation as well as fairly high latitude, contain glaciers, as shown in *Figure 1*.

Geographic Features

Geographic features, like mountain ranges, lakes, and oceans, affect the climate of a region. As shown in *Figure 2*, mountains can have a dramatic effect on precipitation in nearby areas. The **windward** side of a mountain chain often receives much more rainfall than the leeward side. As wind approaches the mountains, it is forced upwards. When the air rises, it cools, and water vapor condenses into clouds, which produce precipitation. Conversely, the **leeward** side of a mountain range is in what is called a **rain shadow**. It often receives very little rain. That is because the air has already lost much of its

Figure 1 Mountains at high elevation and high latitudes often contain glaciers.

moisture on the windward side. When the air descends the leeward slope of the mountain, it warms up as the greater air pressure compresses it. That causes clouds to evaporate and the humidity of the air to decrease. The deserts of the southwestern United States have low rainfall because they are in the rain shadow of the Sierra Nevada and other mountain ranges along the Pacific coast.

Figure 2 The rain shadow effect. Most North American deserts are influenced by this effect.

Geo Words

heat capacity: the quantity of heat energy required to increase the temperature of a material or system; typically referenced as the amount of heat energy required to generate a 1°C rise in the temperature of 1 g of a given material that is at atmospheric pressure and 20°C.

Large bodies of water can also affect climate dramatically. The ocean has a moderating effect on nearby communities. Temperatures in coastal communities vary less than inland communities at similar latitude. This is true both on a daily basis and seasonally. The effect is especially strong where the coast faces into the prevailing winds, as on the West Coast of the United States. Kansas City's average temperature is 79°F in July and 26°F in January. San Francisco's average temperature is 64°F in July and 49°F in January. On average, New York City's January temperatures vary only 11°F during a day, whereas Omaha's January temperatures vary 20°F during a day. In each of these two cases the difference between the two cities' climates is too great to be related to their latitude, which is only different by less than about 1.5°. Instead, the differences in climate in these two places are because water has a much higher **heat capacity** than soil and rock. That means that much more heat is needed to raise the temperature of water than to raise the

Geo Words

lake-effect snow: the snow that is precipitated when an air mass that has gained moisture by moving over a relatively warm water body is cooled as it passes over relatively cold land. This cooling triggers condensation of clouds and precipitation.

global climate: the mean climatic conditions over the surface of the Earth as determined by the averaging of a large number of observations spatially distributed throughout the entire region of the globe.

Little Ice Age: the time period from mid-1300s to the mid-1400s AD. During this period, global temperatures were at their coldest since the beginning of the Holocene.

Check Your Understanding

1. What is the difference between weather and climate?

2. What is the difference between regional climate and global climate?

3. Compare the climate of a city along the Pacific coast with that of a city with a similar latitude but located inland.

4. Explain how there can be snow on the top of a mountain near the Equator.

5. What is the "Little Ice Age"?

temperature of soil or rock. In the same way, water cools much more slowly than soil and rock. Land areas warm up quickly during a sunny day and cool down quickly during clear nights. The ocean and large lakes, on the other hand, change their temperature very little from day to day. Because the ocean absorbs a lot of heat during the day and releases it at night, it prevents daytime temperatures in seaside communities from climbing very high and prevents nighttime temperatures from falling very low (unless the wind is blowing from the land to the ocean!). By the same token, oceans store heat during the summer and release it during the winter, keeping summers cooler and winters warmer than they would be otherwise.

Lake-effect snow is common in late autumn and early winter downwind of the Great Lakes in north–central United States. Cold winds blow across the still-warm lake water, accumulating moisture from the lake as they go. When they reach the cold land, the air is cooled, and the water precipitates out of the clouds as snow. The warm oceans also supply the moisture that feeds major rainstorms, not just along the coast but even far inland in the eastern and central United States.

Global Climate

Climates differ from one region to another, depending on latitude, elevation, and geographical features. However, the entire Earth has a climate, too. This is called **global climate**. It is usually expressed as the year-round average temperature of the entire surface of the Earth, although average rainfall is also an important part of global climate. Today, the average temperature on the surface of the Earth is about 60°F. But the Earth's climate has changed continually over geologic time. During the Mesozoic Era (245–65 million years ago), when the dinosaurs roamed the Earth, global climate was warmer than today. During the Pleistocene Epoch (1.6 million–10,000 years ago), when mastodons and cave people lived, global climate seesawed back and forth between cold glacial intervals and warmer interglacial intervals. During glacial intervals, huge sheets of glacier ice covered much of northern North America. Just a few hundred years ago, the climate was about 3°F cooler than now. The time period from about the mid-1300s to the mid-1800s is called the **Little Ice Age**, because temperatures were generally much colder than today, and glaciers in many parts of the world expanded. Global temperatures have gradually increased since then, as the Earth has been coming out of the Little Ice Age.

Over the next several activities, you will be looking at what causes these changes in global climate, and how human activity may be causing global climate change.

Understanding and Applying What You Have Learned

1. What is the nearest body of water to your community? In what ways does it affect the physical environment of your community?

2. Identify one physical feature in or near your community and explain how it affects the climate. You may need to think regionally. Is there a mountain range, a large lake, or an ocean in your state?

3. How would changing one feature of the physical environment near your community affect the climate? Again, you may need to think on a regional scale. Name a feature and tell how the climate would be different if that feature changed. How would this change life in your community?

4. Can you think of any additional reasons to explain the differences in climate between your community and the other community you looked at in the **Investigate** section?

Preparing for the Chapter Challenge

1. Clip and read several newspaper articles about scientific topics.

2. Using a style of writing appropriate for a newspaper, write a few paragraphs in which you:

   - explain the term climate;
   - describe the climate of your community (including statistics about seasonal temperatures, rainfall, and snowfall);
   - explain what physical factors in your community or state combine to produce this climate;
   - explain the difference between regional climate and global climate, and
   - describe the Earth's global climate.

Inquiring Further

1. **Weather systems and the climate of your community**

   Investigate how weather systems crossing the United States affect the climate in your community. In many places, weather systems travel in fairly regular paths, leading to a somewhat predictable series of weather events.

2. **Jet stream**

   Do some research on the jet stream. How does its position affect the climate in your community?

Activity 2   Paleoclimates

Goals

In this activity you will:

- Understand the significance of growth rings in trees as indicators of environmental change.

- Understand the significance of ice cores from glaciers as indicators of environmental change.

- Investigate and understand the significance of geologic sediments as indicators of environmental change.

- Examine the significance of glacial sediments and landforms as evidence for climate change.

- Investigate and understand the significance of fossil pollen as evidence for climate change.

Think about It

The cross section of a tree trunk shows numerous rings.

- What do you think the light and dark rings represent?
- What might be the significance of the varying thicknesses of the rings?

What do you think? Record your ideas about these questions in your *EarthComm* notebook. Be prepared to discuss your responses with your small group and the class.

Investigate

Part A: Tree Rings

1. Examine the photo that shows tree growth rings from a Douglas fir. Notice the arrow that marks the 550-year-old growth ring.

a) Where are the youngest and the oldest growth rings located?

b) Not all the growth rings look identical. How are the rings on the outer part of the tree different from those closer to the center?

c) Mark the place on a copy of the picture where the change in the tree rings occurs.

2. Using the 550-year arrow as a starting point, count the number of rings to the center of the tree. Now count the number of rings from the arrow to where you marked the change in the way the rings look.

a) Record the numbers.

b) Assuming that each ring represents one year, how old is the tree?

c) Assume that the tree was cut down in the year 2000. What year did the tree rings begin to look

different from the rings near the center (the rings older than about 550-years old)?

3. Compare the date you calculated in **Step 2 (c)** to the graph that shows change in temperature for the last 1000 years.

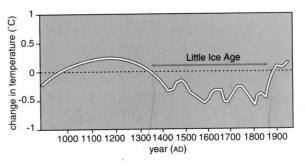

a) What was happening to the climate during that time?

b) From these observations, what would you hypothesize is the correlation between the thickness of tree rings and climate?

4. Examine the diagram that shows temperature change for the last 150,000 years.

a) How does the duration of the Little Ice Age compare to the duration of the ice age (the time between the two interglacial periods) shown in this figure?

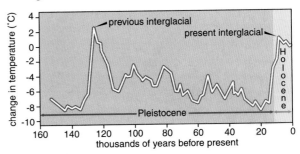

Part B: Fossil Pollen

1. Using blue, red, green, and yellow modeling clay, put down layers in a small container. You may put them down in any order and thickness. The container represents a lake or pond, and the clay represents sediment that has settled out over a long time.

2. When you have finished laying down your "sediments," use a small pipe to take a core. Push the pipe straight down through all of the layers. Then carefully pull the pipe back up. Use a thin stick to push the core of sediments out of the pipe.

 Place folded paper towels or other padding between your hand and the upper end of the pipe before pushing it into the clay.

   a) Draw a picture of the core in your notebook. Note which end is the top.

   b) Measure and record the thickness of each layer of sediment to the nearest tenth of a centimeter.

3. The different colors of clay represent sediments that have settled out of the lake water at different times. For this exercise, imagine that each centimeter of clay represents the passage of 1000 years.

   a) How many years does your core represent from top to bottom?

   b) How many years does each layer represent?

4. Imagine that the different colors of clay represent the following:

   • Blue: sediments containing pollen from cold-climate plants like spruce and alder trees.

   • Red: sediments containing pollen from warm-climate plants, like oak trees and grasses.

   • Green: sediments containing mostly spruce and alder pollen, with a little oak and grass pollen.

   • Yellow: sediments containing mostly oak and grass pollen, with a little spruce and alder pollen.

   a) How do you think the pollen gets into the lake sediments?

   b) Describe what the climate around the lake was like when each layer of sediment was deposited.

   c) Write a paragraph describing the climate changes over the period of time represented by your core. Make sure you say at how many years before the present each climate change occurred. Note whether transitions from one type of climate to another appear to have happened slowly or quickly.

Reflecting on the Activity and the Challenge

You will need to explain some of the ways that geologists know about climates that existed in the geologic past. The activity helped you understand two of the ways that geologists find out about ancient climates. Geologists study tree growth rings. They relate the thickness of the tree rings to the climate. Geologists also collect cores from layers of sediments and study the kinds of pollen contained in the sediments. The pollen shows what kinds of plants lived there in the past, and that shows something about what the climate was like.

Digging Deeper

HOW GEOLOGISTS FIND OUT ABOUT PALEOCLIMATES

Direct Records and Proxies

A **paleoclimate** is a climate that existed sometime in the past: as recently as just a few centuries ago, or as long as billions of years ago. For example, in the previous activity you learned that the world was warmer in the Mesozoic Era (245 – 65 million years ago) and experienced periods of glaciation that affected large areas of the Northern Hemisphere continents during the Pleistocene Epoch (1.6 million–10,000 years ago). At present the Earth is experiencing an interglacial interval—a period of warmer climate following a colder, glacial period. The Earth today has only two continental ice sheets, one covering most of Greenland and one covering most of Antarctica.

The last retreat of continental glaciers occurred between about 20,000 years ago and 8000 years ago. That was before the invention of writing, so there is no direct record of this change. Systematic records of local weather, made with the help of accurate weather instruments, go back only about 200 years. A global network of weather stations has existed for an even shorter time. Historical accounts exist for individual places, most notably in China. For certain places in China records extend back 2000 years. They are useful, but more extensive information is required to understand the full range of climate variability. **Paleoclimatologists** use a variety of methods to infer past climate. Taken together, the evidence gives a picture of the Earth's climatic history.

Unfortunately, nothing gives a direct reading of past temperature. Many kinds of evidence, however, give an indirect record of past temperature. These are called **climate proxies**. Something that represents something else indirectly is called a proxy. In some elections, a voter can choose another person to cast the vote, and that vote is called a proxy. There are many proxies for past climate, although none is perfect.

Fossil Pollen

Pollen consists of tiny particles that are produced in flowers to make seeds. Pollen is often preserved in the sediments of lakes or bogs, where it is blown in by the wind. For example, a layer of sediment may contain a lot of pollen from spruce trees, which grow in cold climates. From that you can infer that the climate around the lake was cold when that layer of sediment was being deposited. Geologists collect sediment from a succession of

Geo Words

paleoclimate: the climatic conditions in the geological past reconstructed from a direct or indirect data source.

paleoclimatologist: a scientist who studies the Earth's past climate.

climate proxy: any feature or set of data that has a predictable relationship to climatic factors and can therefore be used to indirectly measure those factors.

sediment layers. They count the number of pollen grains from different plants in each layer. Then they make charts that can give an idea of the climate changes that have taken place. (See *Figure 1*.) Pollen is easy to study because there is so much of it. Geologists also study fossil plants and insects to reconstruct past climates.

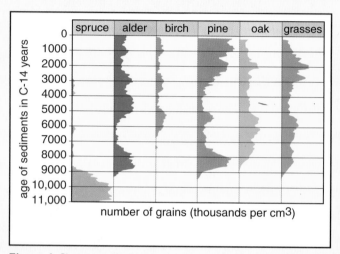

Figure 1 Changes over time in the relative amounts of different types of pollen from various trees and grasses give clues as to how climate has changed in the past.

Ice Cores

Figure 2 Scientists are able to obtain clues into past climatic conditions from air bubbles trapped in ice cores.

In recent years, study of cores drilled deep down into glaciers, like the one shown in *Figure 2*, has become a very powerful technique for studying paleoclimate. Very long cores, about 10 cm (4 in.) in diameter, have been obtained from both the Greenland and Antarctic ice sheets. The longest, from Antarctica, is almost 3400 m (about 1.8 mi.) long. Ice cores have been retrieved from high mountain glaciers in South America and Asia.

Glaciers consist of snow that accumulates each winter and does not melt entirely during the following summer. The snow is gradually compressed into ice as it is buried by later snow. The annual layers can be detected by slight changes in dust content. The long core from Antarctica provides a record of climate that goes back for more than 400,000 years. See *Figure 3*.

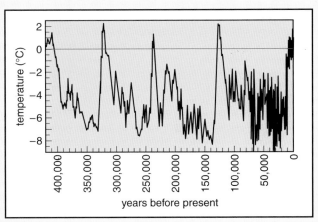

Figure 3 Temperature variation over the past 420,000 years, relative to the modern surface temperature at Vostok (−55.5°C).

Geo Words

isotope: one of two or more kinds of atoms of a given chemical element that differ in mass because of different numbers of neutrons in the nucleus of the atoms.

Bubbles of air trapped in the ice contain samples of the atmosphere from the time when the snow fell. Paleoclimatologists study the oxygen in the water molecules in the ice. Almost all of the oxygen atoms in the atmosphere are in two forms, called **isotopes**. The two isotopes are oxygen-16 (written ^{16}O) and oxygen-18 (written ^{18}O). They are the same chemically, but they have slightly different weights. ^{18}O is slightly heavier than ^{16}O. The proportion of these two isotopes in snow depends on average global temperatures. Snow that falls during periods of warmer global climate contains a greater proportion of ^{18}O, and snow that falls during periods of colder global climate contains a smaller proportion. The ratio of ^{18}O to ^{16}O can be measured very accurately with special instruments. Another important way of using the glacier ice to estimate global temperature is to measure the proportions of the two naturally occurring isotopes of hydrogen: ^{1}H, and ^{2}H (which is called deuterium).

The air bubbles in the ice contain carbon dioxide. The amount of carbon dioxide in the glacier ice air bubbles depends on the amount of carbon dioxide in the air at that time. The amount of carbon dioxide in the atmosphere can be correlated to global temperatures. During times when the paleoclimate is thought to have been warm, the ice core record shows relatively higher levels of atmospheric carbon dioxide compared to times of interpreted colder climate. Measurements of carbon dioxide taken from the cores give a global picture, because carbon dioxide is uniformly distributed in the global atmosphere.

A third component of the ice that yields clues to paleoclimates is dust. During colder climates, winds tend to be stronger. The stronger winds erode more dust, and the dust is deposited in small quantities over large areas of the Earth.

Geo Words

foraminifera: an order of single-celled organisms (protozoans) that live in marine (usually) and freshwater (rarely) environments. Forams typically have a shell of one or more chambers that is typically made of calcium carbonate.

loess: the deposits of wind-blown silt laid down over vast areas of the mid-latitudes during glacial and postglacial times.

Check Your Understanding

1. How do preserved tree rings indicate changes in climate?

2. List three ways that sediments in the ocean help scientists understand ancient climates.

3. Imagine an ice core taken from the Antarctic ice sheet. A layer of ice called "A" is 100 m below the surface. A layer of ice called "B" is 50 m below the surface. Explain why layer "A" represents the atmospheric conditions of an older climate than layer "B."

Deep-Sea Sediments

Sand-size shells of a kind of single-celled animal called **foraminifera** ("forams," for short) accumulate in layers of ocean-bottom sediment. During warm climates, the shells spiral in one direction, but during cold climates, the shells spiral in the opposite direction. Also, the shells consist of calcium carbonate, which contains oxygen. Geologists can measure the proportions of the two oxygen isotopes to find out about paleoclimates. The shells contain more ^{18}O during colder climates than during warmer climates.

Glacial Landforms and Sediments

Glaciers leave recognizable evidence in the geologic record. Glacial landforms are common in northern North America. Glaciers erode the rock beneath, and then carry the sediment and deposit it to form distinctive landforms. Cape Cod, in Massachusetts, and Long Island, in New York, are examples of long ridges of sediment deposited by glaciers. Similar deposits are found as far south as Missouri.

Fine glacial sediment is picked up by the wind and deposited over large areas as a sediment called **loess**. There are thick deposits of loess in central North America. The loess layers reveal several intervals of glaciation during the Pleistocene Epoch.

Glaciers also leave evidence in the ocean. When glaciers break off into the ocean, icebergs float out to sea. As the icebergs melt, glacial sediment in the icebergs rains down to the ocean bottom. The glacial sediment is easily recognized because it is much coarser than other ocean-bottom sediment.

Tree Rings

Paleoclimate is also recorded in the annual growth rings in trees. Trees grow more during warm years than during cold years. A drawback to tree rings is that few tree species live long enough to provide a look very far in the past. Bristlecone pines, which can live as long as 5000 years, and giant sequoias, which are also very long-lived, are most often used.

Figure 4 A glacier carries ground-up pieces of rock and sediment into lakes and oceans.

Understanding and Applying What You Have Learned

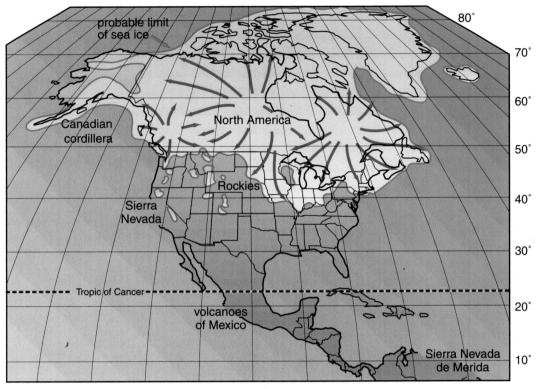

The approximate extent of the ice sheets in North America during the last Pleistocene glaciation.

1. Using evidence from glacial landforms and sediments, geologists have pieced together the maximum advance of glaciers about 18,000 years ago, which is shown in the figure above.

   a) Was your community located under ice during this time period? If not, describe how far your part of the country was from the ice sheet.

   b) What do you think the climate was like in your part of the country during the glacial maximum?

2. Use colored pencils and a ruler to draw a hypothetical series of lake-bottom sediments representing the sequence of climates given on the following page. Use the same colors as you used in the **Investigate** section to represent layers containing different kinds of pollen. Again, assume that it takes 1000 years to deposit 1 cm of sediment.

- 7000–5000 years ago: Warm climate supporting grasses and oaks.
- 5000–3000 years ago: Moderate climate supporting mostly grasses and oaks, with some spruce and alder.
- 3000–2000 years ago: Colder climate supporting mostly spruce and alder, with some grasses and oaks.
- 2000–1500 years ago: Moderate climate supporting mostly grasses and oaks, with some spruce and alder.
- 1500 years ago to the present: Warm climate supporting grasses and oaks.

a) Describe what the climate around the lake was like when each layer of sediment was deposited.

b) From this data, what time period marks the coldest climate recorded in the lake bottom sediments?

c) Did the climate cool at the same rate as it warmed?

d) Think of a hypothesis that might explain your answer to **Part (c)**. What additional observations might help you test this hypothesis?

Preparing for the Chapter Challenge

Using a style appropriate for a newspaper article, write a paragraph or two about each of the following topics, explaining how geologists use them to find out about paleoclimates:

- deep-sea sediments;
- glacial landforms and sediments;
- ice cores from Antarctica;
- pollen studies, and
- tree rings.

Inquiring Further

1. **GISP2 (Greenland Ice Sheet Project)**

   Research GISP2 (Greenland Ice Sheet Project), a project that is collecting and analyzing ice cores. What are the most recent discoveries? How many ice cores have been collected? How many have been analyzed? How far into the past does the data currently reach? Visit the *EarthComm* web site to help you start your research.

2. **Dating deep-sea sediments**

   Investigate some of the techniques geologists use to date deep-sea

   sediments: carbon-14 dating, isotope dating of uranium, fission-track dating of ash layers, and geomagnetic-stratigraphy dating.

3. **Paleoclimate research in your community**

   Investigate whether any of the paleoclimate techniques discussed in this activity have been used near your community or in your state to research paleoclimates.

Activity 3

How Do Earth's Orbital Variations Affect Climate?

Goals

In this activity you will:

- Understand that Earth has an axial tilt of about 23 1/2°.

- Use a globe to model the seasons on Earth.

- Investigate and understand the cause of the seasons in relation to the axial tilt of the Earth.

- Understand that the shape of the Earth's orbit around the Sun is an ellipse and that this shape influences climate.

- Understand that insolation to the Earth varies as the inverse square of the distance to the Sun.

Think about It

When it is winter in New York, it is summer in Australia.

- Why are the seasons reversed in the Northern and Southern Hemispheres?

What do you think? Write your thoughts in your *EarthComm* notebook. Be prepared to discuss your responses with your small group and the class.

Investigate

Part A: What Causes the Seasons?
An Experiment on Paper

1. In your notebook, draw a circle about 10 cm in diameter in the center of your page. This circle represents the Earth.

   Add the Earth's axis of rotation, the Equator, and lines of latitude, as shown in the diagram and described below. Label the Northern and Southern Hemispheres.

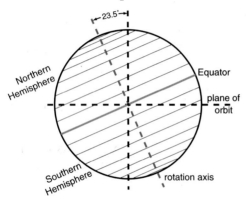

   Put a dot in the center of the circle. Draw a dashed line that goes directly up and down from the center dot to the edge of the circle. Use a protractor to measure 23 1/2° from this vertical dashed line. Use a blue pen or pencil to draw a line through the center of the "Earth" at 23 1/2° to your dashed line. This blue line represents the Earth's axis of rotation. Use your protractor to draw a red line that is perpendicular to the axis and passes through the center dot. This red line represents the Equator of the Earth. Label the Northern and Southern Hemispheres. Next you need to add lines of latitude. To do this, line your protractor up with the dot in the center of your circle so that it is parallel with the Equator.

   Now, mark off 10° increments starting from the Equator and going to the poles. You should have eight marks between the Equator and pole for each quadrant of the Earth. Use a straight edge to draw black lines that connect the marks opposite one another on the circle, making lines that are parallel to the Equator. This will give you lines of latitude in 10° increments so you can locate your latitude fairly accurately. Note that the lines won't be evenly spaced from one another because latitude is measured as an angle from the center of the Earth, not a linear distance.

2. Imagine that the Sun is directly on the left in your drawing. Draw horizontal arrows to represent incoming Sun rays from the left side of the paper.

3. Assume that it is noon in your community. Draw a dot where your community's latitude line intersects the perimeter of the circle on the left. This dot represents your community.

   a) Explain why this represents noon.

   b) At any given latitude, both north and south, are the Sun's rays striking the Northern Hemisphere or the Southern Hemisphere at a larger angle relative to the local vertical to the Earth's surface?

   c) Which do you think would be warmer in this drawing—the Northern Hemisphere or the Southern Hemisphere? Write down your hypothesis. Be sure to give a reason for your prediction.

   d) What season do you think this is in the Northern Hemisphere?

4. Now consider what happens six months later. The Earth is on the opposite side of its orbit, and the sunlight is now coming from the right side of the paper. Draw horizontal arrows to represent incoming Sun's rays from the right.

5. Again, assume that it is noon. Draw a dot where your community's latitude line intersects the perimeter of the circle on the right.

   a) Explain why the dot represents your community at noon.

   b) Are the Sun's rays striking the Northern Hemisphere or the Southern Hemisphere more directly?

   c) Which do you think would be warmer in this drawing—the Northern Hemisphere or the Southern Hemisphere? Why?

   d) What season do you think this is in the Northern Hemisphere?

Part B: What Causes the Seasons? An Experiment with a Globe

1. Test the hypothesis you made in **Part A** about which hemisphere would be warmer in which configuration. Find your city on a globe. Using duct tape, tape a small thermometer on it. The duct tape should cover the thermometer bulb, and the thermometer should be over the city. With a permanent black marking pen, color the duct tape black all over its surface.

2. Set up a light and a globe as shown.

⚠️ Use only alcohol thermometers. Place a soft cloth on the table under the thermometer in case it falls off. Be careful not to touch the hot lamp.

3. Position the globe so that its axis is tilted 23 1/2° from the vertical, and the North Pole is pointed in the direction of the light source.

4. Turn on the light source.

   a) Record the initial temperature. Then record the temperature on the thermometer every minute until the temperature stops changing.

5. Now position the globe so that the axis is again tilted 23 1/2° from the vertical but the North Pole is pointing away from the light source. Make sure the light source is the same distance from the globe as it was in **Step 4**. Turn on the light source again.

   a) Record the temperature every minute until the temperature stops changing.

6. Use your observations to answer the following questions in your notebook:

   a) What is the difference in the average temperature when the North Pole was pointing toward your "community" and when it was pointing away?

   b) What caused the difference in temperature?

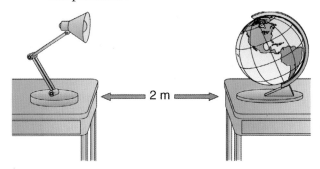

2 m

Part C: What Would Happen if the Earth's Axial Tilt Changed? An Experiment on Paper

1. Repeat the experiment you did in **Part A**, except this time use an axial tilt of 10°.

   a) Compared to an axial tilt of 23 1/2°, would your hemisphere experience a warmer or colder winter?

   b) Compared to an axial tilt of 23 1/2°, would your hemisphere experience a hotter or cooler summer?

2. Repeat the experiment you did in **Part A**, except this time use an axial tilt of 35°.

   a) Compared to an axial tilt of 23 1/2°, would your hemisphere experience a warmer or colder winter?

   b) Compared to an axial tilt of 23 1/2°, would your hemisphere experience a hotter or cooler summer?

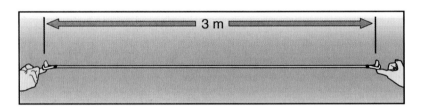

Part D: The Earth's Elliptical Orbit around the Sun

1. Tie small loops in each end of a rope, as shown in the diagram above.

2. Pick a point in about the middle of the floor, and put the two loops together over the point. Put a dowel vertically through the loops, and press the dowel tightly to the floor.

3. Stretch out the rope from the dowel until it is tight, and hold a piece of chalk at the bend in the rope, as shown in the diagram below. While holding the chalk tight against the rope, move the chalk around the dowel.

   a) What type of figure have you constructed?

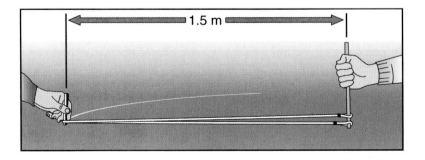

4. Draw a straight line from one edge of the circle that you just made to the opposite edge, through the center of the circle. This line represents the diameter of the circle. Mark two points along the diameter, each a distance of 20 cm from the center of the circle. Put the loops of the rope over the two points, hold them in place with two dowels, and use the chalk to draw a curve on one side of the straight line. Move the chalk to the other side of the line and draw another curve.

a) What type of figure have you constructed?

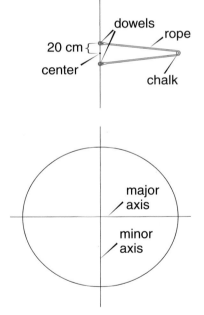

5. Using different colors of chalk, make a few more curved figures in the same way. Choose sets of dowel points that are farther and farther away from the center.

a) Describe the shapes of the figures you constructed. Make sketches in your *EarthComm* notebook.

b) What would be the shape of the curve when the dowel points are spaced a distance apart that is just equal to the length of the rope between the two loops?

Part E: How Energy from the Sun Varies with Distance from the Sun

1. Using scissors and a ruler, cut out a square 10 cm on a side in the middle of a poster board.

2. Hold the poster board vertically, parallel to the wall and exactly two meters from it.

3. Position a light bulb along the imaginary horizontal line that passes from the wall through the center of the hole in the poster board. See the diagram.

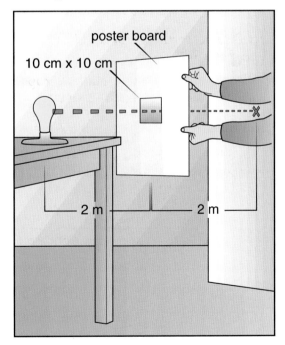

 Avoid contact with the hot light bulb. Do not look directly into the light.

4. Turn on the light bulb, and turn off the lights in the room. If the room is not dark enough to see the image on the wall, close any curtains or shades, or cover the windows with dark sheets or blankets.

5. With the chalk, trace the edge of the image the hole makes on the wall.

   a) Measure and record the length of the sides of the image you marked with the chalk.

   b) Divide the length of the image on the wall by the length of the sides of the square in the poster board. Now divide the distance of the light bulb from the wall by the distance of the poster board from the wall. What is the relationship between the two numbers you obtain?

   c) Compute the area of the image on the wall, and compute the area of the square hole in the poster board. Divide the area of the image by the area of the hole. Again, divide the distance of the light bulb from the wall by the distance of the poster board from the wall. What is the relationship between the two numbers you obtain?

6. Repeat **Part E** for other distances.

   a) What do you notice about the relationship between the area of the image and the area of the hole?

Reflecting on the Activity and the Challenge

In this activity you modeled the tilt of the Earth's axis to investigate the effect of the angle of the Sun's rays. You discovered that the axial tilt of the Earth explains why there are seasons of the year. You also discovered that if the tilt were to vary, it would affect the seasons.

You also modeled the Earth's elliptical orbit around the Sun. This will help you to understand one of the main theories for explaining why the Earth's climate varies over time. You will need to explain this in your newspaper articles.

Digging Deeper

THE EARTH'S ORBIT AND THE CLIMATE

The Earth's Axial Tilt and the Seasons

The Earth's axis of rotation is tilted at about 23 1/2° away from a line that is perpendicular to the plane of the Earth's orbit around the Sun (*Figure 1*). This tilt explains the seasons on Earth. During the Northern Hemisphere summer, the North Pole is tilted toward the Sun, so the Sun shines at a high angle overhead. That is when the days are warmest, and days are longer than nights. On the summer solstice (on or about June 22) the Northern Hemisphere experiences its longest day and shortest night of the year. During the Northern Hemisphere winter the Earth is on the other side of its orbit. Then the North Pole is tilted away from the Sun, and the Sun shines at a lower angle. Temperatures are lower, and the days are shorter than the nights. On the winter solstice (on or about December 22) the Northern Hemisphere experiences its shortest day and longest night of the year.

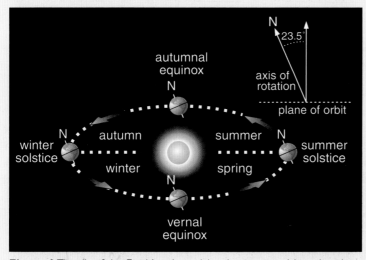

Figure 1 The tilt of the Earth's axis explains the seasons. Note that the Earth and Sun are not shown to scale.

How Do Earth's Orbital Variations Affect Climate?

In **Activity 2** you saw that paleoclimatologists have developed a good picture of the Earth's climatic history. The advances and retreats of the continental ice sheets are well documented. Nevertheless, questions remain.

Geo Words

eccentricity: the ratio of the distance between the foci and the length of the major axis of an ellipse.

obliquity: the tilt of the Earth's rotation axis as measured from the perpendicular to the plane of the Earth's orbit around the Sun. The angle of this tilt varies from 22.5° to 24.5° over a 41,000-year period. Current obliquity is 23.5°.

precession: slow motion of the axis of the Earth around a cone, one cycle in about 26,000 years, due to gravitational tugs by the Sun, Moon, and major planets.

orbital parameters: any one of a number of factors that describe the orientation and/or movement of an orbiting body or the shape of its orbital path.

insolation: the direct or diffused shortwave solar radiation that is received in the Earth's atmosphere or at its surface.

inverse-square law: a scientific law that states that the amount of radiation passing through a specific area is inversely proportional to the square of the distance of that area from the energy source.

Why does Earth's climate sometimes become cold enough for ice sheets to advance? Why does the climate later warm up and cause ice sheets to retreat? The answers to these questions are not yet entirely clear. Most climatologists believe that variations in the geometry of the Earth's orbit around the Sun are the major cause of the large variations in climate. These variations have caused the advance and retreat of ice sheets in the past couple of million years.

If the Earth and the Sun were the only bodies in the solar system, the geometry of the Earth's orbit around the Sun and the tilt of the Earth's axis would stay exactly the same through time. But there are eight other known planets in the solar system. Each of those planets exerts forces on the Earth and the Sun. Those forces cause the Earth's orbit to vary with time. The Moon also plays a role. The changes are slight but very important. There are three kinds of changes: **eccentricity**, **obliquity**, and **precession**. These three things are called the Earth's **orbital parameters**.

Eccentricity

The Earth's orbit around the Sun is an ellipse. The deviation of an ellipse from being circular is called its eccentricity. A circle is an ellipse with zero eccentricity. As the ellipse becomes more and more elongated (with a larger major diameter and a smaller minor diameter), the eccentricity increases. The Earth's orbit has only a slight eccentricity.

Even though the eccentricity of the Earth's orbit is very small, the distance from the Earth to the Sun varies by about 3.3% through the year. The difference in **insolation** is even greater. The word insolation (nothing to do with insUlation!) is used for the rate at which the Sun's energy reaches the Earth, per unit area facing directly at the Sun. The seasonal variation in insolation is because of what is called the **inverse-square law**. What you found in **Part E** of the investigation demonstrates this. The area of the image on the wall was four times the area of the hole, even though the distance of the wall from the bulb was only twice the distance of the hole from the bulb. Because of the inverse-square law, the insolation received by the Earth varies by almost 7° between positions on its orbit farthest from the Sun and positions closest to the Sun.

Because of the pull of other planets on the Earth–Sun system, the eccentricity of the Earth's orbit changes with time. The largest part of the change in eccentricity has a period of about 100,000 years. That means that one full cycle of increase and then decrease in eccentricity takes 100,000 years. During that time, the difference in insolation between the date of the shortest distance to the Sun and the date of the farthest distance to the Sun ranges from about 2° (less than now) to almost 20° (much greater than now!).

The two points you used to make ellipses in **Part D** of the investigation are called the foci of the ellipse. (Pronounced "FOH-sigh". The singular is focus.) The Sun is located at one of the foci of the Earth's elliptical orbit. The Earth is closest to the Sun when it is on the side of that focus, and it is farthest from the Sun when it is on the opposite side of the orbit. (See *Figure 2*.) Does it surprise you to learn that nowadays the Earth is closest to the Sun on January 5 (called **perihelion**) and farthest from the Sun on July 5 (called **aphelion**)? That tends to make winters less cold and summers less hot, in the Northern Hemisphere.

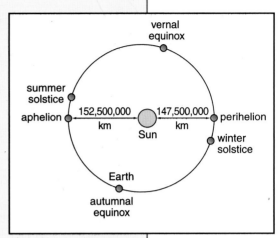

Figure 2 Schematic diagram showing occurrence of the aphelion and perihelion.

Obliquity

The tilt of the Earth's axis relative to the plane of the Earth's orbit is called the obliquity. The axis is oblique to the plane rather than perpendicular to it. In the investigation you discovered that a change in the obliquity would cause a change in the nature of the seasons. For example, a smaller obliquity would mean warmer winters and cooler summers in the Northern Hemisphere. This might result in more moisture in the winter air, which would mean more snow. In cooler summers, less of the snow would melt. You can see how this might lead to the buildup of glaciers.

Geo Words

perihelion: the point in the Earth's orbit that is closest to the Sun. Currently, the Earth reaches perihelion in early January.

aphelion: the point in the Earth's orbit that is farthest from the Sun. Currently, the Earth reaches aphelion in early July.

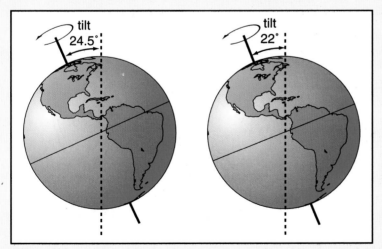

Figure 3 The angle of tilt of the Earth's axis varies between about 24.5° and 22°, causing climatic variations over time.

Geo Words

Milankovitch cycles: the cyclical changes in the geometric relationship between the Earth and the Sun that cause variations in solar radiation received at the Earth's surface.

axial precession: the wobble in the Earth's polar axis.

orbital precession: rotation about the Sun of the major axis of the Earth's elliptical orbit.

Again, because of the varying pull of the other planets on the Earth–Sun system, the Earth's obliquity changes over a period of about 40,000 years. The maximum angle of tilt is about 24 1/2°, and the minimum angle is about 22°. At times of maximum tilt, seasonal differences in temperature are slightly greater. At times of minimum tilt angle, seasonal differences are slightly less.

Precession

Have you ever noticed how the axis of a spinning top sometimes wobbles slowly as it is spinning? It happens when the axis of the top is not straight up and down, so that gravity exerts a sideways force on the top. The same thing happens with the Earth. The gravitational pull of the Sun, Moon, and other planets causes a slow wobbling of the Earth's axis. This is called the Earth's **axial precession**, and it has a period of about 26,000 years. That's the time it takes the Earth's axis to make one complete revolution of its wobble.

There is also another important kind of precession related to the Earth. It is the precession of the Earth's orbit, called **orbital precession**. As the Earth moves around the Sun in its elliptical orbit, the major axis of the Earth's orbital ellipse is rotating about the Sun. In other words, the orbit itself rotates around the Sun! The importance of the two precession cycles for the Earth's climate lies in how they interact with the eccentricity of the Earth's orbit. This interaction controls how far the Earth is from the Sun during the different seasons. Nowadays, the Northern Hemisphere winter solstice is at almost the same time as perihelion. In about 11,000 years, however, the winter solstice will be at about the same time as aphelion. That will make Northern Hemisphere winters even colder, and summers even hotter, than today.

Milankovitch Cycles

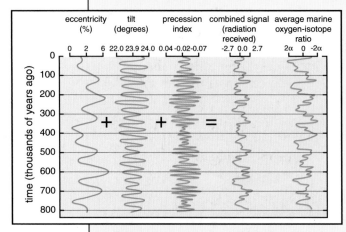

Figure 4 Interpretation of Milankovitch cycles over the last 800,000 years.

Early in the 20th century a Serbian scientist named Milutin Milankovitch hypothesized that variations in the Earth's climate are caused by how insolation varies with time and with latitude. He used what is known about the Earth's orbital parameters (eccentricity, obliquity, and precession) to compute the variations in insolation. Later scientists have refined the computations. These insolation cycles are now called **Milankovitch cycles**. (See *Figure 4*.)

Climatologists now generally agree that Milankovitch cycles are closely related to the glacial–interglacial cycles the Earth has experienced in recent geologic time. *Figure 3* in **Activity 2**, based on a long Antarctic ice core, shows how temperature has varied over the past 420,000 years. There is a clear 100,000-year periodicity, which almost exactly matches the eccentricity cycle. Temperature variations seem to have been controlled by the 100,000-year eccentricity cycle during some time intervals but by the 41,000-year obliquity cycle during other time intervals.

Climatologists are trying to figure out how Milankovitch cycles of insolation trigger major changes in climate. The Milankovitch cycles (the "driver" of climate) are just the beginning of the climate story. Many important climate mechanisms must be taken into account. They involve evaporation, precipitation, snowfall, snowmelt, cloud cover, greenhouse gases, vegetation, and sea level. What makes paleoclimatology difficult (and interesting!) is that these factors interact with one another in many complicated ways to produce climate.

Check Your Understanding

1. Explain why the days are longer than the nights during the summer months. Include a diagram to help you explain.

2. What are the three factors in Milankovitch cycles?

3. Explain how Milankovitch cycles might cause changes in global climate.

Understanding and Applying What You Have Learned

1. You have made a drawing of winter and summer in the Northern Hemisphere showing the tilt of Earth.

   a) Make a drawing showing Earth on or about March 21 (the vernal equinox). Indicate from which direction the Sun's rays are hitting the Earth.

   b) Explain why the daytime and nighttime last the same length of time everywhere on the Earth on the vernal equinox and on the autumnal equinox.

2. In **Part E** of the **Investigate** section you explored the relationship between energy from the Sun and distance to the Sun. How would you expect the area of light shining on the wall to change if the light source was moved farther away from the wall (but the cardboard was left in the same place)?

3. The tilt of the Earth varies from about 22° to about 24.5° over a period of 41,000 years. Think about how the solar radiation would change if the tilt was 24.5°.

   a) What effect would this have on people living at the Equator?

   b) What effect would this have on people living at 30° latitude?

   c) What effect would this have on people living at 45° latitude?

   d) What modifications in lifestyle would people have to make at each latitude?

Preparing for the Chapter Challenge

Use a style of writing appropriate for a newspaper to discuss the following topics:

- How does the tilt of the Earth's axis produce seasons?

- How does a variation in this tilt affect the nature of the seasons?
- How might a variation in the tilt affect global climate?
- How does the shape of the Earth's orbit influence climate?

Inquiring Further

1. **Sunspots and global climate**

   Do sunspots affect global climate? There is disagreement over this in the scientific community. Do some research to find out what sunspots are and how the activity of sunspots has correlated with global climate over time. Why do some scientists think sunspot activity affects global climate? Why do some scientists think that sunspot activity does NOT affect global climate?

2. **Milutin Milankovitch**

   Write a paper on Milutin Milankovitch, the Serbian scientist who suggested that variations in the Earth's orbit cause glacial periods to begin and end. How were his ideas received when he first published them?

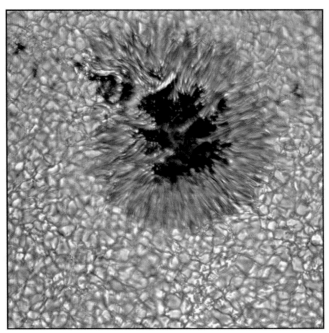

False color telescope image of a sunspot.

Activity 4

How Do Plate Tectonics and Ocean Currents Affect Global Climate?

Goals

In this activity you will:

- Model present and ancient land masses and oceans to determine current flow.

- Explain how ocean currents affect regional and global climate.

- Understand how ocean currents are affected by Earth's moving plates.

- Understand the relationship between climate and Earth processes like moving plates, mountain building, and weathering.

Think about It

Ocean currents help to regulate global climate by transferring heat and moisture around the globe.

- How would a change in the position of a land mass influence global climate?

What do you think? Record your ideas about this question in your *EarthComm* notebook. Be prepared to discuss your responses with your small group and the class.

Investigate

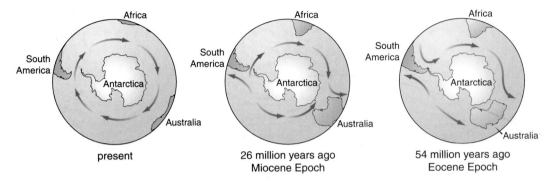

present

26 million years ago
Miocene Epoch

54 million years ago
Eocene Epoch

1. Divide your class into three groups. Each group will investigate the flow of water at one of these three periods of time:

   Group 1: The present.

   Group 2: During the Miocene Epoch, 26 million years ago.

   Group 3: During the Eocene Epoch, 54 million years ago.

2. Obtain a copy of the map for your assigned time period. Put this map under a clear plastic container.

3. Using clay, construct the correct land masses inside the container using the map as a template. Make the land masses at least 3 cm high.

4. Remove the map and add water to the container up to the level of the land masses.

5. Obtain a blue-colored ice cube. Place this as close to the South Pole as possible.

   a) As the ice cube melts and the cold water flows into the clear water, draw arrows on the map to record the direction of flow.

 Use only food coloring to dye the ice. Clean up spills immediately. Dispose of the water promptly.

   b) Write a paragraph in which you describe your observations.

6. Present your group's data to the class.

   a) Compare the direction of current flow on your map to those presented by the other groups. How does the current change as the land masses change from the Eocene Epoch to the Miocene Epoch to the present?

7. Use the results of your investigation to answer the following:

   a) Based on the map that shows the position of Australia in the Eocene Epoch and your investigation, what tectonic factors do you think are most important to consider when contemplating Australia's climate in the Eocene Epoch? How might Australia's Eocene Epoch climate have been different from its climate today?

   b) What tectonic factor(s) (for example, the position of the continents, occurrence of major ocean currents, mountain ranges, etc.) is/are most important in affecting the climate in your community today?

8. Examine the map of ocean surface currents carefully.

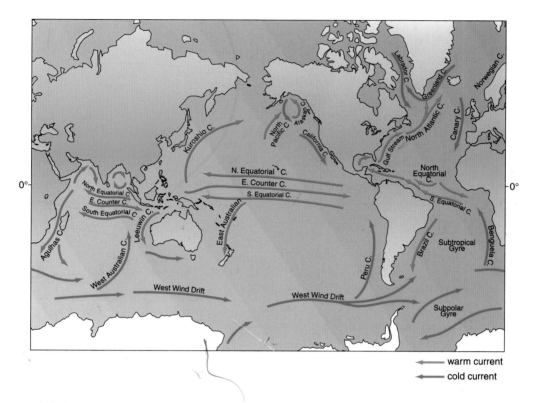

a) How do you think surface ocean currents modify the climatic patterns in the United States?

b) What changes in the surface-current patterns might arise if North America and South America split apart from one another, leaving an open passageway from the Atlantic Ocean to the Pacific Ocean?

c) How might the climate of the East Coast of the United States change if tectonic forces changed the positions of the continents so that the Gulf Stream no longer flowed north?

d) How might some other parts of the world (including your community) be affected if the Gulf Stream stopped flowing north?

Reflecting on the Activity and the Challenge

Ocean currents play a large role in global climate. This activity helped you see how ocean currents change in response to movements of the Earth's lithospheric plates.

Geo Words

thermohaline circulation:
the vertical movement of
seawater, generated by density
differences that are caused by
variations in temperature and
salinity.

Digging Deeper

CHANGING CONTINENTS, OCEAN CURRENTS, AND CLIMATE

How Ocean Currents Affect Regional Climates

A community near an ocean has a more moderate climate than one at the same latitude inland because water has a much higher heat capacity than rocks and soil. Oceans warm up more slowly and cool down more slowly than the land. Currents are also an important factor in coastal climate. A coastal community near a cold ocean current has cooler weather than a coastal community near a warm ocean current. For example, Los Angeles is located on the Pacific coast near the cold California Current. The city has an average daily high temperature in July of 75°F. Charleston, South Carolina, is located at a similar latitude, but on the Atlantic coast near the warm Gulf Stream. (See *Figure 1*.) Charleston's average daily high temperature in July is 90°F.

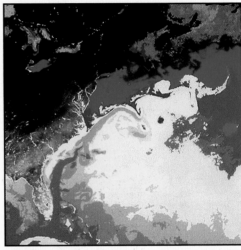

Figure 1 This thermal infrared image of the northwest Atlantic Ocean was taken from an NOAA satellite. The warm temperatures (25°C) are represented by red tones, and the cold temperatures (2°C) by blue and purple tones.

How Ocean Currents Affect Global Climate

Patterns of ocean circulation have a strong effect on global climate, too. The Equator receives more solar radiation than the poles. However, the Equator is not getting warmer, and the poles are not getting colder. That is because oceans and winds transfer heat from low latitudes to high latitudes. One of the main ways that the ocean transfers this heat is by the flow of North Atlantic Deep Water (abbreviated NADW). It works like this: In the northern North Atlantic, the ocean water is cold and salty, and it sinks because of its greater density. It flows southward at a deep level in the ocean. Then at low latitudes it rises up toward the surface as it is forced above the even denser Antarctic Bottom Water. Water from low latitudes flows north, at the ocean surface, to replace the sinking water. As it moves north, it loses heat. This slow circulation is like a "conveyor belt" for transferring heat. This kind of circulation is usually called **thermohaline circulation**. (*thermo* stands for temperature, and *haline* stands for saltiness.)

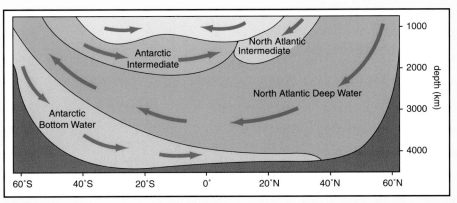

Figure 2 Circulation cell formed by the movement of deep-water masses in the ocean.

Geo Words

lithospheric plate: a rigid, thin segment of the outermost layer of the Earth, consisting of the Earth's crust and part of the upper mantle. The plate can be assumed to move horizontally and adjoins other plates.

plate tectonics: the study of the movement and interaction of the Earth's lithospheric plates.

When this conveyor belt is disturbed, the entire global climate is affected. For example, about 12,000 years ago, glaciers were melting rapidly, because the Earth was coming out of a glacial age. The melting glaciers discharged a lot of fresh water into the North Atlantic in a short time. The fresh water decreased the salinity of the ocean water thus reducing its density. This decrease was so much that the production of NADW was decreased. This seems to have plunged the world back into a short cold period, which lasted about 1000 years.

How Plate Tectonics Affects Global Climate

The positions of the continents on the Earth change as the Earth's **lithospheric plates** move. (**Plate tectonics** is the study of the movement and interaction of the Earth's lithospheric plates.) The arrangement of the continents has a strong effect on the Earth's climate. Think about the requirements for the development of large continental ice sheets. Glaciers form only on land, not on the ocean. For an ice sheet to develop there has to be large land areas at high latitudes, where snow can accumulate to form thick masses of ice. Where oceans occupy polar areas, accumulation of snow is limited by melting in the salty ocean waters. Polar oceans, like the Arctic Sea, around the North Pole, are mostly covered by pack ice. This ice is no more than several meters thick.

Today, the two continental landmasses with permanent ice sheets are Antarctica, in the Southern Hemisphere, and Greenland, in the Northern Hemisphere. The continent of Antarctica has not always been centered on the South Pole. About two hundred million years ago, all of the Earth's continents were welded together. They formed a single continent, called the supercontinent of **Pangea**. Pangea was eventually rifted apart into several large pieces. One of the pieces, the present Antarctica, moved slowly southward. Eventually it moved close enough to the South Pole for ice sheets to form. In recent geologic time, Antarctica has been directly over the South Pole, so the Antarctic ice sheet has remained in existence even during interglacial periods. We know that because otherwise global sea level would have been much higher during the interglacial periods of the past million years.

Figure 3 An ice-core station in Antarctica.

At present, most of the Earth's continental land area is in the Northern Hemisphere. Much of North America and Eurasia is at a high latitude. Ice sheets can form during the parts of Milankovitch cycles that are favorable for decreased global temperatures. During times of increased global temperatures, the North American and Eurasian ice sheets have melted away completely. The picture is very different in the Southern Hemisphere. Except for Antarctica, there is not enough continental land area at high latitudes for large continental glaciers to form.

Figure 4 Mt. St. Helens is an example of a volcano associated with a plate boundary.

Plate tectonics affects climate in other ways besides changing the positions of the continents. Volcanoes like the one shown in *Figure 4* from along active plate margins. Increased activity at these margins causes increased volcanic activity. Volcanoes release carbon dioxide, which is a gas that traps heat in the atmosphere. (You'll learn more about carbon dioxide in the following activity.) In this way, plate tectonics might cause global climate to warm. However, volcanic eruptions also add dust to the atmosphere, which blocks out some solar radiation. This tends to decrease global temperatures.

Continent–continent collisions create huge mountain ranges. The Himalayas and the Alps are modern examples. Many scientists believe that the weathering of such mountain ranges uses up carbon dioxide from the Earth's atmosphere because some of the chemical reactions that break down the rock use carbon dioxide from the atmosphere. This causes global climate to cool. For example, the collisions between continents that produced the supercontinent Pangea resulted in high mountain ranges like the one at the present site of the Appalachian Mountains. The Appalachians were much taller and more rugged when they first formed—perhaps as tall as the Himalayas shown in *Figure 5*. Three hundred million years of erosion have given them their lower and well-rounded appearance. On a global scale, all that weathering (which uses up carbon dioxide) may have contributed to the period of glaciation that began about 300 million years ago and ended about 280 million years ago.

Figure 5 The geologically young Himalayan mountains formed when India collided with Asia.

Check Your Understanding

1. Explain how North Atlantic Deep Water circulates.

2. Why do glaciers form only on continents and not in oceans?

3. Explain how plate tectonics can affect global climate.

Understanding and Applying What You Have Learned

1. In the **Investigate** section, you made models designed to demonstrate how ocean currents were different during the Eocene, Miocene, and today.

   a) Assuming that the maps were accurate, in what ways was your model helpful in exploring possible differences in oceanic currents?

   b) What are some of the drawbacks or problems with your model (how is a model different than the "real world"?).

   c) What improvements could you make to the model so that it would behave in a more accurate way?

2. Increased weathering of rocks uses up carbon dioxide. Decreasing carbon dioxide in the atmosphere contributes to global cooling. Reconstructions of the collision between India and Asia suggest that India first collided with Asia during the Late Eocene but that most of the mountain building took place during the Miocene and later.

a) When would you expect to observe the greatest changes in weathering rate?

b) Why?

3. Melting glaciers discharged a lot of fresh water into the North Atlantic in a short period of time about 12,000 years ago. Adding fresh water "turned off" the North Atlantic Deep Water current for about 1000 years.

a) What other changes could disturb the NADW?

b) In the event that this happened, what effect would it have had on global climate?

c) How would this change affect your community? Even if you don't live near the Atlantic Ocean, your physical environment might still be greatly affected.

Preparing for the Chapter Challenge

Using a style of writing appropriate for a newspaper, write several paragraphs containing the following material:

• Explain how the locations of the continents on the Earth affect global climate.

• Explain how ocean currents affect global climate.

• Explain how moving continents change ocean currents.

Inquiring Further

1. **Modeling North Atlantic Deep Water flow**

Make a physical model of the flow of North Atlantic Deep Water. Experiment with several ideas. Think of how you might do it using actual water, and how you might do it using other materials. If your model idea is large and expensive, draw a diagram to show how it would work. If your model idea is small and simple, construct the model and see if it works.

Activity 5

How Do Carbon Dioxide Concentrations in the Atmosphere Affect Global Climate?

Goals

In this activity you will:

- Compare data to understand the relationship of carbon dioxide to global temperature.

- Evaluate given data to draw a conclusion.

- Recognize a pattern of information graphed in order to predict future temperature.

- Understand some of the causes of global warming.

Think about It

"What really has happened to winter?" You may have heard this type of comment.

- What causes "global warming?"

What do you think? Write down your ideas to this question in your *EarthComm* notebook. Be prepared to discuss your responses with your small group and the class.

Investigate

Part A: Atmospheric Carbon Dioxide Concentrations over the Last Century

Data on 10-year Average Global Temperature and Atmospheric Carbon Dioxide Concentration		
time interval	average global temperature (°F)	atomospheric carbon dioxide (ppm)
1901–1910	56.69	297.9
1911–1920	56.81	301.6
1921–1930	57.03	305.19
1931–1940	57.25	309.42
1941–1950	57.24	310.08
1951–1960	57.20	313.5
1961–1970	57.14	320.51
1971–1980	57.26	331.22
1981–1990	57.71	345.87
1991–2000*	57.87	358.85

*carbon dioxide data only through 1998.

1. Graph the concentration of carbon dioxide in the atmosphere from 1900 to 2000. Put the year on the *x* axis and the CO_2 levels (in parts per million) on the *y* axis.

2. On the same graph, plot the global average temperature for the same period. Put another *y* axis on the right-hand side of the graph and use it for global average temperature.

   a) Is there a relationship between carbon dioxide concentration and global average temperature? If so, describe it.

   b) What do you think is the reason for the relationship you see?

Part B: Atmospheric Carbon Dioxide Concentrations over the Last 160,000 Years

1. Look at the figure showing data from an ice core in Antarctica. The graph shows changes in concentrations of carbon dioxide and methane contained in trapped bubbles of atmosphere within the ice, and also temperature change over the same

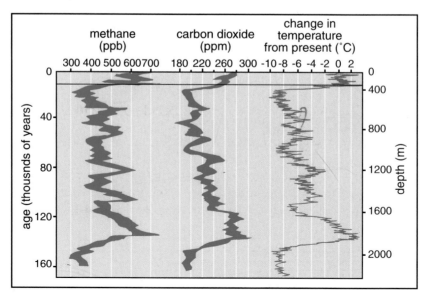

time interval. Data was obtained from the study of an ice core from the Antarctic Ice Sheet. The core was approximately 2200 m long. It was analyzed for methane concentrations (in parts per billion—left graph), carbon dioxide concentrations (in parts per million—middle graph), and inferred change in temperature from the present (in °C—right graph), over the last 160,000 years.

2. Obtain a copy of the graph. Use a straightedge to draw horizontal lines across the three maximum temperatures and the three minimum temperatures.

   a) Describe the correlation between these temperature events and changes in levels of carbon dioxide.

   b) Label likely glacial intervals (low temperatures) and interglacial intervals (higher temperatures).

   c) When did the most recent glacial interval end, according to these graphs?

Part C: The Greenhouse Effect

The phrase "greenhouse effect" is used to describe a situation in which the temperature of an environment (it could be any environment like a room, a car, a jar or the Earth) increases because incoming solar energy gets trapped because heat energy cannot easily escape. The incoming energy easily enters into the environment, but then, once it has been absorbed and is being re-radiated, it is harder for the energy to escape back out of the environment.

1. Work as a group to design an experiment to demonstrate the greenhouse warming in the atmosphere. The experiment should be simple in design, include a control element, and be performed in a short period of time (for example, a class period). The experiment will be presented to the community as a way to show the greenhouse effect.

   a) Record your design in your *EarthComm* notebook. Remember to include a hypothesis. Be sure to also include any safety concerns.

2. Decide on the materials you will use. The materials should be inexpensive and easy to get. The following is a possible list:

   • two identical 2-L plastic bottles with labels removed and tops cut off or two identical beakers

   • water

   • a clear plastic bag

   • a thermometer

   • ice cubes

   • a sunny windowsill or two similar lamps

   a) Record your list in your *EarthComm* notebook.

3. Decide on the measurements that you will make.

   a) Prepare a data table to record your observations.

4. With the approval of your teacher, conduct your experiment.

 Have the design of your experiment checked carefully by your teacher for any safety concerns.

5. Use the results of your experiment to answer the following questions:

   a) How did this experiment demonstrate (or fail to demonstrate) the greenhouse effect?

   b) How can this experiment serve as an analogy for atmospheric greenhouse effects?

   c) Was there any difference observed between the greenhouse experiment and the control?

   d) If there was a difference (or differences) describe it (them) in both qualitative and quantitative terms.

   e) How did the data in each case change through time during the experiment?

   f) Did the experiment reach a point of equilibrium where continuing changes were no longer observed? (Note: To answer this question, it may take longer than the class period, or, alternatively, you could hypothesize an answer to this question based on the trends of the data that you were able to gather.)

Reflecting on the Activity and the Challenge

In this activity you designed an experiment to demonstrate the greenhouse effect. You also examined the concentration of atmospheric carbon dioxide to see if it is correlated with changes in global average temperature. You discovered that an increase in carbon dioxide seems to be correlated with an increase in global average temperature. You will need this information to begin writing your article on "What is Global Warming?"

Digging Deeper

CARBON DIOXIDE AND GLOBAL CLIMATE

Correlation Studies

The relationship between carbon dioxide and global climate was mentioned in previous activities. When there is more carbon dioxide in the atmosphere, global temperatures are higher. When there is less carbon dioxide in the atmosphere, temperatures are lower. A scientist would say that there is a **correlation** between carbon dioxide concentration and global temperature. You might think, "Oh, that's because carbon dioxide concentration affects global temperature." And you might be right—but you might be wrong.

It is important to keep in mind always that a correlation does not, by itself, prove cause and effect. There are three possibilities: (1) carbon dioxide affects temperature; (2) temperature affects carbon dioxide; and (3) both are affected by a third factor, and are independent of one another! Any one of these three possibilities is consistent with the observations. It is the scientists' job to try to figure out which is the right answer. There are good reasons to think that the first possibility is the right one. That is because carbon dioxide is a "greenhouse gas."

What Are Greenhouse Gases?

The reason that the Earth is warm enough to support life is that the atmosphere contains gases that let sunlight pass through. Some of these gases absorb some of the energy that is radiated back to space from the Earth's surface. These gases are called **greenhouse gases**, because the effect is in some ways like that of a greenhouse. Without greenhouse gases, the Earth would be a frozen wasteland. Global temperatures would be much lower. Water vapor is the most important contributor to the greenhouse effect. Other greenhouse gases include carbon dioxide, methane, and nitrogen oxides.

How do greenhouse gases work? Most solar radiation passes through the clear atmosphere without being absorbed and is absorbed by the Earth's surface (unless it's reflected back to space by clouds first). There is a law in physics that states that all objects radiate electromagnetic radiation. The wavelength of the radiation depends on the objects' surface temperature. The hotter the temperature, the shorter the wavelength. The extremely hot surface of the Sun radiates much of its energy as visible light and other shorter-wavelength radiation. The much cooler surface of the Earth radiates energy too, but at much longer wavelengths. Heat energy is in the infrared range (*infra-* means "below," and the color red is associated with the longest wavelength in the color spectrum.) See *Figure 1*.

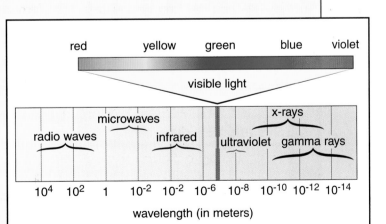

Figure 1 The spectrum of electromagnetic radiation.

Geo Words

greenhouse gases: gases responsible for the greenhouse effect. These gases include: water vapor (H_2O), carbon dioxide (CO_2), methane (CH_4), nitrous oxide (N_2O), chlorofluorocarbons (CF_xCl_x), and tropospheric ozone (O_3).

Greenhouse gases are those that absorb some of the outgoing infrared radiation. None of them absorb all of it, but in combination they absorb much of it. They then re-radiate some of the absorbed energy back to the Earth, as shown in *Figure 2.* That is what keeps the Earth warmer than if there were no greenhouse gases.

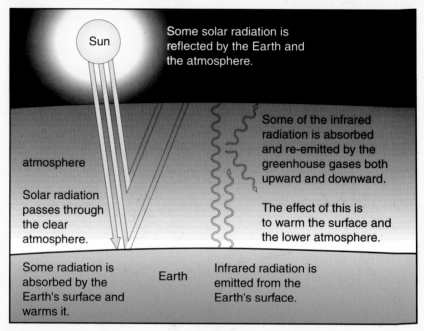

Some solar radiation is reflected by the Earth and the atmosphere.

Sun

atmosphere

Solar radiation passes through the clear atmosphere.

Some of the infrared radiation is absorbed and re-emitted by the greenhouse gases both upward and downward.

The effect of this is to warm the surface and the lower atmosphere.

Some radiation is absorbed by the Earth's surface and warms it.

Earth

Infrared radiation is emitted from the Earth's surface.

Figure 2 Schematic diagram illustrating how the greenhouse effect works.

The Carbon Cycle

Carbon dioxide is put into the atmosphere in two main ways: during volcanic eruptions, and by oxidation of organic matter. Oxidation of organic matter happens naturally in the biosphere. It occurs when plant and animal tissue decays. The organic matter is converted back to carbon dioxide and water. It also happens when animals breathe (and when plants respire too!). When you breathe, you take in oxygen, which you use to oxidize organic matter — your food. Then you breathe out carbon dioxide. Organic matter is also oxidized (more rapidly!) when it is burned. Carbon dioxide is released into the atmosphere whenever people burn wood or fossil fuels like gasoline, natural gas, or coal.

Plants consume carbon dioxide during photosynthesis. It is also consumed during the weathering of some rocks. Both land plants and algae in the ocean use the carbon dioxide to make organic matter, which acts as a storehouse for carbon dioxide. Carbon dioxide is constantly on the move from place to place. It is constantly being transformed from one form to another. The only way that it is removed from the "active pool" of carbon dioxide at or near the Earth's surface is to be buried deeply with sediments. Even then, it's likely to reenter the Earth–surface system later in geologic time. This may be a result of the uplift of continents and weathering of certain carbon-rich rocks. This transfer of carbon from one reservoir to another is illustrated in the carbon cycle shown in *Figure 3*.

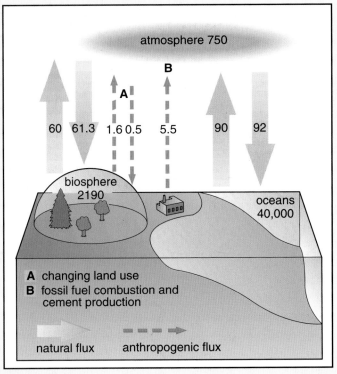

Figure 3 Global carbon cycle. Fluxes are given in billion metric tons per year and reservoirs in billion metric tons.

Carbon Dioxide and Climate

It appears that the more carbon dioxide there is in the environment, the warmer global temperatures are. Scientists have determined this from geologic data like the kind you worked with in the investigation. To what extent is this because carbon dioxide in the atmosphere acts as a greenhouse gas?

It is valuable to look at this question on two different time scales. On a scale of hundreds of thousands of years, carbon dioxide and global temperature track each other very closely. This correlation occurs through several glacial–interglacial cycles (*Figure 4*). It is not easy to develop a model in which carbon dioxide is the cause and global temperature is the effect. It's much more likely that variations are due to Milankovitch cycles. They may well explain the variation in both global temperature and carbon dioxide. On a scale of centuries, however, the picture is different. It seems very likely that the increase in carbon dioxide has been the cause of at least part of the recent global warming.

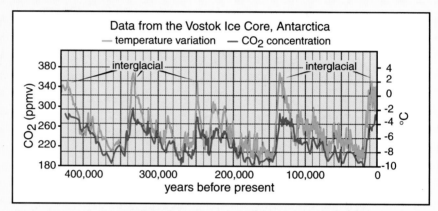

Figure 4 Variations in temperature and carbon dioxide (CO_2) concentration in parts per million by volume (ppmv) over the past 420,000 years interpreted from Antarctic ice cores. Temperature change is relative to the modern surface temperature at Vostok (−55.5°C).

Human emissions of greenhouse gases contribute significantly to the total amount of greenhouse gases in the atmosphere. For a long time humans have been adding a lot of carbon dioxide to the atmosphere by the burning of fossil fuels. This has especially increased in the past couple of centuries. Before the Industrial Revolution, carbon dioxide concentrations in the atmosphere were approximately 300 ppm (parts per million). As of 1995, carbon dioxide concentrations were almost 360 ppm. Scientists are concerned that the temperature of the Earth may be increasing because of this increasing concentration of carbon dioxide in the atmosphere.

Many nations have a commitment to reduce the total amount of greenhouse gases produced. It is their effort to reduce the risk of rapid global temperature increase. The trouble is that the size of the effect is still uncertain. Some people take the position that the increase in carbon dioxide should be reversed. They believe this is necessary even though the size of the contribution to global warming is not certain. It is their belief that the consequences would be very difficult to handle. Other people take a different position. They consider that it would be unwise to disrupt the world's present economy. They consider the future danger to be questionable. The big problem is that no one is certain that rapid global warming will take place. If it does, it may be too late to do anything about it!

Not all of the carbon dioxide released by burning of fossil fuels stays in the atmosphere. Carbon dioxide is also dissolved in ocean water. As carbon is put into the atmosphere, some of it is absorbed by the oceans. That lessens the impact of burning of fossil fuels on climate. Some people have even suggested that enormous quantities of carbon dioxide should be pumped into the oceans. That would tend, however, to just postpone the problem until later generations. Carbon dioxide is also stored by **reforestation**. Reforestation is the growth of forests on previously cleared farmland. Did you know that there is a lot more forested land in the eastern United States now than at the time of the Civil War? The Civil War took place almost 150 years ago. By some estimates, the United States is a sink, rather than a source, for carbon dioxide. Extensive reforestation is occurring east of the Mississippi, despite the continuing expansion of suburbs and shopping malls!

Geo Words

reforestation: the replanting of trees on land where existing forest was previously cut for other uses, such as agriculture or pasture.

Figure 5 Clear-cut forest area in Olympic National Forest, Washington.

Check Your Understanding

1. List four greenhouse gases. Which gas contributes most to the greenhouse effect?

2. Explain how greenhouse gases make it possible for humans to live on Earth.

3. What are two ways in which carbon dioxide is put into the Earth's atmosphere?

Understanding and Applying What You Have Learned

1. Which of the following activities produce carbon dioxide? Which consume carbon dioxide? Explain how each can influence global climate.

   a) cutting down tropical rainforests
   b) driving a car
   c) growing shrubs and trees
   d) breathing
   e) weathering of rocks
   f) volcanic eruptions
   g) burning coal to generate electricity
   h) heating a house using an oil-burning furnace

2. Describe the carbon cycle in your community. List the ways that carbon dioxide is produced and used up and the organisms responsible for cycling.

3. What are some difficulties involved with predicting concentrations of atmospheric carbon dioxide into the future?

4. Examine the graph your group prepared. You have gathered data through the year 2000. You have seen that this data has changed over time. Using additional graph paper, try to continue this pattern for the next 10 years.

5. The United States has a population of about 280 million people (according to the 2000 census) and uses about 70 billion gigajoules of energy a year. India has a population of about 835 million people (1990) and uses about 7 billion gigajoules of energy a year.

   a) Divide the United States' total yearly energy use by its population to find out the yearly energy use per person.
   b) Calculate the yearly energy use per person for India.
   c) Give as many reasons as you can to explain the difference.
   d) Do you think you use more or less energy than the typical American? Explain.
   e) If you wanted to use less energy, what would you do?
   f) Why is how much energy you use important when considering how much carbon dioxide is in the air?

6. Determine one source of greenhouse gas emission in your community.

   a) What gas is being produced?
   b) How is it produced?
   c) Can you think of a way to determine the level of the gas that is being produced by your community?
   d) Propose a means for limiting emissions of this gas.

Preparing for the Chapter Challenge

1. Using a newspaper style of writing, write several paragraphs in which you:

   • explain how humans have increased the concentration of carbon dioxide in the atmosphere;
   • explain why scientists think that increased carbon dioxide levels might lead to global climate change.

2. Clip and read several newspaper articles containing quotations.

3. Interview a member of your community about global warming. Is this person concerned about global warming? What does he or she think people should do about it? Look over your notes from your interview. Pick out several quotations from the community member that might work well in a newspaper article.

Inquiring Further

1. **Intergovernmental Panel on Climate Change (IPCC)**

   The Intergovernmental Panel on Climate Change (IPCC) is a group of more than 100 scientists and economists from many countries that is investigating the possibility of global warming and proposing ways that the nations of the world should respond. Do some research on the IPCC and what they have reported.

2. **Earth Summit**

   Investigate the 1997 United Nations Earth Summit in New York. What did the world's nations agree to at the Summit? Have the nations stuck to their promises?

Activity 6

How Might Global Warming Affect Your Community?

Goals

In this activity you will:

- Brainstorm the ways that global warming might influence the Earth.

- List ways that global warming might affect your community.

- Design an experiment on paper to test your ideas.

- Explain some of the effects of global warming that computer models of global climate have predicted.

- Understand positive and negative feedback loops and their relationship to climate change.

- Evaluate and understand the limitations of models in studying climate change through time.

Think about It

Some scientists think that the average global temperature may increase by several degrees Fahrenheit by the end of the 21st century.

- How do you think global warming could affect your community?

What do you think? List several ideas about this question in your *EarthComm* notebook. Be prepared to discuss your ideas with your small group and the class.

Investigate

1. In small groups, brainstorm as many effects of higher global temperatures (a few degrees Fahrenheit) as you can. Each time you come up with a possible result of global warming, ask yourselves what effect that result might have. For example, if you think glaciers will recede, ask yourself what the implications of that would be. At this point, do not edit yourself or criticize the contributions of others. Try to generate as many ideas as possible. Here are a few ideas to get your discussion going.

   How might higher temperatures affect the following processes?

   • evaporation

   • precipitation

   • glacial activity

   • ocean circulation

   • plant life

   • animal life.

   a) List all the ideas generated.

2. As a group, review your list and cross off those that everyone in the group agrees are probably incorrect or too far-fetched. The ideas that remain are those that the group agrees are possible (not necessarily proven or even likely, but possible). It's okay if some of the ideas are contradictory. Example: More cloud cover might block out more solar radiation (a cooling effect) vs. More cloud cover might increase the greenhouse effect (a warming effect).

   a) Make a poster listing the ideas that remain. Organize your ideas on the poster using the following headings:

   • geosphere

   • hydrosphere

   • atmosphere

   • cryosphere

   • biosphere.

   b) On a separate piece of paper, write down how each of the possible results might affect your community.

3. Imagine that your group is a group of scientists who are going to write a proposal asking for grant money to do an experiment. Pick one of the ideas on your poster that you would like to investigate.

   a) On paper, design an experiment or project to test the idea. Choose ONE of the following:

   • Design an experiment that you could do in a laboratory that would model the process. Draw a diagram illustrating the model. Tell what materials you would need and how the model would work. Describe what the results would mean. Tell which parts of the experiment would be difficult to design or run, and explain why.

 If you plan to perform your experiments do so only under careful supervision by a knowledgeable adult.

- Design a project in which you would gather data from the real world. Include a diagram or sketches illustrating how you would gather data. Tell what kind of data you would gather, how you would get it, how frequently and how long you would collect it, and how you would analyze it. Tell which parts of the project would be difficult to design or carry out, and explain why.

4. Present your poster and your proposal for an experiment or project to the rest of the class.

Reflecting on the Activity and the Challenge

In this activity, you brainstormed ways in which an increase in global temperatures might affect the geosphere, the hydrosphere, the atmosphere, the cryosphere, the biosphere, and your community. Then you designed an experiment or a project for how you might test one of your ideas. This process modeled the way in which scientists begin to think about how to investigate an idea. This will help you to explain which possible effects of global warming would have the greatest impact on your community, and also why it is difficult for scientists to accurately predict climate change.

Geo Words

urban heat-island effect: the observed condition that urban areas tend to be warmer than surrounding rural areas.

Digging Deeper

EFFECTS OF GLOBAL WARMING IN YOUR COMMUNITY
Problems with Making Predictions

Many scientists believe that the world's climate is becoming warmer as a result of the greenhouse gases (carbon dioxide, methane, and nitrogen-oxide compounds) that humans are adding to the atmosphere. Because the world's climate naturally experiences warmer years and colder years, it is hard to say for sure whether global average temperature has been increasing. Nowadays, remote sensing of the land and ocean surface by satellites makes it easy to obtain a good estimate of global temperature. The problem is that such techniques didn't exist in the past. Therefore, climatologists have to rely on conventional weather records from weather stations. That involves several problems. Thermometers change. The locations of the weather stations themselves often have to be changed. The move is usually away from city centers. As urban areas have been developed, they become warmer because of the addition of pavement and the removal of cooling vegetation. That is called the **urban heat-island effect**. Climatologists try to make corrections for these effects. The consensus is that global average temperature really is increasing. The questions then become: how much of the warming is caused by humankind, and how much is natural? It is known that there have been large variations in global temperature on scales of decades, centuries, and millennia long before humankind was releasing large quantities of carbon dioxide into the atmosphere (*Figure 1*).

Geo Words

feedback loops: the processes in which the output of a system causes positive or negative changes to some measured component of the system.

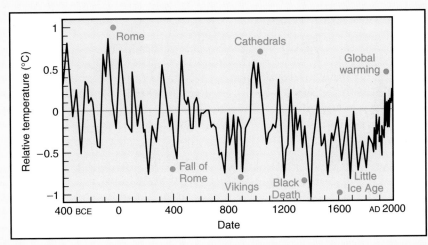

Figure 1 Relative global temperature from 400 BCE to the present.

Scientists who study global warming use very complicated computer models to try to predict what might happen. These computer models do not simply look at carbon dioxide and global temperature. They also do calculations based on many other factors that might be involved in climate change— everything from how much moisture is held in the Earth's soils to the rate at which plants transpire (give off water vapor). The physics of clouds is an especially important but also especially uncertain factor. The workings of the Earth's atmosphere are still much more complex than any computer model. Climatologists are hard at work trying to improve their models.

Drawbacks to the Computer Models

As you have seen, many factors influence the climate on Earth: carbon dioxide and other greenhouse gases, Milankovitch cycles, ocean currents, the positions of continents, weathering of rocks, and volcanic activity. Many of these factors interact with each other in ways that scientists do not fully understand. This makes it hard to make accurate predictions about how the atmosphere will respond to any particular change. The ways that different factors interact in global climate change are called **feedback loops**.

Feedback may be positive or negative. Positive feedback occurs when two factors operate together and their effects add up. For example, as the climate cools, ice sheets grow larger. Ice reflects a greater proportion of the Sun's radiation, thereby causing the Earth to absorb less heat. This results in the Earth becoming cooler, which leads to more ice forming. Ice cover and global cooling have a positive feedback relationship.

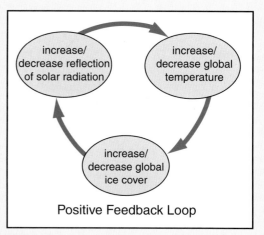

Positive Feedback Loop

Figure 2 An example of a positive feedback loop.

In a negative feedback relationship, two variables operate in opposition with each other. Each tends to counteract the effects of the other. Weathering and carbon dioxide are one such negative feedback pair. Weathering uses up carbon dioxide, which causes the temperature to drop. When the temperature drops, weathering rates slow down, using up less carbon dioxide, and slowing the rate of temperature decrease. In this sense, weathering acts as a negative feedback for global cooling. The Earth's global climate involves many feedback loops like these. Understanding of such feedback loops is extremely important in understanding how the Earth's physical environment changes through time.

How many feedback loops are there? How do they work? These are questions that scientists are working on every day. The uncertainty about feedback loops is one thing that makes it hard to predict how the Earth's climate might respond to an increase in carbon dioxide. Another major unknown in global warming is clouds. With warmer temperatures, there will be more evaporation and therefore more clouds. Clouds reflect incoming solar radiation into space—a cooling effect. But clouds also act like a blanket to hold in heat—a warming effect. Which effect predominates? Scientists aren't yet sure.

Figure 3 How can clouds influence climate?

What Do the Computer Models Say?

Scientists continue working on their computer models of global climate. They learn as they go and make improvements all the time. Because some of the models have been used for years, scientists can test some of the predictions of past years against weather data collected recently. This helps them make changes to the computer models to make them work better.

Computer climate models have come up with some possible scenarios that may result from the increased concentration of greenhouse gases in the atmosphere. Remember, however, that these scenarios are theoretical outcomes, not certainties.

Changes in Precipitation

Warmer temperatures lead to more clouds. More clouds lead to more rain. Some models predict more rain with global warming. Others predict a change in rainfall patterns—more precipitation in the winter and less in the summer, for example. Some areas of the world would receive more rain, others less. In that respect, some countries would be winners, and others, losers. With the increase in evaporation brought on by warmer temperatures, an increase in extreme events (stronger hurricanes and winter snowstorms) might be likely.

Figure 4 Global warming may cause an increase in the number of extreme winter snowstorms.

Changes in Sea Level

Glaciers around the world have been shrinking in recent years. If the Earth's climate continues to warm, more and more glacier ice sheets will melt. Meltwater is returned to the ocean. This would result in a worldwide rise in sea level. Some models predict a sea-level rise of as much as a meter by 2100.

Changes in Agriculture

In the Northern Hemisphere, where most of the world's cropland is located, warmer temperatures would cause a northward shift of the regions where certain crops are grown. Agriculture would also be affected by changes in rainfall patterns. Some regions might become too dry to support present crops. Other places might become too wet to support present crops. Many areas might continue growing traditional crops but experience declines in productivity. In other words, farmers might still grow corn in Iowa but produce fewer bushels per year. An example of a change that might decrease crop productivity is an increase in nighttime temperatures. Corn and some other grain crops do best when the temperature drops below 70°F at night. Another change that could reduce productivity (or increase costs) is a switch to wetter winters and drier summers.

Changes in Ocean Circulation

The addition of fresh meltwater from glaciers into the North Atlantic could disturb the production of North Atlantic Deep Water. The same thing happened 12,000 years ago (see **Activity 4**). The circulation of North Atlantic Deep Water helps distribute heat from solar radiation evenly around the globe. If this flow is disturbed, there might be far-reaching effects on global climate.

Check Your Understanding

1. Explain how ice cover and global cooling work as a positive feedback loop.

2. How might global warming lead to increased precipitation?

3. Why is it hard to predict how the global climate might react to an increase of carbon dioxide in the atmosphere?

Understanding and Applying What You Have Learned

1. Using the information in **Digging Deeper**, add to the poster you made in the **Investigate** section.

2. For each new item you added to your poster, hypothesize how your community would be affected by that outcome.

3. Using what you learned in **Digging Deeper**, modify the experiment or model you proposed in the **Investigate** section OR design another experiment or model.

Preparing for the Chapter Challenge

1. Using a style of writing appropriate for a newspaper, write a paragraph on each of the following possible effects of global warming. Make sure you make it clear that these are only possible scenarios, not certainties:

   • changes in rainfall patterns
   • increase in extreme events
   • changes in sea level
   • changes in ocean currents
   • changes in agriculture.

2. Write an editorial about how you think your community should respond to global warming. Should your community wait for further research? Should your community take action? What kind of action should be taken? Would these actions benefit your community in other ways, in addition to slowing global warming?

Inquiring Further

1. **Community energy use**

   Make a plan for calculating how much energy your school uses for heating, air conditioning, lights, and other electrical uses. Make a plan for calculating the energy used in gasoline for students, teachers, staff, and administrators to travel to and from school each day. How could you test your estimates to see how accurate they are? What are some ways your school could reduce its energy use? How can a reduction in energy use influence climate?

2. **"CO_2-free" energy sources**

   Investigate some sources of energy that do not produce carbon dioxide, like solar and wind power.

3. **Climate change and crops**

   Call your state's cooperative extension service and find out what are the top three crops grown in your state. Visit the *EarthComm* web site to determine if your state's cooperative extension service has a web site. What are the optimal climatic conditions for maximizing productivity of these crops? How might climate changes due to global warming affect farmers who grow these crops in your state?

Earth Science at Work

ATMOSPHERE: *Plant Manager*
Some companies are providing their workers with retraining to use new equipment that has been designed to reduce the emission of greenhouse gases and control global warming.

BIOSPHERE: *Farmer*
Agriculture is an area of the economy that is very vulnerable to climate change. Climate change that disturbs agriculture can affect all countries in the world. However, there are also steps that farmers can take to reduce the amount of carbon dioxide and other greenhouse gases.

CRYOSPHERE: *Mountaineering Guide*
Regions where water is found in solid form are among the most sensitive to temperature change. Ice and snow exist relatively close to their melting point and frequently change phase from solid to liquid and back again. This can cause snow in mountainous areas to become unstable and dangerous.

GEOSPHERE: *Volcanologist*
Volcanoes can emit huge amounts of carbon dioxide gas as well as sulfur dioxide gas into the atmosphere with each eruption. Both of these substances can have adverse effects on the atmosphere, including global warming as a possible result.

HYDROSPHERE: *Shipping Lines*
Even under "normal" climate conditions, ocean circulation can vary. A changing climate could result in major changes in ocean currents. Changes in the patterns of ocean currents and storm patterns will have important consequences to shipping routes.

How is each person's work related to the Earth system, and to Climate Change?

3

Changing Life
...and Your Community

Changing Life
...and Your Community

Getting Started

When you travel across the continental United States by land, you can see obvious changes in the plants and animals. For example, you would expect to find cactus in the Southwest but not in Oregon, alligators in Florida but not in Maine, and sea otters in California but not in Michigan. Organisms live in particular areas because they are adapted to a range of climate conditions. If the range is exceeded, that organism can no longer live in that area.

• Do the plants and animals that live in your community also live in other areas of your state or region? If so, over what geographic area?

• What would happen to these plants and animals in your community, state, or region if climate or geological setting changed?

What do you think? In your *EarthComm* notebook write down the factors that affect what plants and animals live in your community. Consider both the climate and the geography. Be prepared to discuss your ideas with your working group and the class.

Scenario

Scientists have recognized that there are short-term and long-term changes in plants and animals during Earth's history. The United Nations is interested in changes in the number of different organisms and where they live. A special task force has been organized to make recommendations on what should be done over different time scales (decades, centuries, millennia) to maintain the ecosystem in your community. Your class has been asked to help the task force by explaining how and why plants and animals in your community have changed over time. This information will help the task force to make predictions about how life might change in the future. Can the *EarthComm* team meet this challenge?

Chapter Challenge

You have been asked to create a display that illustrates the biological changes your community has experienced over several scales of geologic time. You will need to address:

- Evidence that there has been change in the life forms (trees, shrubs, herbivores, carnivores, etc.) and biodiversity (numbers of different organisms) of your community over time.

- Short-term and long-term factors that have influenced biological changes in your community.

- The natural processes that have been responsible for the appearance and disappearance of life forms throughout geologic time.

- Suggestions as to what could be done to reduce biodiversity loss caused by natural changes in Earth systems.

Assessment Criteria

Think about what you have been asked to do. Scan ahead through the chapter activities to see how they might help you to meet the challenge. Work with your classmates and your teachers to define the criteria for assessing your work. Record all of this information. Make sure that you understand the criteria as well as you can before you begin. Your teacher may provide you with a sample rubric to help you get started.

Activity 1   The Fossil Record and Your Community

Goals

In this activity you will:

• Understand the process of fossilization.

• Determine which plant and animal parts have the highest and lowest potential for becoming fossilized and understand why this is the case.

• Determine which organisms in your community are most likely to become preserved in the fossil record.

• Determine where fossils may be forming within your community.

• Understand the hierarchy of a food chain and how this affects the likelihood that an organism will be preserved in the fossil record.

Think about It

Imagine that it is hundreds of thousands of years into the future. A geologist has just discovered your community and is planning an excavation.

• What evidence would the geologist find to know that life had existed in your community?

What do you think? Record your ideas about this question in your *EarthComm* notebook. Be prepared to discuss your response with your small group and the class.

Investigate

Part A: How Fossils Form

1. With a paper towel, smear petroleum jelly all over the inside of a container.

2. Following the directions on the package, mix plaster in a mixing bowl. Complete **Steps 3** through **6** immediately after this, so that the plaster does not set while you are still preparing the "rock."

3. Fill the container half full of the plaster.

4. With a paper towel, smear a thin coating of petroleum jelly on both surfaces of a clamshell. Place the clamshell in the middle of the container and press it gently into the plaster.

5. Sprinkle some confetti onto the rest of the surface of the plaster, enough to cover about 50% of the surface.

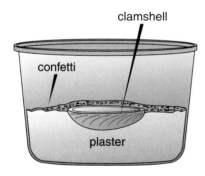

6. Fill the rest of the container with more of the plaster.

7. Let the plaster harden overnight. In the next class, remove the plaster "rock" from the container by turning the container upside down and banging it down against the floor or tabletop.

 Wear goggles throughout Part A.

8. Set the plaster on its edge on a hard surface. Hit it gently with the hammer, at about the level where the confetti was sprinkled. It should split along the plane where the clamshell was placed.

Cover the plaster cast with a towel before hitting it with the hammer.

a) Why did the "rock" break along the plane where the fossil is located rather than somewhere else?

b) Do you think that a rock would usually break through the locations of fossils? Why or why not?

c) Clams have two parts to their shell. The parts are called valves. Each valve has an inner surface and an outer surface. How many different kinds of imprints might be seen when the valves of a clam are buried and fossilized as in this investigation?

d) If you had not seen the original shell that went into the plaster and did not see it when the "rock" was split open, how might you reconstruct what the shell looked like, just from studying the fossil evidence?

Part B: Fossils in Your Community

1. Natural ecosystems have different energy levels called trophic levels. Plants belong to the first level because the chemical energy they store comes directly from solar energy. They are primary producers. Organisms that eat only plants are at a higher level. They are called primary consumers or herbivores. Organisms that eat only other animals are higher-order consumers or carnivores. (Omnivores eat both plants and animals.)

   a) Identify the organisms shown at each of these levels in the diagram.

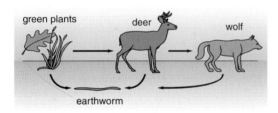

   b) Identify the most common organisms at each of these levels within your community. Try to list at least two or three different organisms for each level.

   c) Draw a diagram that illustrates the connections between each of these organisms. You will have essentially constructed a food web for your community.

2. Think about the organisms and their parts in your community.

   a) Which parts of each organism are the least resistant to decay and decomposition?

   b) Which parts of each organism are the most resistant to decay and decomposition?

3. Compare your list of resistant parts that you have identified for each plant and animal group with others in your group.

   a) Which type of organism has the highest probability of leaving some sort of fossil record?

   b) Why do some plants or animals have a low probability of leaving some sort of fossil record?

   c) How do you think that an organism's position on the food chain affects its likelihood of being fossilized?

Reflecting on the Activity and the Challenge

In this activity you learned how some types of fossils are formed. You also came to understand that not every organism has the same potential for becoming a fossil. Only certain types of parts have a high potential for becoming part of the fossil record. You also realized that the greater the number of parts an organism has, the higher the probability that one individual part may become fossilized at some time if the environmental conditions are right. You are now in a better position to evaluate the kinds of fossil evidence that may be found in your community.

Digging Deeper

FOSSILS

Food Chains and Food Webs

Plants use energy from the Sun to make food, through the process of photosynthesis. Organisms that make their own food are called producers. Other organisms, like animals, are not able to make their own food. They must eat plants, or other animals that eat plants, to obtain energy. Such organisms that rely on plants for food are called consumers. Scientists use a kind of flowchart, called a food chain, to show how organisms are connected to each other by the food they eat. It is a convenient way to show how energy and matter are transferred from producers to the next levels of consumers. In most ecosystems, consumers rely on more than one source of food. Therefore, it is more realistic to show the relationships in the form of a food web. *Figure 1* shows a sample food web.

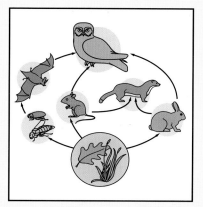

Figure I Can you identify the different trophic levels of this food web?

All living things die. Also, consumers generate waste materials from the food they eat. A special group of consumers, called decomposers, obtain the matter and energy they need from wastes and dead plants and animals. Decomposers play an essential role in food webs.

What is a Fossil?

A **fossil** is any evidence of a past plant or animal contained in a sediment or rock. There are two kinds of fossils: **body fossils** and **trace fossils**. Body fossils, like those shown in *Figure 2*, are the actual organisms or some part of them. They may also be the imprint of the organism or some part of it. Bones, teeth, shells, and other hard body parts are relatively easily preserved as fossils. However, even they may become broken, worn, or even dissolved before they might be buried by sediment. The soft bodies of organisms are relatively difficult to preserve. Special conditions of burial are needed to preserve delicate organisms like jellyfish. Sometimes, such organisms fall into a muddy sea bottom in quiet water. There they might be buried rapidly by more mud. Only in circumstances like these can such organisms be fossilized. For that reason, the fossil record of soft-bodied organisms is far less well known. There is a strong **bias** in the fossil record. Some organisms rarely have the chance of becoming fossilized. Under very specific circumstances, however, even these can become part of the fossil record.

Geo Words

fossil: any remains, trace, or imprint of a plant or animal that has been preserved in the Earth's crust since some past geologic or prehistoric time.

body fossil: any remains or imprint of actual organic material from a creature or plant that has been preserved in the geologic record (like a bone).

trace fossil: a fossilized track, trail, burrow, tube, boring, tunnel or other remnant resulting from the life activities of an animal.

bias: a purposeful or accidental distortion of observations, data, or calculations in a systematic or nonrandom manner.

Figure 2 Dinosaur bones collected in Dinosaur National Monument in Utah.

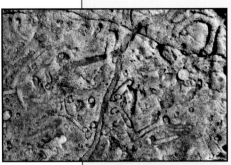

Figure 3 Feeding trails and burrows are kinds of trace fossils. Note the penny for scale.

Trace fossils, like those shown in *Figure 3*, are the record of life activities of organisms rather than the organisms themselves. Tracks, trails, burrows, feeding marks, and resting marks are all trace fossils. Trace fossils are useful for geologists and **paleontologists** because certain kinds of organisms, which live in specific environmental conditions, make distinctive traces.

In relatively young **sediments** and rocks, the actual body parts of an organism are often preserved. You modeled this in **Part A** of the investigation. In older rocks, the body parts are usually dissolved away. They may also be recrystallized or replaced by another kind of mineral. Even so, the imprints of the organisms are still preserved. They can be studied if the rock splits apart in the right place and the right orientation to reveal the imprint. Paleontologists usually collect large numbers of rock pieces. They then split the rock in the laboratory with special mechanical splitting devices to try to find at least a few fossils.

Geo Words

paleontologist: a scientist who studies the fossilized remains of animals and/or plants.

sediments: solid fragmental material that originates from weathering of rocks and is transported or deposited by air, water, or ice, or that accumulates by other natural agents, such as chemical precipitation from solution or secretion by organisms.

Fossilization

Figure 4 Fungi attack a fallen log in the woods.

As you saw when you looked at food chains and food webs, only a very small part of what once lived is spared being a meal for some other organism. There is a very high probability that any organism on Earth will be either consumed by another organism or decomposed by microorganisms following death. Decay affects not only soft body parts but also some of the harder, more resistant body parts. Think of a forest floor like the one in *Figure 4*. Each plant and animal that lives in the forest eventually ends up on the forest floor in some form. Soft tissues of animals, leaves, and flowers are used by decomposers. They decay within several weeks or are used by some other organism as a food source. The most resistant body parts include insect exoskeletons, vertebrate bones, wood, leaf cuticle, seeds, pollen, and spores. They may remain on the forest floor for many years or even centuries. This depends upon the physical and chemical conditions of the soil. A similar situation exists on the ocean floor.

For an organism or body part to become a fossil, it must either live within or be moved to a place where it can be buried. Burial alone does not guarantee that fossilization will occur. Under normal burial conditions all organisms undergo a scientifically predictable decay trend. Hence, there must be other factors operating during or immediately following burial to slow or stop decay. The conditions necessary for fossilization do not exist everywhere all of the time. In fact, they exist in only a few places and for only a tiny fraction of the time.

Despite this, enormous numbers of organisms have become fossilized. The reason lies in the extent of geologic time. It is difficult to imagine how long a million years is. Yet physical, chemical, and biological processes have been operating on Earth not just millions of years but billions of years. *Figure 5* shows a simple geologic time scale that indicates when various kinds of organisms are first seen in the fossil record.

Major Divisions of Geologic Time
(boundaries in millions of years before present)

Era	Period	Event	
Cenozoic	Quaternary	modern humans	
	Tertiary	abundant mammals	1.8
			65
Mesozoic	Cretaceous	flowering plants; dinosaur and ammonoid extinctions	
	Jurassic	first birds and mammals; abundant dinosaurs	145
	Triassic	abundant coniferous trees	213
			248
Paleozoic	Permian	extinction of trilobites and other marine animals	
	Pennsylvanian	fern forests; abundant insects; first reptiles	286
	Mississippian	sharks; large primitive trees	325
	Devonian	amphibians and ammonoids	360
	Silurian	early plants and animals on land	410
	Ordovician	first fish	440
	Cambrian	abundant marine invertebrates; trilobites dominant	505
			544
Proterozoic		primitive aquatic plants	
			2500
Archean		oldest fossils; bacteria and algae	

Figure 5 Important evolutionary events of geologic time. Note that the divisions of geologic time are not drawn to scale. ➞

Geo Words

fossiliferous rock: a rock containing fossils.

sedimentary rock: a rock resulting from the consolidation of accumulated sediments.

Fossiliferous Rocks

A rock, like the one shown in *Figure 6*, that contains fossils is said to be **fossiliferous**. Not all **sedimentary rocks** contain fossils. If you parachuted out of an airplane and landed on sedimentary rock, the chance of your finding a fossil would be rather small.

Figure 6 A fossiliferous limestone composed mostly of brachiopod fossils.

Check Your Understanding

1. What is a food chain, and what role does it play in fossilization?

2. How does the rate of burial relate to the likelihood of fossilization?

3. What proportion of living organisms has the likelihood of becoming fossils?

4. What is the difference between a body fossil and a trace fossil?

5. Which kinds of sedimentary rocks tend to be the most fossiliferous, and which tend to be the least fossiliferous?

Some kinds of sedimentary rocks contain more fossils than others. Limestones are the most fossiliferous sedimentary rocks. That should not be surprising, because most limestones consist in part, or even entirely, of the body parts of shelly marine organisms. Some shales are fossiliferous as well, because certain organisms like to live on muddy sea floors. Sandstones are usually much less fossiliferous than limestones. Fewer kinds of organisms can tolerate the strong currents and shifting sand beds that are typical of areas where sand is being deposited. For the same reason, conglomerates are the least fossiliferous of sedimentary rocks.

Understanding and Applying What You Have Learned

1. A geologic map shows the distribution of bedrock at the Earth's surface. Every geologic map has a legend that shows the kinds of bedrock that are present in the map area. The legend also shows the rock bodies or rock units that these rocks belong to, and their geologic age. Look at a geologic map of your community.

   a) What kinds of rocks are found in your community?

   b) Are fossils likely to be found in these rocks? Why or why not?

2. Revisit the **Think about It** question at the start of the activity.

   a) What evidence do you think the paleontologist would find in your community as proof of past life?

   b) Where would the paleontologist look to find this evidence?

   c) Do the organisms living in your community provide a biological signal that is unique to your area? Explain.

3. Must an organism die as a requirement to be represented in the fossil record? Explain your answer.

4. How are the physical and chemical processes responsible for preservation of plants and soft-bodied animals different from those for organisms that have hard skeletal parts?

5. Why would you expect that organisms living in ponds, lakes, or oceans have a greater chance of becoming part of the fossil record than organisms that live on land?

Preparing for the Chapter Challenge

Write a background summary that introduces fossils and fossilization. Be sure to identify those plant and animal parts in your community that you think are likely to leave some kind of fossil record, and discuss the reasons why you would expect one organism part to be more common than another. Also indicate where you would expect these fossils to be found within your community.

Inquiring Further

1. **Taphonomy**

   Taphonomy is the subdiscipline of paleontology that is concerned with the study of fossilization. The field of forensic science applies these principles to police and detective work. Investigate these subjects further.

2. **Common geological settings for preservation**

   Where on land or in the ocean might an organism be buried "dead or alive?" What are the conditions necessary to preserve soft tissues in these settings? What examples can you find in the fossil record of soft-tissue preservation?

Activity 2   North American Biomes

Goals

In this activity you will:

- Define the major biomes of North America and identify your community's biome.

- Understand that organisms on land and in the ocean have physical and chemical limits to where they live.

- Recognize the most common plants and animals in your community.

- Explore how a change in physical and chemical conditions within your community could alter your community's biome.

- Understand that there are predictable relationships between where the different biomes occur in North America.

Think about It

Humans have adapted to a wide variety of climates. Most plants and animals, too, have a range of climatic tolerances in which they live.

- Why don't the same plants and animals live all over the United States?

What do you think? Record your ideas about this question in your *EarthComm* notebook. Be prepared to discuss your response with your small group and the class.

Investigate

1. A biome is a major biologic community. It is classified according to the main type of vegetation present. The organisms that live in each biome are characteristic of that area. Examine the photographs of the major biomes of North America that have been identified by ecologists.

tundra

taiga

chaparral

desert

grassland

mountain zones

tropical rainforest

temperate deciduous forest

temperate evergreen forest

polar ice

a) Use the photographs above and on the previous page and the *EarthComm* web site to write a short description for each biome, identifying the predominant plants and animals found in the biome.

b) Which biome most closely resembles your community?

c) How were you able to recognize your biome? What characteristic landscape did you use to pick the most representative photograph?

2. Look at the map of North American biomes. Match the photographs of the biomes with their locations shown on the map.

a) How do you think that the climate of your community's biome differs from the climates of other biomes in North America? Consider the temperature and precipitation of the area as well as the temperature and precipitation changes from season to season. Refer also to the map of the climatic regions of the United States on E85.

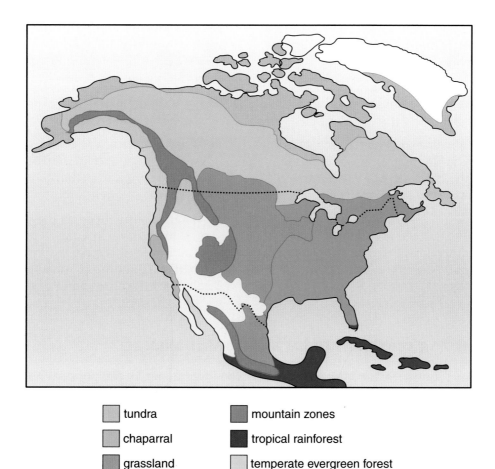

tundra	mountain zones
chaparral	tropical rainforest
grassland	temperate evergreen forest
taiga	temperate deciduous forest
desert	polar ice

3. As a group, think of the common plants and animals that occur naturally in your community. Use any available resources.

   a) Make a list of the most common naturally occurring plants. Identify at least five plants.

   b) Make a list of the most common naturally occurring animals. Identify at least five animals.

4. Share your lists of common plants and animals with the rest of your class using a class discussion format. To make comparisons between groups easier, each group may want to write their lists on the chalkboard.

   a) From the compiled data, develop a single class list of the 10 most common plants and animals in your community. Rank the plants and animals in order from most common to least common.

5. Compare the class list with what scientists have found to be the most common plants and animals in your biome.

   a) How does your class list and ranking compare with the scientific data?

   b) Which plants and animals that you thought were common on the basis of your experiences were the same as those identified by scientists?

   c) What could account for any differences between your observations and the scientific data?

6. Compare the class list with what scientists have found to be the most common plants and animals in a North American biome other than the one in which you live.

   a) How do the plants and animals living in these areas differ?

   b) What are the physical and climatic factors that control the kinds of organisms that live in these two different biomes?

   c) What might happen to the plant and animal life in your community if the physical and chemical conditions suddenly changed to those found in the other biome?

Reflecting on the Activity and the Challenge

You have now seen the interactions between plants and animals in your community and compared these same relationships with another part of North America. You have also seen that different plants and animals characterize other parts of North America because their requirements for life are met by the physical and chemical conditions presently in those regions. You should now be able to begin to explain how biome boundaries can change in response to changing physical and chemical conditions on Earth over time.

Digging Deeper

CLIMATE AND BIOMES

An **ecosystem** is a community of plants and animals together with the physical and chemical environment in which that community exists. In the broadest sense, there are two major kinds of ecosystems on Earth today: aquatic and terrestrial ecosystems. Both of these kinds of ecosystems can be traced far back in geologic time. Each can be split into smaller subdivisions, using different criteria. For example, aquatic ecosystems can be subdivided into two categories using water chemistry: freshwater ecosystems and saltwater ecosystems. Each of these can be further subdivided. The aquatic ecosystem shown in *Figure 1* is a freshwater ecosystem. The terrestrial ecosystem can be divided into many categories, using the tallest plants in the area.

Figure 1 An example of a freshwater ecosystem.

Biological subdivisions on land are called **biomes**. Many present-day biomes parallel the lines of **latitude**. Climate conditions across the globe at these latitudes tend to be similar. In other words, there is a relationship between the physical and chemical processes that operate within latitude belts and the plants and animals that are adapted to these conditions. There is a slight difference in the case of mountains, because temperature decreases with elevation, as shown in *Figure 2*. Often, lowland biomes at high latitudes

Geo Words

ecosystem: a unit in ecology consisting of the environment with its living elements, plus the nonliving factors that exist in it and affect it.

biome: a recognizable assemblage of plants and animals that characterizes a large geographic area on the Earth; a number of different biomes have been recognized, and the distribution of the biomes is controlled mainly by climate.

latitude: a north-south measurement of position on the Earth. It is defined by the angle measured from the Earth's equatorial plane.

Figure 2 How do you think the organisms found at the base of a mountain differ from those found near the top of the mountain?

Geo Words

climate: the characteristic weather of a region, particularly as regards temperature and precipitation, averaged over some significant interval of time.

weather: the condition of the Earth's atmosphere, specifically, its temperature, barometric pressure, wind velocity, humidity, clouds, and precipitation.

(closer to the poles) are very similar to highland biomes at lower latitudes (closer to the Equator). For example, plant communities on the rocky, windswept peaks in the Appalachians are similar to those in many places in subarctic Canada.

Climate involves the long-term characteristics of the **weather** in a given region of the Earth. The most important factors in climate are temperature and precipitation. Both the average values and the deviations from the average are important. Everybody knows that some places are hot and some are cold. Some places are wet and others dry. What is also important is how much temperature and precipitation change from season to season. The average rainfall in an area may be high, but there may also be a long dry season. Plants need adaptations for surviving those dry periods before renewing their growth during the wet season. In areas with rainy seasons and dry seasons, it is also important for plant communities whether the wet season coincides with summer or with winter. You can easily see why climate plays the most important role in the distribution of biomes.

What links common animals with common plants is the dietary requirements of the plant eaters (herbivores). Similarly, the dietary requirements and taste preferences of meat eaters (carnivores) are linked to the specific herbivores that live in a biome. The most common plants, like the ferns, mosses, and trees shown in *Figure 3*, provide food as well as

Figure 3 Temperate evergreen forest, Hoh Rainforest, Washington.

Figure 4 How do you think an organism like an owl responds to climate change?

Geo Words

global climate: mean climatic conditions over the surface of the Earth as determined by the averaging of a large number of observations spatially distributed throughout the entire region of the globe.

shelter for many animals in the biome. When plants and animals die, decomposers break down the dead and discarded organic matter, recycling it to the soils to be used again by plants. The rate of decay and the release of nutrients into the soil are also affected by the climate.

Global climate change is in the news nowadays. There is abundant evidence, however, that climate has changed continually in the past, long before the development of modern human society. These changes have taken place on time scales that range from as short as decades to as long as hundreds of millions of years. **Chapter 2, Climate Change and Your Community**, investigates climate change in greater depth.

How do biomes respond to climate change? Generally, animals in a biome can migrate quite rapidly in response to climate change. Plants migrate much more slowly than animals. Plants are not able to respond immediately when the climate conditions change and the plant's tolerances are exceeded! Plants can shift their range only by dispersal of seeds and spores by the wind or by animals. Keep in mind that all animals depend, directly or indirectly, on plants as their food source. If climate change is slow, biomes can respond without much disruption as they shift in position. If climate change is more rapid, there can be great changes in the makeup of the plant and animal communities in a given area.

Check Your Understanding

1. What are the two major kinds of ecosystems found on Earth?

2. Define, in your own words, the term biome.

3. What factor plays the greatest role in determining the distribution of biomes on Earth?

4. How do biomes respond to changes in climate?

Understanding and Applying What You Have Learned

1. Why might different teams in your class have developed different rankings of the common plants and animals in your community? What role might the location of your home have in what you determined to be the most commonly occurring organisms?

2. Determine the date when your town or city was incorporated.

   a) What plants and animals were common before that date?
   b) How have the common organisms in your community changed since that date?
   c) How do you explain these changes?

3. What are the main climate factors that restrict the distribution of plants and animals within your biome?

4. Refer back to the biome map of North America.

   a) What proportion of the United States lives in the same biome as your community?
   b) What is the relationship between biome distribution and latitude?
   c) What is the relationship between biome distribution and elevation?

5. What changes in the animals and plants might you expect if the climate of your community became colder? Became warmer?

Preparing for the Chapter Challenge

Write a short paper in which you describe the present biome in your community. Indicate which physical and chemical factors determine the limits of your biome, and indicate how variations in these factors could cause changes in the distribution of organisms in your community. For example, suppose that your community is now located in a mild climate. How might a decrease in the yearly average temperature affect the organisms in your community?

Inquiring Further

1. **Herbivores and carnivores in your community**

   What relationships do herbivores and carnivores have with plants in your biome? Do all consumers have the same preference for food, or do different groups of animals use different food sources?

2. **Animal adaptations to climate**

   Animals in Alaska must survive the extreme cold of the arctic and subarctic climate. What adaptations have Alaskan animals developed to survive? How do you think these adaptations might affect how these organisms would be preserved in the fossil record?

Activity 3

Your Community and the Last Glacial Maximum

Goals

In this activity you will:

- Investigate how changes in climate are linked to shifts in the distribution of oak and spruce trees in North America, 20 ka (20,000 years ago) to the present.

- Understand how scientists can use data collected from pollen and spores to reconstruct past environments.

- Understand how the climate of your community has changed over the past 18,000 years.

- Understand how this climate change has affected the plants and animals of your community.

Think about It

The Earth's climate has varied significantly over geologic time. As recently as 18,000 years ago much of North America was covered by thick glacial ice.

- What plants and animals (if any) lived in your community when large parts of North America were covered by ice?
- As the continental glaciers retreated northward, what changes in the plants and animals happened over time?

What do you think? Record your ideas about these questions in your *EarthComm* notebook. Be prepared to discuss your response with your small group and the class.

Investigate

Part A: Can You Recognize a Forest without the Trees?

1. Examine the maps. Pollen and spore records were recovered from lakes, ponds, and bogs across North America. Coupled with carbon-14 radio-isotopic dating, scientists have reconstructed the changes in plant types over space and time. The maps show sample sites across North America for approximately the last 20,000 years. The percentages of spruce and oak pollen are plotted on each map set.

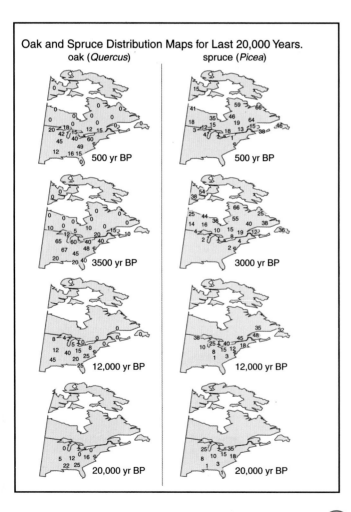

Oak and Spruce Distribution Maps for Last 20,000 Years.
oak (*Quercus*)   spruce (*Picea*)

500 yr BP   500 yr BP

3500 yr BP   3000 yr BP

12,000 yr BP   12,000 yr BP

20,000 yr BP   20,000 yr BP

a) Obtain copies of the maps. Using a different color for each plant, draw the 5% and 20% contour lines neatly across each map.

b) Where is the maximum percentage of spruce found 500, 3000, 12,000 and 20,000 years ago?

c) Where is the maximum percentage of oak found 500, 3500, 12,000 and 20,000 years ago?

2. Oak trees are characteristic of deciduous forest, and spruce trees are representative of the taiga.

a) Do the general trends in oak parallel the changes in spruce? Explain.

b) What other plants and animals might you expect to find in the fossil records in the collection sites 3000 and 20,000 years ago?

Part B: Your Community Biome: Pleistocene to Present

1. Develop a hypothesis concerning the plants and animals that may have lived in your community when North America experienced the transition from a glacial period to the present day (nonglacial period).

a) Record your prediction and the reason for your prediction in your *EarthComm* notebook.

2. Visit the *EarthComm* web site to find a list of databases and animations regarding pollen distribution from the Late Pleistocene to the present.

a) Make a list of plants that have been found in your community from approximately 18,000 years ago to the present.

b) How does this list compare to the list of plants commonly found in your community, which you developed in **Activity 2**?

c) How do you account for the differences between the plants found in your community today and the plants that were found in your community in the past?

3. Databases also exist that document the fossil animals found across North America through time. Visit the *EarthComm* web site to find a list of databases that show animal distribution in North America.

a) Why are fossil animal records not as comprehensive as pollen records?

b) Make a list of animals that have been found in your community from approximately 18,000 years ago to the present.

c) How does this list compare to the list of animals commonly found in your community, which you developed in **Activity 2**?

d) How do you account for the differences between the animals found in your community today and the animals that were found in your community in the past?

4. Evaluate the hypothesis you generated at the beginning of **Part B** of the investigation.

a) Do the data you have collected verify or refute your hypothesis?

b) What modification(s) to your hypothesis must be made, in light of the data you found? Revise your hypothesis according to your limited data set.

Reflecting on the Activity and the Challenge

You have learned that the plants and animals that once lived in your community were probably very different than today. As changes in climate accompanied the retreat of the glaciers, there were changes in the composition of the ecosystem. Compiling information on past communities helped you to think about the potential change in plants and animals in your state, region, and community under future changes in climate.

Digging Deeper

ORGANISM RESPONSE TO CLIMATE CHANGE

Pollen and Spores

The reproduction in plants is different from that in animals. As part of the plant life cycle, **spores** (from mosses, ferns, and horsetails) or **pollen** (from most other kinds of plants) are produced in the hundreds of thousands per individual plant each year. Spores and pollen can be dispersed in a number of ways. The most common way is by wind. This is made easier by the very small size of individual pollen or spore grains, generally less than 50 μm (0.05 mm). *Figure 1* shows a 15 μm pollen grain magnified 1600 times its actual size.

Figure 1A
Transmitted-light image of a pollen grain (of the genus *Cupuliferoipollenites*), 15 μm in diameter.

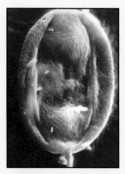

Figure 1B Scanning electron microscope image of the same pollen grain.

All species are genetically unique. The genes of an organism control its specific growth and development. When plants reproduce, each plant species produces a unique spore or pollen grain. Spores and pollen grains differ greatly in their shape, size, and surface features. Some plants produce spores that are triangular, and others produce spores that are football shaped, as shown in *Figure 2*. Some spores are covered with short spines or club-shaped structures, and

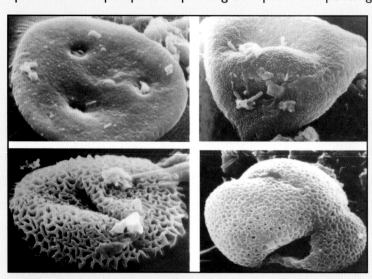

Figure 2 Scanning electron microscope image of four different pollen grains, ranging in diameter from 18 to 38 μm.

others are perfectly smooth. All plants of the same species produce the same type of pollen each year throughout each generation. The pollen grains are transported to ponds, lakes, and rivers where they settle with the sediment and are buried.

Pollen and spores are very resistant to decay. Pollen and spores can be preserved for hundreds of millions of years under the right burial conditions. This resistance to decay is the main reason why spores and pollen can be extracted not only from recently deposited sediments but also from ancient sedimentary rocks from the geologic past.

Paleoclimate

Paleoclimatology is the study of the Earth's past climates. Climatologists know from several kinds of evidence that the Earth's climate has changed continually, and substantially, through geologic time. Over the past million years (a short time, geologically!) there have been several colder periods when vast ice sheets, as much as a few kilometers thick, expanded to cover much of northern and central North America and Eurasia. In between these **glacial periods**, there were shorter periods, called **interglacials**, when global temperature was much warmer and ice sheets disappeared from North America and Eurasia. *Figure 3* shows temperature changes over the past 420,000 years as interpreted from data recovered from the Vostok ice core (Antarctica).

Geo Words

paleoclimatology: the scientific study of the Earth's climate during the past.

glacial period: an interval in time that is marked by one or more major advances of glacier ice. Note that the time interval is not necessarily of the same magnitude as the "Period" rank of the geologic time scale.

interglacial period: the period of time during an ice age when glaciers retreated because of milder temperatures.

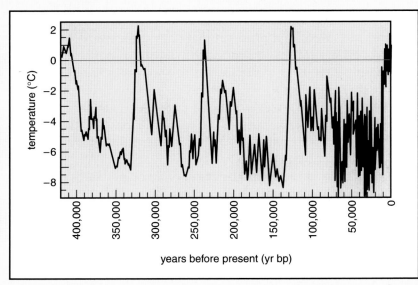

Figure 3 Temperature variation over the past 420,000 years relative to the modern surface temperature at Vostok (−55.5°C).

Geo Words

steppe: an extensive, treeless grassland found in semiarid mid-latitude regions. Steppes are typically considered to be drier than the prairie.

Glacial periods last longer than interglacials. Ice sheets build up slowly over several tens of thousands of years, and then retreat rapidly from their maximum advance over a brief period of several thousand years. Interglacials last only 20,000 to 25,000 years. The last glacial maximum was about 20,000 years ago. By about 7000 years ago, almost all of the Northern Hemisphere continental ice sheets, except for the Greenland ice sheet, had melted away. Since then, global climate has been relatively warm, although with significant fluctuations over decades, centuries, and millennia.

The Response of Biomes to Climate Change

Each glacial advance modified the climate across North America. In response to these climatic changes, there was a change in biome boundaries. Each plant species has evolved to be adapted to a particular range of climatic conditions. Outside of that range of conditions, the climate is too cold or warm, or too wet or too dry, for that species to survive over the long term. As climatic belts shift during times of global climate change, plant species shift accordingly in their range of distribution. If the change is too rapid, they become extinct. The animals that rely upon specific kinds of plants for food or shelter are similarly affected. Some of the organisms that lived during the most recent glacial and interglacial periods continue to exist today in North America. Some of the organisms that lived in the past are now extinct.

The distribution of biomes during the last glacial period, as determined from the fossil record across North America, was very different from the present distribution. For example, much of the southeastern United States was covered in an open woodland or forest that graded westward into forest **steppe** and open, dry treeless steppe at the glacial maximum. Fossil evidence indicates that parts of the Florida peninsula may have been desertlike. At the same time a variety of forest types persisted in the northernmost part of the state. To the east of the Appalachians, cool-climate pine forests and prairie herbs existed. The central Rocky Mountains were covered in cold-tolerant conifer woodlands. Farther south there was a mixture of semidesert scrub and sparse conifer woodland. Where there are dry desert conditions in the southwest, temperate open woodlands or grasslands covered the region during glacial maximum.

Not only was biome distribution different in response to the shift in climate belts across North America, but many of the organisms within them were also different. Fossil evidence indicates that some associations between plants and animals, particularly among ice-age North American mammals that exist today did not exist in the Pleistocene. For example, the snowshoe hare still found in Minnesota and Wisconsin is known from fossil evidence in

Missouri, Kentucky, and Virginia when these states were covered in taiga. It's known that extinction of large mammals in North America occurred at the time when the last continental ice sheets melted. Two hypotheses have been proposed to account for this. One hypothesis proposes that ecological changes at the end of the Pleistocene disrupted the biological balance. This hypothesis suggests that at the time of biome readjustment, a large number of species were unable to adapt. The other hypothesis, the "overkill model," proposes that

the expansion of human migrants from Asia into North America resulted in overhunting and depletion of the mammal populations. Some authors suggest that humans killed everything in their path, whereas others hypothesize that humans reduced mammal populations to low numbers. Such low populations, in turn, were unable to maintain birthrates high enough for the species to survive. Whatever the reason (or reasons), North America today is very different from the North America of just 10,000 years ago.

Check Your Understanding

1. What are the two hypotheses to account for the extinction of some animals at the end of the Pleistocene?

2. Why are pollen and spores conducive to long-term preservation?

3. How was the climate of North America different during the last full glacial episode? What impact did this have on organisms in the area?

Understanding and Applying What You Have Learned

1. A scientist is like a detective. Rarely do detectives have all of the information to solve the case. However, they usually get enough evidence to show beyond a reasonable doubt what happened and when it happened. Use evidence that you have gathered to answer the following questions:

   a) How can you demonstrate that the biome in which you now live was different during and after the last glacial maximum?

   b) How many different kinds of fossil data have been found in your community or region?

   c) What do these fossil data tell you about the plants and animals that once lived where you do?

   d) What happened to the Late Pleistocene plants and animals that today are not found in your community?

2. It has been stated that the fossil record is biased. What biases might have affected the Late Pleistocene fossil record of your community's recent past?

3. How good is the Pleistocene fossil record? How much data have been collected and used to characterize the North American Pleistocene?

4. a) For the Pleistocene plants and animals that no longer live in your community and survived the Pleistocene extinction, what part(s) of the food web do they occupy? Why might they no longer be found in your community naturally?

b) For the Pleistocene plants and animals that lived in your community but didn't survive the Pleistocene extinction, what part(s) of the food web did they occupy? Why might they have become extinct?

Preparing for the Chapter Challenge

Think about what you have learned about the plants and animals in the present and past biome of your area. Prepare an illustration that shows the relationships between the organisms of the past and present. Can you document a progression from the organisms of the past to the organisms of the present? Include a narrative in which you explain why the organisms changed through time.

Inquiring Further

1. **Carbon-14 dating techniques**

   Search your library and the web for information about how it is possible to determine the carbon-14 age of organic matter. Prepare a report for the class on the physical and chemical principles upon which the technique is based, and how advances in analytical equipment have reduced the uncertainty in the age estimates.

2. **Late Pleistocene extinctions**

   Approximately 11,000 years ago, a variety of animals across North America became extinct. These were mostly large mammals (over 50 kg), like saber-toothed cats, mammoths, mastodons, and giant beavers. What mechanisms have been proposed to have caused the extinctions in North America? Did Late Pleistocene extinctions occur in places other than North America? If so, where and what types of organisms became extinct?

Activity 4

The Mesozoic–Cenozoic Boundary Event

Goals

In this activity you will:

- Understand how changes in the Earth's climate have affected organisms throughout geologic time.

- Understand that the organisms that dominate the continents today differ from the organisms that dominated the Earth in the deep geologic past.

- Understand that severe ecological disruptions alter the history of life, resulting in extinction followed by the evolution and appearance of new organisms.

- Understand that newly evolved organisms develop similar body features that allow them to use the same resources as those organisms that became extinct.

Think about It

Perhaps no other interval of geologic time has captured the attention of popular culture as much as the Mesozoic Era. This was the time when dinosaurs roamed the Earth.

- If the dinosaurs were such successful creatures, what happened to them, and why?

What do you think? Record your ideas about this question in your *EarthComm* notebook. Be prepared to discuss your ideas with your working group and the class.

Investigate

Part A: Changes in Climate and Life at the End of the Mesozoic Era

1. Look at the geologic time scale. Familiarize yourself with the terms used to name different geologic time intervals. The boundary between the Mesozoic Era and the Cenozoic Era, about 65 million years ago, represents one of the most catastrophic extinction events in Earth history. In this part of the investigation you will focus on the changes in climate and organisms between the end of the Cretaceous Period (the end of the Mesozoic), and the beginning of the Tertiary Period (the beginning of the Cenozoic). You may sometimes see different names used to refer to the Cenozoic Periods. That is because there are two alternative ways that the Cenozoic Era can be subdivided into periods. In the older terminology, the Cenozoic is subdivided into the Tertiary and Quaternary Periods.

Major Divisions of Geologic Time
(boundaries in millions of years before present)

	Epoch	Period		Era	Eon
.01	Holocene	Neogene	Quat.	Cenozoic	Phanerozoic
1.8	Pleistocene				
5.3	Pliocene		Tertiary		
24	Miocene				
34	Oligocene	Paleogene			
56	Eocene				
65	Paleocene				
145		Cretaceous		Mesozoic	
213		Jurassic			
248		Triassic			
286		Permian		Paleozoic	
325		Pennsylvanian			
360		Mississippian			
410		Devonian			
440		Silurian			
505		Ordovician			
544		Cambrian			
2500				Proterozoic	Cryptozoic (Precambrian)
				Archean	

Note that the divisions of geologic time are not drawn to scale. Quat. = Quaternary

The newer terminology, however, subdivides the Cenozoic Era into the Paleogene and Neogene Periods. It is important to note, as is shown in the diagram on p. 174, that the Period boundaries are not in the same place for the two different terminologies.

2. In your group, visit the *EarthComm* web site to collect data on paleoclimate from the pre-boundary time interval (the Late Cretaceous) and the post-boundary time interval (the earliest Tertiary, also known as the Paleogene Period).

   a) How did the climate change at the end of the Mesozoic?

   b) What evidence is there on how fast the climate changed?

   c) From your findings, what do you think are the dominant plants and animals in North America before the boundary?

   d) From your findings, what do you think are the dominant plants and animals in North America after the boundary?

3. In your group, visit the *EarthComm* web site to collect data on the fossil record of organisms from the pre-boundary time interval (the Late Cretaceous) and the post-boundary time interval (the Paleogene).

   a) How accurate were your predictions on the dominant plants and animals in North America before and after the boundary? Explain any differences.

   b) How do you think that the interactions between organisms differed before and after the boundary? Why?

   c) Which organisms from the fossil record are still living (extant) and which ones are no longer known to be alive on Earth today (extinct)?

   d) Why do you think that some organisms survived beyond the boundary, but others did not?

   e) How do you think that the dominant plants and animals in your community differed before and after the boundary? Why?

Part B: Consumers of the Mesozoic and Cenozoic

The adaptions of organisms that have evolved to function within a given ecosystem appear to have several common features that allow success. You have now seen that plants before and after the extinction between the Cretaceous and Tertiary Periods (the K/T extinction) were very similar but that the dominant animals were very different. Or were they?

1. Examine the photographs of the skull and jaw structure of both a hare (rabbit) and a wolf (shown on the next page.

Hare skull.

Wolf skull.

a) What are the differences in the organization of teeth in these animals?

b) Which animal is a carnivore and which is a herbivore?

c) How does the tooth arrangement reflect their levels within the ecosystem?

2. Examine the photographs of extinct fossil mammal skulls collected from Paleogenic rocks of North America.

a) How are these skulls similar to modern rabbits and wolves?

b) In which level(s) of the ecosystem would you predict that each of these animals existed? That is, which ones were herbivores and which ones were carnivores? How can you make these interpretations?

3. Examine the photographs of dinosaur skulls collected from Mesozoic rocks of North America.

a) What features do these skulls have that are similar to the modern rabbits and wolves, and to the extinct mammals from the Tertiary Period?

b) Which dinosaurs exhibit skull, jaw, and teeth similar to the herbivores?

c) Which dinosaurs exhibit skull, jaw, and teeth similar to the carnivores?

d) In which level(s) of their ecosystem would you predict that each of these animals existed? How can you make these interpretations?

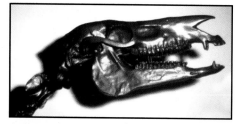

Archaeohippus (an early horse).

Smilodon *californicus* (saber-toothed tiger).

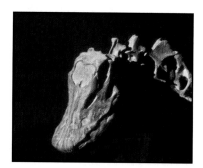

Diplodocus.

Tyrannosaurus *rex*.

Reflecting on the Activity and the Challenge

This activity gave you the chance to explore the fact that life forms that dominated Earth in the deep past differ in several ways from what exists at the present. However, these extinct life forms occupied all the parts of the same ecological levels that exist today. It also showed you that at certain times in the geologic past, climate and life changed over very short geological times. New organisms evolved to take the ecological place of those that became extinct. How did this activity change your ideas about life on Earth? You will need to explain the appearance of new animals and plants in Paleogenic (post-boundary) rocks that have no fossil record in Cretaceous (pre-boundary) rocks as part of your **Chapter Challenge.**

Digging Deeper

THE EXTINCTION OF SPECIES

The success or failure of a particular species through time is impossible to predict. Many physical and biological factors interact with one another in complicated ways over a long time to determine success or failure. Additionally, the data from the fossil record seem to indicate that different kinds of organisms have different rates of overall success. Paleontologists have documented that some species have persisted for tens of millions of years. Others span only a few million years, or even only a few hundred thousand years.

The Extinction Event at the End of the Mesozoic

You have learned that there was a marked difference in the landscapes of the Mesozoic Era and the Cenozoic Era. (The terms come from the Greek *meso-*, meaning middle, and *kainos-*, meaning new.) The groups of animals that dominated Earth for nearly 130 million years during the Mesozoic in the pre-boundary biosphere mysteriously disappeared. The disappearance was sudden; almost overnight, in terms of geologic time. This extinction affected some plants and many groups of animals that lived on land. It similarly affected much of the food web in the oceans. Groups from lowly **phytoplankton** to top carnivores disappeared from the fossil record, never to be seen again except as fossil material. The post-boundary biosphere, which became established early in the Paleogene was very different in its aspect. It took several million years for the plant and animal groups

Geo Words

phytoplankton: small photosynthetic organisms, mostly algae and bacteria, found inhabiting aquatic ecosystems.

known to exist at present to evolve and fill all of the ecological spaces opened by the end-of-the-Mesozoic extinction event.

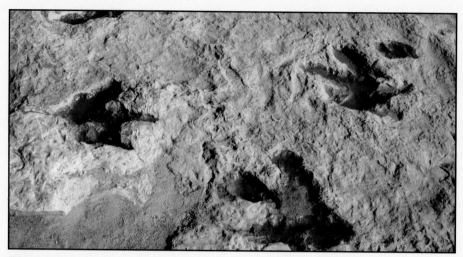

Figure 1 Dinosaur tracks provide evidence for these prehistoric life forms.

If you were to examine the post-boundary fossil record in more detail, you would find that changes in the kinds of animals now extinct are related to the appearance and disappearance of their food source(s). The fossil record indicates that when evolution changes the basic composition of plants in a community, those dependent organisms must find a new food source, change how they process food for nutrition, or face extinction. For example, there is no physical evidence in the extensive fossil record, to date, for many grazing animals until the mid-Cenozoic. The first evidence for the evolution and appearance of grasslands appears at about this time. Following this, many new groups of animals whose diets include these plants are found for the first time in the fossil record, not before. In North America such animals include camels, rhinoceroses, horses, and a wealth of other mammals that are now known to be extinct. The extinction of a few species now and then appears to be a normal phenomenon. Scientists refer to the appearance and disappearance of a few species at any time as **background extinction**. When the fossil record documents a significant change in Earth's **biodiversity**, these events are termed **mass extinctions**. There have been five major mass extinctions during the history of life. During these mass extinctions up to 90% of the known biodiversity was lost. The extinction event at the end of the Paleozoic Era, between the Permian and the Triassic Periods, was even more devastating to life on Earth than the extinction at the end of the Mesozoic. The general patterns of evolution and recovery in each of the post-extinction worlds are similar, including the appearance of new organisms with similar adaptions for living. Understanding these patterns may provide insight into how the Earth's biosphere responds to severe trauma.

Figure 2 The woolly mammoth became extinct near the end of the Pleistocene Epoch.

Incidentally, are you aware that the subdivision of geologic time into the Paleozoic, Mesozoic, and Cenozoic Eras at the particular places in the span of geologic time was adopted just because of the magnitude and abruptness of the extinctions? To a great extent, the accepted scheme of subdivision of geologic time isn't just arbitrary; it has a natural basis.

The Cause of the Extinction

Geologists and paleontologists have known for more than 150 years about the mass extinction at the end of the Mesozoic. The cause, or causes, of the extinction, however, remained obscure until very recently. In the 1970s a scientist name Luis Alvarez and his coworkers proposed that the extinction was caused by collision of a gigantic asteroid with the Earth. They based that hypothesis on studies of cores and outcrop sections through sedimentary rocks whose deposition spanned the Mesozoic–Cenozoic boundary. In several such sections they found geochemical evidence, in the form of unusually high concentrations of the chemical element iridium, that pointed toward a catastrophic collision. Iridium is known to be introduced into the Earth system during certain meteorite and asteroid impacts. Later, what most geoscientists consider to be the "smoking gun" was found in the Yucatán Peninsula of Mexico: the remnants of a colossal impact structure, called the Chicxulub crater. The idea is that the collision placed such quantities of dust and ash into the atmosphere that the climate became dramatically cooler and it is believed that light was unable to reach Earth's surface. The Earth's ecosystems were stressed for long times after the collision, leading to widespread extinction of species of many kinds of organisms. In the Gulf of Mexico, evidence of sediment movement and deposition by a gigantic sea wave, presumably caused by the impact, has strengthened the hypothesis.

Check Your Understanding

1. How long do species last?

2. What happens to animal species when the food sources of the animals change?

3. How can you document that as different groups of organisms evolved they developed similar structures, allowing them to occupy a position in the ecological hierarchy?

4. What is the difference between background extinction and mass extinction?

5. What kinds of evidence can be used to document a major meteorite or asteroid impact in the geologic past?

Figure 3 The Chicxulub Crater, on the Yucatan Peninsula of Mexico, provides evidence for a large impact event at the end of the Cretaceous. Here the crater is magnified using detailed measurements of the Earth's gravitational field and is revealed as the roughly circular feature in the center of this image.

Many aspects of the extinction remain unclear. Extinction of species continued for geologically long times after the collision. One needs to appeal to long-term ecological effects to explain this circumstance. In addition, there is also good evidence for increased volcanic activity around the time of the Mesozoic–Cenozoic boundary. A minority of geoscientists favor an alternative hypothesis for the great extinction, having to do with climate change induced by the volcanism. Evidence is still being gathered to resolve the details of the extinction and its causes.

Understanding and Applying What You Have Learned

1. Think about the Mesozoic and Cenozoic fossil records you have uncovered. How do the organisms of the deep geologic past differ from those in your present community? Why?

2. What is the probability of one or more of the organisms that lived just before or just after the time of the Mesozoic–Cenozoic boundary still existing today somewhere in the world? Explain your answer.

3. If you were to examine the rock record of another planet, how would you identify that a mass extinction occurred when you were unfamiliar with that planet's life forms?

4. How are new data discovered, where are these data reported, and what is the purpose of independent review of a scientist's data and ideas?

Preparing for the Chapter Challenge

With your group, develop a poster presentation that illustrates both the Cretaceous (pre-boundary) and Paleogene (post-boundary) organisms within their ecological context. Indicate on the poster all of the data sources you consulted, the approximate duration of time that is represented by your fossil communities (how many millions of years), and the major differences between pre-boundary and post-boundary biodiversity. Compare these data to the data you collected for the last glacial maximum to the present. Over how many years is it thought that both of these extinction events occurred? Consider which organisms or types of life strategies appear to have been affected most by the extinction events.

Inquiring Further

1. **Hypotheses to explain the Mesozoic–Cenozoic boundary event**

   Using available resources, investigate further the hypotheses that have been proposed to explain the Mesozoic–Cenozoic boundary event. (It would be useful to know that the event has often been called the "Cretaceous–Tertiary boundary event," because in earlier usage, which still exists today, the Cenozoic was divided into the Tertiary and Quaternary periods.) How do the hypotheses differ? What scientific evidence and data exist to support each hypothesis?

2. **Other mass-extinction events**

   Research other mass extinctions that paleontologists have identified in the rock record. When in time did these occur? What groups of organisms were affected?

Activity 5

How Different Is Your Community Today from that of the Very Deep Past?

Goals

In this activity you will:

- Understand that many different plants and animals evolved and became extinct during the Phanerozoic.

- Recognize that plant and animal fossil assemblages of the very deep geologic past (for example, in the Paleozoic) are unlike organisms alive today.

- Describe the variety of plants and animals that once lived in your community.

- Relate the increases and decreases in the numbers of different organisms during the Phanerozoic to geologic causes.

- Describe several lines of fossil evidence to support the theory of evolution based on the fossil record.

Think about It

You have been learning about how life has been changing throughout geologic time.

- If you could be transported back in time, would you recognize your community?

What do you think? Record your ideas in your *EarthComm* notebook. Be prepared to discuss your ideas with your working group and the class.

Investigate

1. Examine a geologic map of your region.

   a) Which geologic time periods are represented by the rocks in your community?

   b) Choose one of these periods as your "target" in the geologic past. Make sure that all of the time periods represented by the rock record in your community are selected by one or more of your classmates.

2. Using available resources, including textbooks, encyclopedias, the *EarthComm* web site, and museum displays (if possible), collect data on the kinds of plants and animals that have been found as fossils in your target geologic period.

3. Construct either a natural habitat (for land-dwelling animals) and aquarium (for marine-dwelling organisms), or a botanical garden (for land plants) diorama depicting your community during your selected interval of geologic time. Your display should present the biodiversity of the single period of time you chose to investigate.

4. Once you and your classmates have constructed your displays, assemble them in your classroom in order according to the geologic time scale.

   a) How has your community changed over time? Take notes on the similarities and differences between adjacent "exhibits."

 Have your teacher approve the materials you plan to use to construct your diorama.

Reflecting on the Activity and the Challenge

You may have seen that some major groups of organisms are restricted to one or two geologic periods. Other groups may have lived during several geologic periods. You may also find that some geological periods do not show evidence for one or more particular groups of organisms. This may be a result of the kinds of sedimentary rocks preserved in your region. Check the geologic map of your area, again, to see if all the geologic periods are represented by rock. Once you have finished comparing and contrasting the data, decide for yourself if you could recognize your community at any given point in geologic time on the basis of the plants and animals known from its fossil record.

Earth System Evolution Changing Life

Digging Deeper

BIODIVERSITY AND CLIMATE CHANGE

The classification of plants and animals into **species**, and the grouping of species into related groups, is called **taxonomy**. The species is the basic taxonomic unit. A species can be defined as a population of organisms that can interbreed to produce fertile offspring. Species that seem to be closely related, in terms of how they evolved, are grouped into a higher taxonomic unit called a genus (plural: genera). In turn, genera that are thought to be closely related are grouped into families, and so on; see *Figure 1*. In today's world, biologists can (in theory, at least!) determine what a species really is. Paleontologists can't do that, because individuals of the species are no longer alive. Paleontologists try to recognize features using both external appearances (**morphology**) and internal structures (**anatomy**). Keep in mind also that genera and higher taxonomic units cannot be directly verified, either for fossil organisms or for living organisms.

All evolutionarily related species and genera (for example, *Homo sapiens*) are placed into the next highest larger category called a family (*H. sapiens* belongs to the family Hominidae). Related families are grouped into a higher category called an order (Hominidae belong to the order Primates). Hence, there can be many families in any order and many genera within any family. Paleontologists have tried to construct graphs, called biodiversity curves that show biodiversity as a function of geologic time. These **biodiversity curves** are based on the fossil record of higher-order taxonomic units like families or orders. That is, rather than using the number of species or genera known from an interval in geologic time, paleontologists have used the number of families or orders that have been identified.

Your community's biodiversity as reflected in the fossil record is related both to the geologic period you have examined and to the physical and chemical environment that existed there. There is

Geo Words

species: a group of organisms, either plant or animal, that may interbreed and produce fertile offspring.

taxonomy: the theory and practice of classifying plants and animals.

morphology: the (study of the) features that comprise or describe the shape, form, and structure of an object or organism.

anatomy: the (study of the) internal structure of organisms.

biodiversity curve: a graph that shows changes in the diversity of organisms as a function of geologic time.

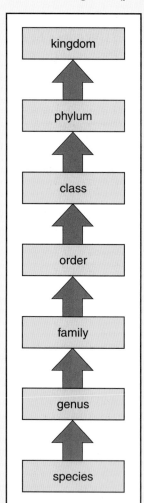

Figure 1 The hierarchy of taxonomic units.

kingdom — phylum — class — order — family — genus — species

incontrovertible evidence that the number, diversity, and complexity of both marine and terrestrial organisms found in the fossil record have changed through the hundreds of millions of years of Earth's history. Many of the "big groups" that are found today in your community have fossil records that extend deep into the past. You can certainly identify vertebrates in your community, and vertebrates certainly have a fossil record that is first found in the Paleozoic. You have also discovered in this activity, however, that there are many strange and interesting creatures that once lived but are no longer found on Earth today.

Figure 2 Reconstruction of what life may have been like 540 million years ago in British Columbia, Canada, based on the fossils found within the Burgess Shale.

New fossil data are published weekly all over the globe. These data do not originate only from scientists working in North America, nor are the scientific journals in which they are found published only here. Rather, there are thousands of paleontologists (in China alone, for example) studying Earth's fossil record on all continents, including Antarctica, and there are nearly 100 different scientific journals that publish data on fossils. The results of these scientists' investigations continue to support and reinforce the general trends you have analyzed in this activity.

One principle of scientific inquiry is that a hypothesis may be falsified sometime in the future if some new, scientifically reviewed and published data are found. These new investigations may challenge certain specifics concerning an individual fossil or the group to which it belongs.

One recent example of this is the controversy about whether or not feathers are only found in birds or if non-avian reptiles also evolved feathers. Nevertheless, the overall evolutionary pattern of life on Earth has not been dramatically altered or changed because of new scientific data.

Figure 3 Fossil of *Archaeopteryx*, which is considered to be the first ancestor to modern birds. *Archaeopteryx* is about 150 million years old.

Many different organisms have had the same or similar life strategies throughout Earth history. Some of these groups that dominated the landscape for several million years have gone extinct or have been placed into a minor role, following some change in global conditions. For example, "club moss" trees, which grew to heights greater than about 40 m (about 120 ft.), are the plants that formed the Mississippian and Pennsylvanian Period coals of North America, Europe, and China. (These two periods are sometimes jointly referred to as the Carboniferous Period because of the extensive hydrocarbon desposits of this time.) These fossil trees are known to have lasted in peat swamps for nearly 30 million years without change. Without these trees in the very deep past, there would have been no coal. Imagine how many trees must have lived over an interval of 30 million years to result in the vast resources of coal that the United States relies on now for electricity. At one time heating, cooking, and steam engines were all powered by coal. So, why are "club moss" trees, like the ones reconstructed in the coal swamp shown in *Figure 4*, not found outside of your school today? If they were successful for 30 million years, why aren't these trees living in your community or somewhere, anywhere, on Earth?

Figure 4 Reconstruction of middle to late Carboniferous tropical coal swamp showing different plant communities.

The loss of biodiversity in the recent past and the deep geologic past appears to be related to changes in global climate. In the case of the club moss trees, their extinction is associated with climate change associated with Late Paleozoic ice ages. These trees were replaced across the Northern Hemisphere by the gymnosperm trees that reproduced by seeds. Seed plants are better adapted to dry environments, similar to the environments that are interpreted to have accompanied global deglaciation and the assembly of Pangea. Some of these same gymnosperm families are still living today, like the cycads and ginkgos, but most are extinct. Distant relatives of the club moss trees are found today as groundcover in the north temperate woodlands and elsewhere. (Change in global climate is not the only factor that contributes to the loss of biodiversity. Many species are endangered or extinct through the actions of humans.)

Figure 5 Photograph of a ginkgo tree in autumn.

Check Your Understanding

1. What factors influence biodiversity as reflected in the fossil record?

2. Why did the "club moss" tree become extinct?

3. How does the work of scientists contribute to the understanding of how life has changed through time?

Understanding and Applying What You Have Learned

1. Large-scale changes in biodiversity due to extinctions and evolution of new organisms thereafter have altered the aspects of your community through geologic time.

   a) How different was your community biome in the record of the deep geologic past you investigated?

   b) Are the common plants and animals you identified in your present community the same as in the fossil record? Explain.

   c) How many times during Earth's history has there been a major change in the biodiversity of your community?

2. When a group of organisms is no longer found in the fossil record, how do new organisms adapt to take its place in the ecosystem?

3. If all soft-bodied organisms and those with hard skeletons that lived in your community in the deep geologic past had been fossilized, how would this change your perspective about life on Earth?

4. What would your present community be like if one or more of the extinction events in the deep geologic past had not occurred?

Preparing for the Chapter Challenge

As a group, synthesize what you have learned about the changes in biodiversity over geologic time and the causes proposed for the mass extinction events documented in the fossil record. Review your notes on how your community has changed over time. Write an essay in which you explain whether organisms with similar life strategies have similar fossil records (i.e., do organisms with the same life strategies respond the same). Explain any differences.

Inquiring Further

1. **Extinctions**

   Is extinction common throughout Earth history, or are extinctions limited to only the "Big Ones?" One paleontologist has asked the question whether extinction is "bad timing, or bad luck?" What do you think? How do mass extinctions change the balance of Earth's ecosystems?

2. **Originations**

   What natural mechanisms are responsible for the evolution and origination of new organisms following extinction events? Is the rate of origination of new organisms slow or rapid following an extinction event? What kinds of organisms appear first in the fossil record following a mass extinction event?

Earth Science at Work

ATMOSPHERE: *Birdwatcher*
Climate change might change the distribution of birds in North America. Birdwatchers can help scientists determine if the range of a given species of bird has changed, or if there has been a change in the time of bird migration.

BIOSPHERE: *Paleontologist*
When detectives investigate a murder, they do not just look at the dead body. They look at a great deal of other evidence. Similarly, when paleontologists find a dinosaur's bones, they can pick up extra clues from trace fossils. These clues to lifestyles help scientists conjure a much richer picture of prehistoric life.

CRYOSPHERE: *Park Ranger*
The Arctic ecosystem is in a very delicate balance and is particularly vulnerable to climate change. Climate change is likely to threaten both marine and terrestrial wildlife. From plankton to polar bears, many species could suffer or disappear entirely.

GEOSPHERE: *Urban Planner*
Urban expansion can result in deforestation of large areas. Also, pollution can make existing trees more susceptible to freeze injury and in turn to drought and insects. Urban planning needs to take into account not such social and economic factors, but environmental factors as well.

HYDROSPHERE: *Fishing Industry*
Fisheries already face the problems of overfishing, diminishing wetlands, pollution, and competition among fleets for uses of aquatic ecosystems. The industry is constantly monitoring seafood supplies for any further changes.

How is each person's work related to the Earth system, and to Changing Life?

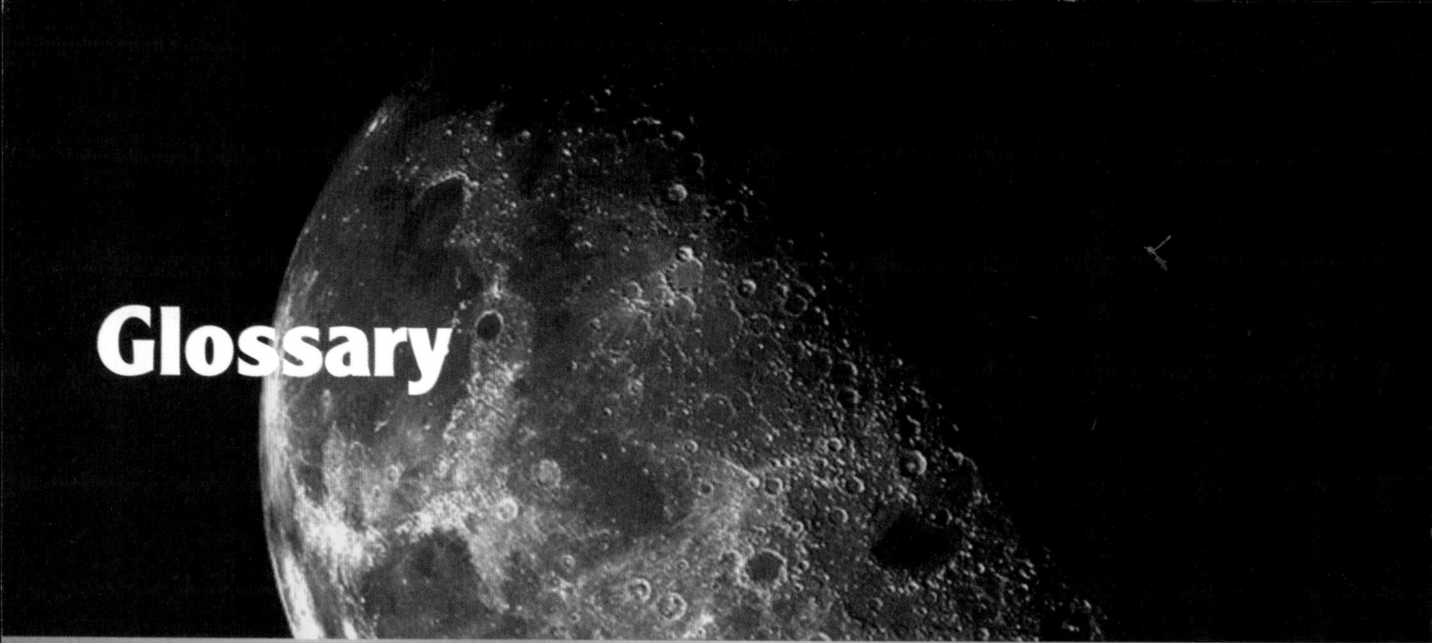
Glossary

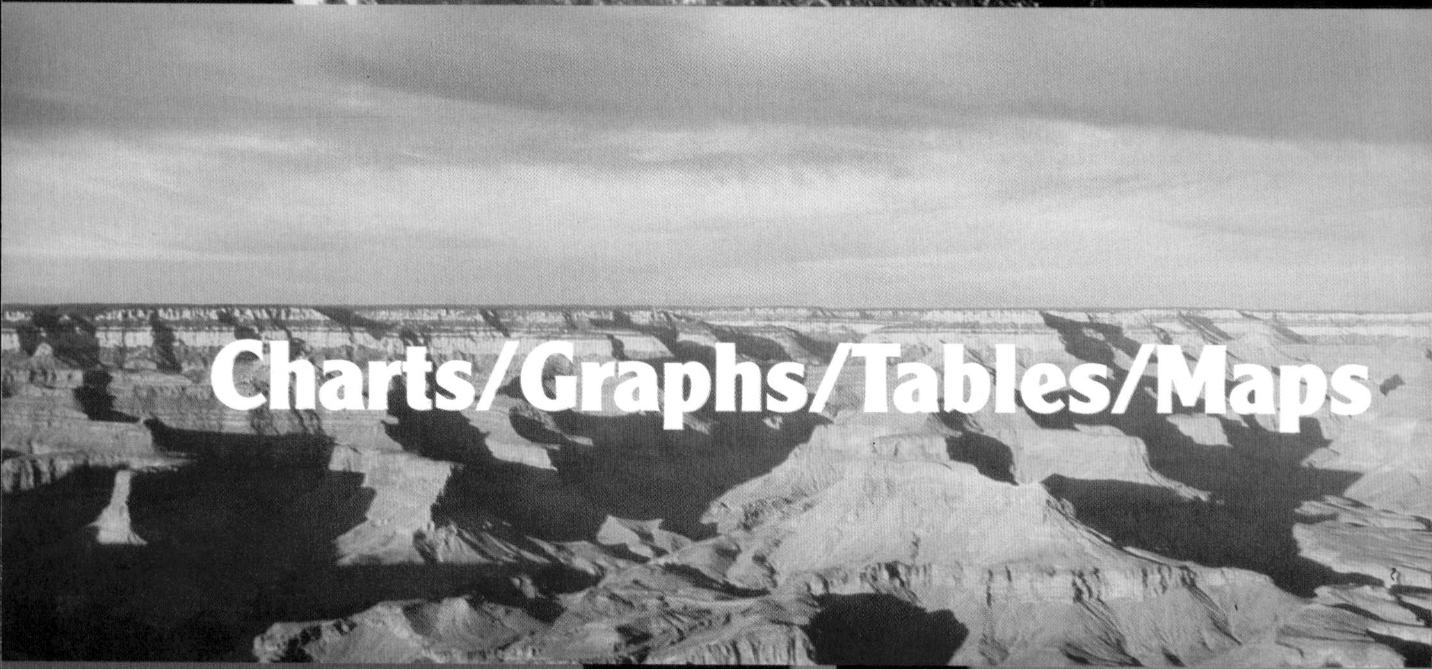
Charts/Graphs/Tables/Maps

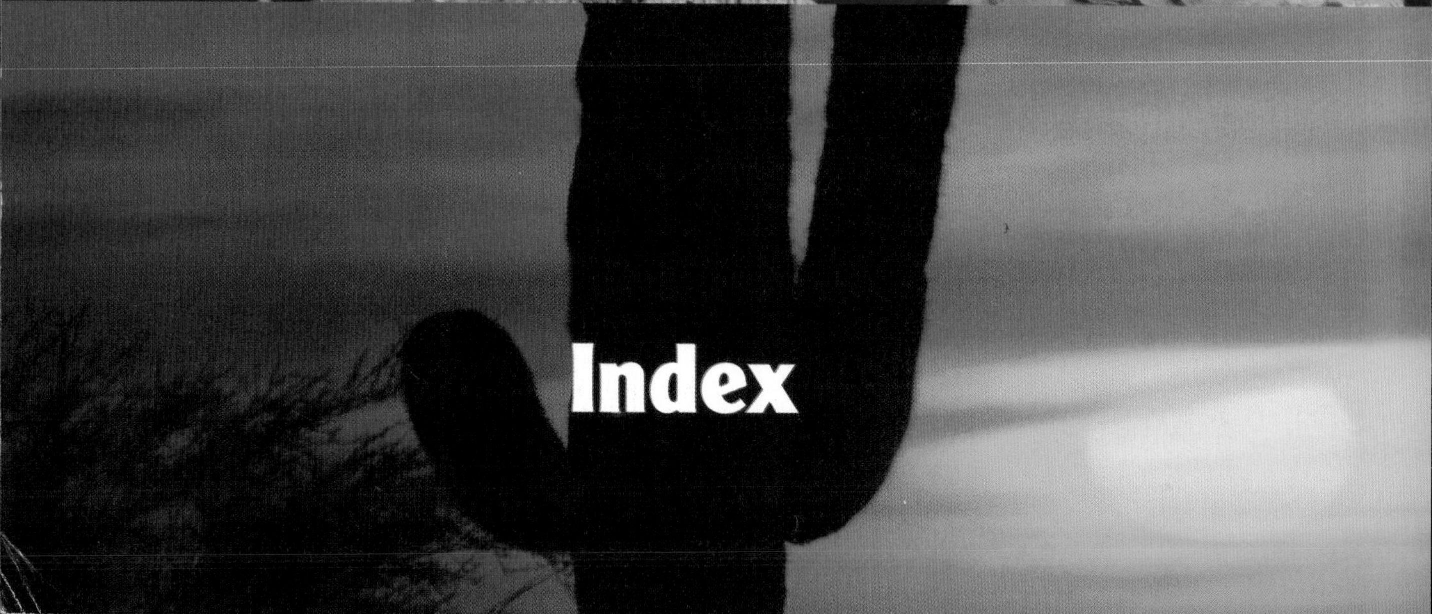
Index

Glossary

absorption spectrum: a continuous spectrum interrupted by absorption lines or a continuous spectrum having a number of discrete wavelengths missing or reduced in intensity.

accretion: the process whereby dust and gas accumulated into larger bodies like stars and planets.

albedo: the reflective property of a non-luminous object. A perfect mirror would have an albedo of 100% while a black hole would have an albedo of 0%.

anatomy: the (study of) internal structure of organisms.

aphelion: the point in the Earth's orbit that is farthest from the Sun. Currently, the Earth reaches aphelion in early July.

asteroid: a small planetary body in orbit around the Sun, larger than a meteoroid (a particle in space, less than a few meters in diameter) but smaller than a planet. Many asteroids can be found in a belt between the orbits of Mars and Jupiter.

astronomical unit: a unit of measurement equal to the average distance between the Sun and Earth, i.e., about $149,600,000$ (1.496×10^8) km.

aurora: the bright emission of atoms and molecules near the Earth's poles caused by charged particles entering the upper atmosphere.

axial precession: the wobble in the Earth's polar axis.

background extinction: normal extinction of species that occurs as a result of changes in local environmental conditions.

bias: a purposeful or accidental distortion of observations, data, or calculations in a systematic or nonrandom manner.

biodiversity: the diversity of different biologic species and/or the genetic variability among individuals within each species.

biodiversity curve: a graph that shows changes in the diversity of organisms as a function of geologic time.

biome: a recognizable assemblage of plants and animals that characterizes a large geographic area of the Earth; a number of different biomes have been recognized, and the distribution of the biomes is controlled mainly by climate.

body fossil: any remains or imprint of actual organic material from a creature or plant that has been preserved in the geologic record (like a bone).

chromosphere: a reddish layer in the Sun's atmosphere, the transition between the outermost layer of the Sun's atmosphere, or corona.

climate: the general pattern of weather conditions for a region over a long period of time (at least 30 years).

climate proxy: any feature or set of data that has a predictable relationship to climatic factors and can therefore be used to indirectly measure those factors.

coma: a spherical cloud of material surrounding the head of a comet. This material is mostly gas that the Sun has caused to boil off the comet's icy nucleus. A cometary coma can extend up to a million miles from the nucleus.

comet: a chunk of frozen gasses, ice, and rocky debris that orbits the Sun.

constellation: a grouping of stars in the night sky into a recognizable pattern. Most of the constellations get their name from the Latin translation of one of the ancient Greek star patterns that lies within it. In more recent times, more modern astronomers introduced a number of additional groups, and there are now 88 standard configurations recognized.

corona: the outermost atmosphere of a star (including the Sun), millions of kilometers in extent, and consisting of highly rarefied gas heated to temperatures of millions of degrees.

correlation: a mutual relationship or connection.

cosmologist: a scientist who studies the origin and dynamics of the universe.

eccentricity: the ratio of the distance between the foci and the length of the major axis of an ellipse.

ecosystem: a unit in ecology consisting of the environment with its living elements, plus the nonliving factors that exist in it and affect it.

electromagnetic radiation: the energy propagated through space by oscillating electric and magnetic fields. It travels at 3×10^8 m/s in a vacuum and includes (in order of increasing energy) radio, infrared, visible light (optical), ultraviolet, x-rays, and gamma rays.

elevation: the height of the land surface relative to sea level.

emission spectrum: a spectrum containing bright lines or a set of discrete wavelengths produced by an element. Each element has its own unique emission spectrum.

feedback loops: the processes where the output of a system causes positive or negative changes to some measured component of the system.

foraminifera: an order of single-celled organisms (protozoans) that live in marine (usually) and freshwater (rarely) environments. Forams typically have a shell of one or more chambers that is typically made of calcium carbonate.

fossil: any remains, trace, or imprint of a plant or animal that has been preserved in the Earth's crust since some past geologic or prehistoric time.

fossiliferous rock: a rock containing fossils.

gas giant planets: the outer solar system planets: Jupiter, Saturn, Uranus, and Neptune, composed mostly of hydrogen, helium and methane, and having a density of less than 2 gm/cm^2.

glacial period: an interval in time that is marked by one or more major advances of glacier ice. Note that the time interval is not necessarily of the same magnitude as the "Period" rank of the geologic time scale.

glacier: a large long-lasting accumulation of snow and ice that develops on land and flows under its own weight.

global climate: the mean climatic conditions over the surface of the Earth as determined by the averaging of a large number of observations spatially distributed throughout the entire region of the globe.

greenhouse gases: gases responsible for the greenhouse effect. These gases include: water vapor (H_2O), carbon dioxide (CO_2); methane (CH_4); nitrous oxide (N_2O); chlorofluorocarbons (CF_xCl_x); and tropospheric ozone (O_3).

heat capacity: the quantity of heat energy required to increase the temperature of a material or system; typically referenced as the amount of heat energy required to generate a 1°C rise in the temperature of 1 g of a given material that is at atmospheric pressure and 20°C.

inclination: the angle between the orbital plane of the solar system and the actual orbit of an object around the Sun.

infrared: electromagnetic radiation with wavelengths between about 0.7 to 1000 μm. Infrared waves are not visible to the human eye.

insolation: the direct or diffused shortwave solar radiation that is received in the Earth's atmosphere or at its surface.

interglacial period: the period of time during an ice age when glaciers retreated because of milder temperatures.

inverse-square law: a scientific law that states that the amount of radiation passing through a specific area is inversely proportional to the square of the distance of that area from the energy source.

ion: an atom with one or more electrons removed (or added), giving it a positive (or negative) charge.

ionosphere: the part of the Earth's atmosphere above about 50 km where the atoms are significantly ionized and affect the propagation of radio waves.

isotope: one of two or more kinds of atoms of a given chemical element that differ in mass because of different numbers of neutrons in the nucleus of the atoms.

lake-effect snow: the snow that is precipitated when an air mass which has gained moisture by moving over a relatively warm water body is cooled as it passes over relatively cold land. This cooling triggers condensation of clouds and precipitation.

latitude: a north-south measurement of position on the Earth. It is defined by the angle measured from the Earth's equatorial plane.

leeward: the downwind side of an elevated area like a mountain, opposite of windward.

light-year: a unit of measurement equal to the distance light travels in one year, i.e., 9.46×10^{12} km.

lithospheric plate: a rigid, thin segment of the outermost layer of the Earth, consisting of the Earth's crust and part of the upper mantle. The plate can be assumed to move horizontally and adjoins other plates.

Little Ice Age: the time period from 1450 to 1850 AD. During this period, global temperatures were at their coldest since the beginning of the Holocene.

loess: the deposits of wind-blown silt laid down over vast areas of the mid-latitudes during glacial and postglacial times.

luminosity: the total amount of energy radiated by an object every second.

mass extinction: a catastrophic, widespread perturbation where major groups of species become extinct in a relatively short time compared to normal background extinction.

meteor: the luminous phenomenon seen when a meteoroid enters the atmosphere (commonly known as a shooting star).

meteorite: a part of a meteoroid that survives through the Earth's atmosphere.

meteoroid: a small rock in space.

Milankovitch cycles: the cyclical changes in the geometric relationship between the Earth and the Sun that cause variations in solar radiation received at the Earth's surface.

molecular cloud: a large, cold cloud made up mostly of molecular hydrogen and helium, but with some other gases, too, like carbon monoxide. It is in these clouds that new stars are born.

morphology: the (study of the) features that comprise or describe the shape, form, and structure of an object or organism.

neap tide: the tides of decreased range occurring semimonthly near the times of the first and last quarter of the Moon.

nebula: a general term used for any "fuzzy" patch on the sky, either light or dark; a cloud of interstellar gas and dust.

neutron star: the imploded core of a massive star produced by a supernova explosion.

nuclear fusion: a nuclear process that releases energy when lightweight nuclei combine to form heavier nuclei.

obliquity: the tilt of the Earth's rotation axis as measured from the perpendicular to the plane of the Earth's orbit around the Sun. The angle of this tilt varies from 22.5° to 24.5° over a 41,000-year period. Current obliquity is 23.5°.

orbital parameters: any one of a number of factors that describe the orientation and/or movement of an orbiting body or the shape of its orbital path.

orbital plane: (also called the ecliptic or plane of the ecliptic). A plane formed by the path of the Earth around the Sun.

orbital precession: rotation about the Sun of the major axis of the Earth's elliptical orbit.

paleoclimate: the climatic conditions in the geological past reconstructed from a direct or indirect data source.

paleoclimatologist: a scientist who studies the Earth's past climate.

paleoclimatology: the scientific study of the Earth's climate during the past.

paleontologist: a scientist who studies the fossilized remains of animals and/or plants.

Pangea: Earth's most recent supercontinent, which was rifted apart about 200 million years ago.

parsec: a unit used in astronomy to describe large distances. One parsec equals 3.26 light-years

peak wavelength: the wavelength of light with the most electromagnetic energy emitted by any object.

perihelion: the point in the Earth's orbit that is closest to the Sun. Currently, the Earth reaches perihelion in early January.

photosphere: the visible surface of the Sun, lying just above the uppermost layer of the Sun's interior, and just below the chromosphere.

phytoplankton: small photosynthetic organisms, mostly algae and bacteria, found inhabiting aquatic ecosystems.

planetesimal: one of the small bodies (usually micrometers to kilometers in diameter) that formed from the solar nebula and eventually grew into protoplanets.

plasma: a state of matter wherein all atoms are ionized; a mixture of free electrons and free atomic nuclei.

plate tectonics: the study of the movement and interaction of the Earth's lithospheric plates.

pollen: a collective term for pollen grains, which are microspores containing the several-celled microgametophyte (male gametophyte) of seed plants.

precession: slow motion of the axis of the Earth around a cone, one cycle in about 26,000 years, due to gravitational tugs by the Sun, Moon, and major planets.

protoplanetary body: a clump of material, formed in the early stages of solar system formation, which was the forerunner of the planets we see today.

radio telescope: an instrument used to observe longer wavelengths of radiation (radio waves), with large dishes to collect and concentrate the radiation onto antennae.

rain shadow: the reduction of precipitation commonly found on the leeward side of a mountain.

reforestation: the replanting of trees on land where existing forest was previously cut for other uses, such as agriculture or pasture.

sedimentary rock: a rock resulting from the consolidation of accumulated sediments.

sediments: solid fragmental material that originates from weathering of rocks and is transported or deposited by air, water, or ice, or that accumulates by other natural agents, such as chemical precipitation from solution or secretion by organisms.

solar wind: a flow of hot charged particles leaving the Sun.

species: a group of organisms, either plant or animal, that can interbreed and produce fertile offspring.

spectroscope: an instrument consisting of, at a minimum, a slit and grating (or prism) which produces a spectrum for visual observation.

spectroscopy: the science that studies the way light interacts with matter.

spore: a typically unicellular reproductive structure capable of developing independently into an adult organism either directly if asexual or after union with another spore if sexual.

spring tide: the tides of increased range occurring semimonthly near the times of full Moon and new Moon.

stellar black hole: the leftover core of a massive single star after a supernova. Black holes exert such large gravitational pull that not even light can escape.

steppe: an extensive, treeless grassland found in semiarid mid-latitude regions. Steppes are typically considered to be drier than the prairie.

supernova: the death explosion of a massive star whose core has completely burned out. Supernova explosions can temporarily outshine a galaxy.

taxonomy: the theory and practice of classifying plants and animals.

terrestrial planets: any of the planets Mercury, Venus, Earth, or Mars, or a planet similar in size, composition, and density to the Earth. A planet that consists mainly of rocky material.

thermohaline circulation: the vertical movement of seawater, generated by density differences that are caused by variations in temperature and salinity.

trace fossil: a fossilized track, trail, burrow, tube, boring, tunnel, or other remnant resulting from the life activities of an animal.

ultraviolet: electromagnetic radiation at wavelengths shorter than the violet end of visible light; with wavelengths ranging from 5 to 400 nm.

urban heat-island effect: the observed condition that urban areas tend to be warmer than surrounding rural areas.

visible spectrum: part of the electromagnetic spectrum that is detectable by human eyes. The wavelengths range from 350 to 780 nm (a nanometer is a billionth of a meter).

weather: the condition of the Earth's atmosphere, specifically, its temperature, barometric pressure, wind velocity, humidity, clouds, and precipitation.

windward: the upwind side or side directly influenced to the direction that the wind blows from, opposite of leeward.

x-ray telescope: instrument used to detect stellar and interstellar x-ray emission. Because the Earth's atmosphere absorbs x-rays, x-ray telescopes are placed high above the Earth's surface.

Charts/Graphs/Tables/Maps

EarthComm

Index